An Illustrated History of
LMS
Locomotives

FRONTISPIECE

The 'Royal Scot' Class is, par excellence, the typical LMS locomotive. The upper picture of No 6130 *Liverpool* (later *The West Yorkshire Regiment*) in parallel boiler configuration at Carlisle in 1929 with its motley collection of pre-group coaches exemplifies the first decade of the company; while, below, taper boiler rebuild No 6103 *Royal Scots Fusilier* at Skipton c1947, with its train of flush sided modern coaches, is equally symbolic of the final LMS period.

Cowan Collection − NRM; Eric Treacy

An Illustrated History of

LMS Locomotives

Volume One: General Review and Locomotive Liveries

by Bob Essery and
David Jenkinson

Oxford Publishing Co.

ISBN 086093 087 4

Typesetting by Gem Graphic Services, Didcot.

Photo reproduction and printing by
The Nuffield Press Ltd, Cowley, Oxford.

Bound in the City of Oxford.

Title Page LMS standard 4—6—0 Class 5XP No. 6010
climbing Camden Bank. *BR LMR*

Above A common sight in early grouping days — pre- and
post-group livery side by side. Two Drummond Caledonian
0—4—4Ts in crimson lake and Caledonian blue livery.
Stephen Collection — NRM

Published by
Oxford Publishing Co
8 The Roundway
Headington, Oxford

Contents

Colour Samples

Colour panels, showing examples of colour shades, lining and cabside layout of lining and numbering, will be found on pages 226, 227, 234 and 235.

NOTES ON THE USE OF THE BOOK

This survey has been planned essentially as a work of reference and is not really designed to be read through from cover to cover — even assuming the reader was willing to try. Each of the main parts is essentially complete in itself and, to avoid the irritation of too much referring backwards or forwards, some fundamental items will be found mentioned several times — but, we hope, not to an excessive extent. We have also tried to make each chapter reasonably self-contained.

Although we have included a variety of summary tables, we have not included a full LMS number list on the conventional 'ABC' pattern for reasons of space. We have, therefore, generally confined ourselves to giving number series which, in most cases, should prove perfectly adequate. Nevertheless, for those who wish to have a full stock list to hand when using this book, we can recommend *Engines of the LMS — built 1923-51* by J.W.P. Rowledge (published 1975 by Oxford Publishing Co.) — a first class summary of numbers, building and withdrawal dates, lot numbers, diagrams etc of all LMS built or LMS designed locomotives.

For the pre-group classes, the comparable book is *Locomotives at the Grouping — No. 3, London Midland and Scottish* by H. C. Casserley and S. W. Johnson (published in 1966 by Ian Allan Ltd. and subsequently re-issued in paperback). This is a formidable piece of work and, although not quite so comprehensive as Rowledge's survey of the LMS standards, still gives full stock lists and much other useful data.

Finally, regarding locomotive liveries, we have replaced our self describing code with a simplified reference system published in this volume, which summarises all the various LMS styles in a simple numerical list and should, except for checking precise details and dimensions, enable the reader to avoid having to refer too often to the livery section. We have used the key numbers on this list to avoid massive repetition of detail in *Volumes II and III* and also on many of the picture captions; the list on page 204 is reproduced as *Table 10* in this volume. Readers wishing to have a separate reference copy of this list should write to the publisher, enclosing a large stamped self addressed envelope.

Authors' Preface

In 1967, we published a book entitled *Locomotive Liveries of the LMS* in which we tried, as best we could, to describe the sundry variations of locomotive painting methods adopted by the largest of Britain's privately owned railway companies. Since that book went out of print we have been asked on numerous occasions when a second edition was going to appear. Consequently, when our present publisher asked us for permission to reprint, we were delighted. When, in addition, he also enquired whether we would like to change the work in any way, we were even more pleased, for we felt that a completely revised and restructured account would enable us not only to improve the presentation and revise the work, but also turn it into an illustrated history as well as a record of livery styles.

It is difficult to decide where to place the emphasis in a locomotive history. Some enthusiasts are interested in performance, others in mechanical details while a third group might be mainly concerned with outward appearances. This latter group will undoubtedly include the growing number of railway modellers anxious to improve the authenticity of their efforts. For our part, we also felt that we should bear in mind the considerable number of authoritative books about the LMS which have been published in more recent years. Since we are neither capable or desirous of competing with acknowledged experts such as E. S. Cox, O. S. Nock, H. A. V. Bulleid and many others in their specialist fields, we have felt it sensible to continue to concentrate on those aspects where we feel ourselves most capable of making a valid contribution and which, to us, seem to have been a little neglected. Thus it is that we have chosen to continue to place more emphasis on the outward appearance of LMS locomotives than on the engineering, mechanical and performance details. For this reason, we have felt it sensible to provide a comprehensive bibliography of sources which we have both consulted and would recommend to our readers.

In this new work, all the essential material originally contained in *Locomotive Liveries* has again been incorporated; but we have managed in the interim period since 1967 to resolve many of our earlier speculations and to considerably simplify both content and presentation of this aspect of the subject – we hope with beneficial effect. Furthermore, this compression has enabled us to find room for a short review of the basic British Railways liveries as applied to LMS locomotives. Most important however and because we have now chosen to call our work a 'history', we have felt it possible to incorporate considerable additional material, particularly in this first volume, relating to LMS locomotive affairs generally. We hope that this, together with the much expanded illustrative content compared with our previous work, will help to produce a more useful document.

In structuring this revised version we decided to perpetuate the sections into which we divided our earlier book but to add to them a fourth part dealing with general locomotive and policy matters. We have also expanded some of the detailed narratives devoted to individual classes to incorporate general as well as painting details and we have abandoned our earlier method of tabulating the locomotive liveries by a self describing code. We now have much more evidence on which to base valid generalisations and the far greater number of pictures we have used has enabled us to illustrate many of the variations we could previously only describe in words. This, of course, has made the whole survey very much larger which is why, at the publisher's suggestion, we shall actually publish the revised work in three physically separate volumes, *Volume I*, therefore, contains all that was in Part I of *Locomotive Liveries* together with the added section on general matters. *Volume II* will deal with the absorbed pre-group classes (excluding Midland) and *Volume III* with the Midland and LMS standard classes, including the London Tilbury and Southend and the Somerset and Dorset Joint Railways.

Taking all three volumes together, we shall try to illustrate every class of locomotive inherited by the LMS and, within each class, as many variations as can reasonably be included. Most pictures have been selected to show locomotives in LMS condition and livery and in some cases historical interest will take precedence over pure pictorial quality. We have also included some pictures in BR colours to complete the story and have also been able to increase the variety of colour work presented in the locomotive livery section. Every effort has been made to avoid mistakes but if the sheer size of the work has caused a few to slip past we apologise for these and would ask readers to inform the publisher, so that at least some of the corrections can be included in *Volumes II or III*.

We do not claim that this work is a fully comprehensive or fully definitive history of all aspects of LMS locomotive affairs but felt that there was a place for a reasonably comprehensive collected review of all LMS locomotives, accompanied by copious illustrations – and this is what we have attempted to produce. We have gained much pleasure in compiling it and will be satisfied if some of this pleasure transmits itself to our readers.

R.J.E.
Orpington
1981

D.J.
Knaresborough
1981

If variety symbolised the LMS of 1923, standardisation was the rule less than 20 years later as is more than evident from this batch of six Stanier 2−8−0s, newly arrived ex-North British Locomotive Company in 1942 and looking for all the world as identical as peas from a pod; save for the Westinghouse pump on loco no. 4 in line − probably a WD example destined for overseas.

NRM

PART I

GENERAL REVIEW

Just as the 'Royal Scots' typified the passenger locomotive of the LMS the Class 4, later Class 4F, was the most commonplace freight engine during the LMS era. No. 4312, photographed at Perth, is one of the very few Class 4s to carry the lined black livery and in this condition is not typical of the class. Livery code B5.

Stephen Collection — NRM

At midnight on 31st December, 1922, the newly formed London Midland and Scottish Railway Company became the largest joint stock corporation operating a railway anywhere in the world. The problems of running this undertaking, an amalgam of once independent and often diametrically opposed companies, were made worse by the very size of the organisation. This is not the place to recount in detail the internal rivalries which occurred, for our concern here is only with locomotive matters. However, internal wranglings did undoubtedly take place and one can often use the locomotive story as the 'litmus paper' of the LMS. It is inevitable, therefore, that some of the conflicts receive mention for, just as in matters of overall policy, the strife between the supporters of its constituent companies lasted longer than on any other of the 'big four' grouped railways, so in locomotive matters too, the LMS took longer to settle down than did its rival concerns. Part of the problem was the sheer size of the inherited locomotive fleet.

In 1923, the LMS found itself the owner of over 10,300 steam locomotives from its constituent and minor companies. This figure was some 3,000 more than that of its largest rival, the LNER and in content, the locomotives varied from the many large classes built by the major constituents to the 'one-off' specimens of the smallest railways included in the group. To these acquired locomotives were later added over 5,000 more units, mainly to LMS standard design, before the eventual supersession of LMS designs by the BR standard equivalents in the early 1950s.

When this latter event took place, the capital stock of LMS constituent or LMS design locomotives had been reduced from the 10,300 figure at grouping to less than 8,000 units. It will thus be seen that in less than thirty years, the locomotive picture had changed from the 100% non-standardisation of 1923 to something like 60% LMS standard design in the early 1950s. If one makes due allowance for the slower rate of new construction during the war years, the re-stocking was even more rapid.

Nothing like this vast turnover occurred in the other three groups. On the GWR lines, the situation was of an unbroken continuation of the standardised procedures developed by Churchward long before grouping. On the LNER system, policy considerations decreed that new construction was less lavish than on the LMS and, of course, this company perpetuated a higher number of pre-group designs than did the LMS. The Southern Railway, as well as being the smallest company after 1922, was also committed to large scale electrification which reduced the need for new *steam* locomotives to even smaller proportionate quantities than on the LNER. Any history of LMS locomotives must, therefore, take due cognisance of this fundamental difference of approach adopted by the LMS management. Although this work is not intended to be a history of the LMS Railway, it is necessary to cover some of the broader trends of company affairs in order to fully understand the locomotive policy adopted.

In 1923, the LMS received its locomotives from a number of constituent and subsidiary companies, the position being summarised at *Table 1*. Locomotives taken into departmental stock, some of which were not numbered in the capital list, are separately summarised at *Table 2*. It should be mentioned that although the LNWR and LYR had carried out their own amalgamation in 1922, the LYR will be regarded throughout this book as a separate company.

The largest constituent of the LMS in terms of locomotive stock, even discounting the amalgamation with the LYR, was the LNWR. Unfortunately for the LNWR, its CME (H. P. M. Beames) had only recently assumed office on the untimely death of C. J. Bowen-Cooke and was, therefore, very junior by comparison with his LYR counterpart, George Hughes. The latter, therefore, became CME of the enlarged LNWR in 1922 and, still being the senior locomotive chief after the 1923 grouping, also inherited the LMS mantle in due course. It must be understood that the question of relative seniority counted for a very great deal in early LMS thinking.

When Hughes retired in 1925, the next senior CME amongst the LMS constituents was Henry Fowler of the Midland who assumed office in succession to Hughes. Thus it was that twice in only three years or so, the head of Britain's largest locomotive building establishment, Crewe Works, had been passed over. But for the death of Bowen-Cooke in 1920 a different locomotive story might well have unfolded on the LMS. Had he lived, he would have been a leading contender for the post of CME to the new company and in this office it is unlikely that he would have played quite the same role as did Hughes and Fowler. Hewitt Beames must have been a saddened man during the 1920s and it speaks volumes for his character that, when passed over yet again on the appointment of William Stanier as CME in 1932, he gave Stanier his whole-hearted support.

◄ **Plate 1 (Opposite)** Standard 5P4F 2—6—0 No. 13088 in immaculate condition. Livery Code A1 (see *Table 10*, page 204). This picture has been selected to illustrate the lining on this class of locomotive and the lining on the buffer bodies and wheels should be noted. The reader's attention is drawn to the fact that the smokebox door numberplate has been painted black, later bright metal finish or white paint was more usual. Note the position of the power classification at the top of the cabside and finally, like the early members of the class, this locomotive has a tender without tender doors. Finally, examination of the original print reveals that lining is evident on the side of the locker on the tender front.

NRM

TABLE 1. LOCOMOTIVES TAKEN INTO LMS RUNNING STOCK FROM THE PRE-GROUPING COMPANIES
1st JANUARY 1923 (Based on official returns)

Several of the locomotives listed below, withdrawn in 1923, were never allotted LMS numbers. Many others, although allotted LMS numbers, were withdrawn from service before receiving the new numbers. For departmental locomotives see Table 2. Steam rail motors are not shown. The two narrow gauge 2–6–4T (note b) were not allotted LMS numbers, neither were the three petrol locomotives (note f).

LMS NUMBER SERIES	1-4026			5000-9645		10000-12994					14000-17997				LMS TOTAL
Pre-Grouping Company	MR	SMJ	NSR	LNWR Div.'A'	WR	LNWR Div.'B'	KER (g)	FR	C&WJ	M&C	CR	G&SW	G&PJ	HR	
Wheel Arrangement				(c)		(c)									
0–10–0	1	—	—	—	—	—	—	—	—	—	—	—	—	—	1
2–8–0	—	—	—	48	—	—	—	—	—	—	—	—	—	—	48
0–8–0	—	—	—	553	—	295	—	—	—	—	8	—	—	—	856
4–6–0	—	—	—	650	—	34	—	—	—	—	65	19	—	50	818
2–6–0	—	—	—	—	—	—	—	—	—	—	5	11	—	—	16
0–6–0	1600	12	47	624	—	540	—	62	—	19	386	177	—	12	3479
4–4–2	—	—	—	—	—	40	—	—	—	—	—	—	—	—	40
4–4–0	386	—	5	299	—	71	—	20	—	—	171	181	—	80	1213
2–4–0	245	1	—	112	—	1	—	1	—	3	—	3	—	3	369
0–4–2	—	—	—	—	—	—	—	—	—	6	20	55	—	—	81
4–2–2	43	—	—	—	—	—	—	—	—	—	—	—	—	—	43
TOTAL TENDER	2275	13	52	2286	—	981	—	83	—	28	655	446	—	145	6964
0–8–2T	—	—	—	30	—	5	—	—	—	—	—	—	—	—	35
0–8–0T	—	—	—	—	—	—	—	—	—	—	6	—	—	—	6
4–6–4T	8	—	—	—	—	—	—	5	—	—	—	6	—	—	19
4–6–2T	—	—	—	47	—	—	—	—	—	—	12	—	—	—	59
2–6–4T	—	—	(b)2	—	—	—	—	—	—	—	—	—	—	—	2
2–6–2T	—	—	—	—	—	18	—	—	—	—	—	—	—	—	18
2–6–0T	—	—	—	—	—	—	1	—	—	—	—	—	—	—	1
0–6–4T	40	—	16	—	2	—	—	—	—	—	—	—	—	8	66
0–6–2T	14	—	36	369	—	(e)21	—	23	—	—	—	28	—	—	(e)491
0–6–0T	353	—	54	313	—	(e)239	3	16	6	1	202	18	—	6	(e)1211
4–4–4T	—	—	—	—	2	—	—	—	—	—	—	—	—	—	2
4–4–2T	70	—	7	50	1	—	—	6	—	—	—	—	—	—	134
4–4–0T	—	—	—	78	—	—	—	—	—	—	12	—	—	8	98
2–4–2T	—	—	6	243	5	329	—	2	—	—	—	—	—	—	585
2–4–0T	—	—	12	15	—	—	—	—	—	—	—	—	—	1	28
0–4–4T	226	—	9	—	7	—	—	—	—	1	141	20	—	5	409
0–4–2T	—	—	—	21	—	—	—	—	—	1	2	—	—	—	24
0–4–0T	33	—	—	17	—	(f)61	—	1	—	2	39	9	2	—	(f)164
TOTAL TANK	744	—	142	1183	17	673	4	53	6	5	414	81	2	28	3352
TOTAL	(a)3019	13	194	(d)3469	17	1654	4	(h)136	6	33	(j)1069	(k)527	2	173	(f)10316

NOTES
(a) MR total includes 2 locomotives ex-S&W 1895, 82 locomotives ex-LTSR 1912, and 12 locomotives of LTSR design delivered direct to MR.

(b) Narrow gauge locomotives ex-Leek & Manifold Railway.

(c) LNWR and L&Y amalgamated 1st January 1922 with title London & North Western Railway. Locomotive stock of two constituent companies continued to be numbered in separate series, being referred to as LNWR Division 'A' (former LNWR) and LNWR Division 'B' (former L&Y).

(d) LNWR Division 'A' total includes 109 locomotives ex-NLR (12 acquired 1909, 97 acquired 1922), and 30 2–8–0's of Great Central Rly design ex-Ministry of Munitions.

(e) Owing to an error in the official returns, the combined LNWR Division 'A' and 'B' figures were given incorrectly as 0–6–2T 391 and 0–6–0T 551, making the LMS totals appear as 0–6–2T 492 and 0–6–0T 1210. This error, which actually occurred in the Division 'B' figures, has been corrected in the above table.

(f) LNWR Division 'B' 0–4–0T total included 3 petrol locomotives, hence LMS steam 0–4–0T total was 161, and LMS steam total 10313.

(g) Knott End Railway was known as Garstang & Knott End Railway until 1908.

(h) FR total includes 2 locomotives ex-WC&E.

(j) Caledonian Railway total includes 2 locomotives ex-Solway Junction Railway: official CR total was 1070, which included 1 G&PJ engine, shown separately in this table.

(k) G&SW official total was 528, which included 1 G&PJ engine, shown separately in this table.

ABBREVIATIONS

CR   Caledonian Railway
C&WJ   Cleator & Workington Junction Railway
FR   Furness Railway
G&PJ   Glasgow & Paisley Joint Railway
G&SW   Glasgow & South Western Railway
HR   Highland Railway
KER   Knott End Railway (g)
L&Y   Lancashire & Yorkshire Railway (c)
LNWR   London & North Western Railway (c)
LTSR   London, Tilbury & Southend Railway
M&C   Maryport & Carlisle Railway
MR   Midland Railway
NLR   North London Railway
NSR   North Staffordshire Railway
SMJ   Stratford-upon-Avon & Midland Junction Railway
S&W   Severn & Wye & Severn Bridge Railway
WC&E   Whitehaven, Cleator & Egremont Railway
WR   Wirral Railway

Compiled by: D.F. TEE 1976

TABLE 2. LOCOMOTIVES TAKEN INTO LMS DEPARTMENTAL STOCK FROM PRE-GROUPING COMPANIES 1st JANUARY 1923

No LMS numbers were allotted to any of the 37 LNWR Division 'A' locomotives, nor to the Division 'B' electric locomotive and the solitary Furness departmental locomotive.

PRE-GROUPING COMPANY	LNWR Div. 'A'	LNWR Div. 'B'	FR	CR	G&SW	LMS TOTAL
WHEEL ARRANGEMENT						
0–6–0	–	–	1	(a)3	–	4
2–4–0	11	–	–	–	–	11
0–4–2	–	–	–	(b)1	–	1
4–2–2	–	–	–	(b)1	–	1
2–2–2	1	–	–	–	–	1
TOTAL TENDER	12	–	1	5	–	18
0–6–2T	–	1	–	–	–	1
0–6–0T	7	5	–	(a)2	–	14
0–4–2T	8	–	–	–	–	8
0–4–0T	10	–	–	1	1	12
TOTAL TANK	25	6	–	3	1	35
TOTAL STEAM	37	6	1	8	1	53
ELECTRIC	–	1	–	–	–	1
TOTAL	37	7	1	8	1	54

NOTES (a) Returned to running stock 1923
(b) Returned to running stock 1925

In addition to the locomotives tabulated above, there were a number of miscellaneous locomotives, including one MR battery electric, and one NSR battery electric, also the Crewe works and Horwich works narrow gauge engines.

For abbreviations see Table 1.

Compiled by
D.F. TEE 1976

So much for some of the leading personalities at the head of locomotive affairs, but when considering motive power, it is wise to remember that this term had two meanings in LMS circles — the locomotives and the organisation which cared for them in service. The latter had a profound effect upon the former and this was probably most prominent in the first and last years of the company's existence from 1923 to 1932 and, again, after 1945.

In 1923, the widely differing locomotive policies inherited from the LNWR, LYR and the Midland can best be summed up in the immortal sentiments of the late D. W. Sanford who, in 1946 wrote:

At Derby the nice little engines were made pets of. They were housed in nice clean sheds and were very lightly loaded. There must have been a Royal Society for the Prevention of Cruelty to Engines in existence. At Horwich they had gone all scientific and talked in 'thous' although apparently some of their work was to the nearest half inch. At Crewe they just didn't care so long as their engines could roar and rattle along with a good paying load, which they usually did.

These comments may seem a little whimsical, but they accurately encapsulate the essential attitudes of the three main sources of influence on LMS locomotives south of the Scottish border. North of this demarcation line, things were very much a law unto themselves and, strangely enough, one Scottish constituent, the Caledonian, had done a considerable amount of work over the period 1909-14 which was to anticipate many of the features of LMS policy after 1944.

Considering all these differences, it is hardly surprising that strong human personalities in both design and motive power departments should attempt to influence the course which company policy should take. This first became apparent when George Hughes retired prematurely, generally believed to have been due to opposition pressure, principally in the person of J. E. Anderson, motive power assistant from the Midland Railway probably acting as mouthpiece for J. H. Follows. These were two of many ex-MR officers who had succeeded to many influential appointments in early LMS days. Hughes, who steadfastly refused to move from Horwich, had already initiated work on the well known 2–6–0 mixed traffic design, eventually introduced in 1926 and was well set to provide the means whereby the LMS could have had — before 1930 — a substantial fleet of modern and efficient locomotives which would have met the needs of the ever-increasing train weights and ever-tightening schedules, particularly on the West Coast services. It is true that his 4–6–0 locomotives lacked somewhat in thermal efficiency but, given the chance, they could have been modified in the light of experience with the 2–6–0s.

When all is said and done, Hughes was one of the pioneers of high-degree superheat (in the rebuilds of Aspinall 0–6–0s and 4–4–0s) and his four 4–4–0 rebuilds in 1908 were the first locomotives in Britain to combine long-lap valves and high-degree superheat. Both of these features, many years later, came to be regarded as the fundamental basis of a modern steam locomotive. However, such things were not to be on the early LMS and the new company was persuaded on a course of action governed not so much by the CME's department as by the traffic side. Here, influenced no doubt by the ex-Midland men, it rather seemed for a while that the new company was hoping that the whole system could be operated on the Midland Railway 'little and often' principle of a frequent service of lightly loaded trains hauled by small engines.

Plate 2 This c1922 picture depicts Hughes 4—6—0 No. 1509 in LYR livery. The locomotive later became 10414 in LMS ownership and carried crimson lake passenger livery with smokebox door number plate. Plate 332, page 209 illustrates another example of one of these locomotives carrying LYR number but with 'LM & SR' in yellow on the tender. Finally it should be noted that a number of tender variations were to be found coupled to this class of locomotive.

Real Photographs

Plate 3 Rebuilt Aspinall 0—6—0 No. 12191 in post-1936 condition but still carrying Ramsbottom safety valves. The probable date of the photograph is c1937 but the location is unknown. Livery Code C15.

Authors 'Collection

Plate 4 LYR 4—4—0 No. 1003, later to become LMS 10126, was an Aspinall 6' 0" and is shown in pre-LMS ownership. Later in its career the locomotive ran in plain black livery, Code C14, prior to withdrawal.

Real Photographs

Plate 5 L&Y 4—4—0 No. 1110 was an Aspinall locomotive rebuilt by Hughes with a superheater and allocated LMS number 10191. The class did not last long in LMS ownership, being extinct by 1926. *Real Photographs*

Thus was perpetuated the Midland Class 4 Compound 4—4—0 as the first LMS standard express type. These were admirable enough locomotives and their limitations lay not so much in poor thermodynamic performance (they were, in fact, remarkably economical by comparison with other pre-group types of similar power) but in lack of absolute size. In the event it proved impossible to operate the erstwhile LNWR main line with Midland size engines and much double-heading continued. Things were not made any better by the LNWR men who had an inherent mistrust of Midland matters in general and compound propulsion in particular (memories of F. W. Webb died hard!).

With the Compounds were continued the Midland Class 4 0—6—0 as the standard large goods engine (this, in spite of the fact that the LNWR and LYR needed hundreds of 0—8—0s to shift their freight), the Midland 0—6—0T (in modified form) as the standard shunter and later (1928), the Class 2 4—4—0 as the standard light passenger tender engine. Faced with all this, it is a little surprising that the Horwich inspired 2—6—0 was built at all, especially after Hughes' retirement.

The results of this course of action by the early LMS management were both predictable and inevitable. In 1926—7, despite Henry Fowler's endorsement of the Horwich 2—6—0 and his attempt to persuade the board to accept a 4—6—2 for West Coast express passenger duty and a 2—8—2 for heavy freight work, management remained obdurately convinced by Anderson's Midland principles, thus precipitating the well known motive power crisis.

Henry (later Sir Henry) Fowler was essentially an administrator rather than a designer and, in consequence, his chief draughtsman, Herbert Chambers, was given a free hand — a situation which, for different reasons and with rather better results, was to be repeated some seven or eight years later with Stanier and Coleman. Chambers was no Coleman but under him was a man called A. E. Owen (the former chief draughtsman of the Furness Railway). According to E. A. Langridge (Eastleigh trained under R. W. Urie), and fortunately for the LMS, Owen managed to persuade his chief that a new design of 2—6—4T should have the long-lap valves used in the successful 2—6—0 and instrumental in the free running and noteworthy economy in coal and water which these engines displayed. Consequently, the new 2—6—4Ts were given these features and eventually established a reputation as the finest of all the engines of this wheel arrangement. It was a close run thing, for two other designs on the drawing board during the late 1920s (the Garratts and the 2—6—2Ts) made use of the old Midland style short-lap valves — similar, in fact, to those fitted to the 2—8—0 locomotives built at Derby for the Somerset and Dorset line. In the case of the Garratt, used entirely on coal train work at low speed, the drawbacks were not so pronounced; but the 2—6—2Ts were a disaster, combining poor steaming qualities with a constipated front end arrangement!

Plate 6 Midland Compound No. 1031 was photographed at Bedford on 1st August, 1937. The locomotive now has replacement Ross pop safety valves, but the chimney and dome are of Midland origin. Note the Deeley tender, distinguished from the more numerous Fowler version by the unequal wheelbase and absence of footplate along its entire length. See also Plate 260 on page 158 for the rear of one of these tenders. Livery Code A5.

Plate 7 Ex-Midland Railway 0–6–0 class 4F No. 3949 photographed at Cricklewood in 1930. The original Ramsbottom safety valves have been replaced by Ross pops but the original MR dome and chimney are being carried. The tender is a 3,500 gallon 'Johnson' style with visible snap head rivets. Livery Code C13.
A.G. Ellis

Plate 8 Large boilered LYR 0–8–0 No. 1437 became LMS 12792 and this picture has been selected to represent the numerous varieties of LYR 0–8–0s which became part of the LMS locomotive stock in 1923. Apart from boiler sizes there were tender variations and cabs with and without side windows. These variations are dealt with in greater depth in *Volume Two*.
Real Photographs

Plate 9 LNWR 0–8–0s came in many styles and this picture illustrates No. 1875, a 'C' Class locomotive later re-numbered 8974 by the LMS. The date is not known but the location is near Leicester and the train of coal is en route from Toton to Willesden. Of particular note is the coal supply on the tender which is piled rather high.
Locomotive and General

Plate 10 The LMS standard shunting tank locomotive was derived from an earlier Midland design. The majority of these locomotives had a 'hole in the tank side' to enable the sandbox to be filled, as shown in this picture of No. 16604. In due course this locomotive was renumbered 7522 under the 1934 renumbering scheme. Note the vacuum pipe — not all were so fitted. The steam is coming from the injector overflow pipe. Livery Code (probably) C5.

Author's Collection

Plate 11 The Class 2P 4—4—0s, 563-700, were considered a standard design and were developed from the Midland Railway '483' Class (see Plate 84, page 61). Chimney heights varied, as did the tenders, but these details are further considered in *Volume III*. This picture shows No. 698 on an up express near Wellow on the SDJR section in 1935. Livery Code almost certainly B4.　　*Locomotive and General*

Plate 12 Three Garratts were built in 1927 with fixed bunkers and smaller front tanks and in 1930 a further thirty locomotives were constructed, also with fixed bunkers but with slightly larger capacity leading water tanks. The original three numbered 4997-9 were followed by Nos. 4967-96 and all were renumbered 7967-99 in 1938 and in due course all except one were equipped with revolving bunkers. 7976 is Livery Code C18.

Author's Collection

Plate 13 Unlike the 2—6—2Ts illustrated in Plate No. 14, the Fowler 2—6—4Ts were most successful and many drivers preferred them to the later Stanier and BR developments. No. 2302 was one of the few turned out in red livery and later, mostly during BR ownership they received outside steam pipes. Photographed at St. Albans in lined black livery. Livery Code B4. *A.G. Ellis*

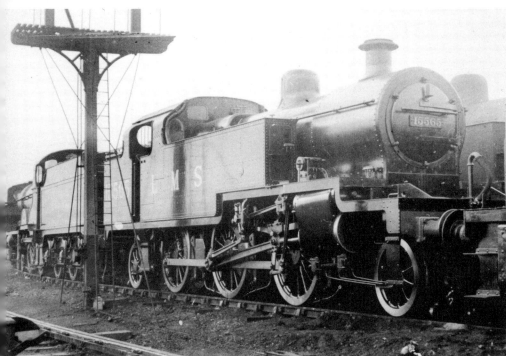

Plate 14 Fowler 2—6—2T No. 15565 probably illustrates the locomotive at Derby following its construction. Note the snap head rivets in the tank sides, only to be found on the final twenty locomotives of the class. In 1934 No. 15565 was renumbered No. 66 and, later still, received outside steam pipes. Livery Code B4. *Authors' Collection*

Plate 15 Ex-SDJR No. 13807 is an example of the large boilered locomotives. Its original LMS number was 9677 but in due course it was renumbered as shown in this picture. The condition of the locomotive is interesting and on the original print it can be clearly seen that the tender, bottom of the cabside, smokebox and below the running plate have been repainted whereas the top half of the cab, boiler and firebox are in a grimy condition. Livery Code C13. *Real Photographs*

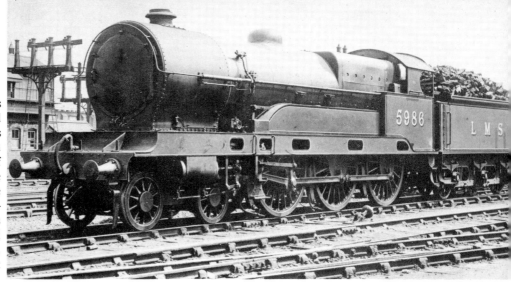

Plates 16 & 17 These two pictures depict the large and small boilered 'Claughtons' and Plate No. 16 shows No. 5986 prior to being fitted with deflectors. Note the large supply of coal on the tender. Livery Code A10. The massive appearance of the reboilered locomotives can be compared with the more elegant looks of these locomotives in their original condition. Plate No. 17 shows No. 5904 on an express train. Livery not clear, probably red.

Authors' Collection

Not surprisingly, the LMS faced the introduction of the new 'Royal Scot' service in 1927 with no express locomotive capable of working it and an approach was made to the Great Western Railway for drawings of the 'Castle' Class 4—6—0. No. 5000 *Launceston Castle* had been tried out in West Coast service — very successfully — but the request was refused. Bearing in mind that R. E. L. Maunsell had, in 1926, produced his 'Lord Nelson' type to do for the Southern Railway just the sort of job which the LMS had in mind (i.e. to handle a 550 ton train at 55 mph schedules), an approach was made to the SR. This time, the request was granted and a set of 'Lord Nelson' drawings was sent to Derby. In view of the limited time available, the contract to build the new engines went to the North British Locomotive Company and the design work was shared between Glasgow and Derby. Fortunately for the LMS, the design turned out to be a 'first timer' and the 50 'Royal Scot' 4—6—0s were put straight into traffic without the need for initial development work. One shudders to think of the results had these locomotives not been successful. Here again, the lessons of the Horwich 2—6—0 were incorporated, aided perhaps by the fact that the 'Lord Nelson' type also embodied long-lap valves and high-degree superheat.

Despite the success of the 'Scots' together with the eventual rebuilding of some of the ex-LNWR 'Claughtons' with larger boilers more suited to their potential (and the subsequent use of this larger boiler on a 'Royal Scot' type chassis to produce the 'Baby Scot' type 4—6—0 later known as the 'Patriot' Class), other engines continued to be turned out incorporating typical Midland weaknesses. Such a type was the Class 7F 0—8—0 which, although it had good valve events, suffered from inadequate journal bearings and big-end and small-end bearings throughout its existence. The class was eventually outlived by some of the locomotives it was intended to replace, namely the ex-LNWR 'Super D' 0—8—0s. At the same time, other classes (e.g. 'Scots', Compounds, etc) were gradually given narrow ring piston valves — a decided improvement. But it was all very piecemeal.

Sir Henry Fowler's retirement from active connection with locomotive matters came in late 1930 with his appointment as an Assistant at Board level. The Chairman, Sir Josiah Stamp, had become convinced that the large number of differing pre-group classes of locomotives were causing maintenance costs to rise unduly and that an even more drastic replacement policy was needed. Thus began the chain of events leading to the appointment of William Stanier in 1932.

Plate 18 (Above) 'Royal Scot' No. 6133 *Vulcan* on a down express passing Oxenholme. Livery Code A1. Although outside the scope of this work, the authors cannot help but draw the reader's attention to the composition of the train which, beginning with an LMS 50' full brake comprises a 50' WCJS corridor composite, three LNWR toplight corridors (brake 3rd, composite, third), WCJS composite diner, LMS standard open 3rd, LNW or WCJS 50' full brake, LMS standard brake composite and, possibly, LNWR composite. *Locomotive and General*

Plate 19 (Below) No. 5521 *Rhyl* heads a passenger train at Birmingham New Street on 7th May, 1938. Livery Code A14. Note the immaculate condition of the locomotive and in particular the smokebox door hinges. *L. Hanson*

Plate 20 The Fowler 0—8—0 Class 7Fs (sometimes referred to as 'Austin 7s') multiplied to 175 units and this picture of No. 9517 reveals the impressive front end of these locomotives. Note the deep front buffer beam, no vacuum pipe, steam brake only, squat chimney and very clean lines. Livery Code probably C13.

Authors' Collection

Before considering Stanier's contribution to LMS motive power affairs — and by any yardstick this was magnificent — we should first consider how it was possible for him to do what he did. The man who made it at all feasible was neither an engineer nor an established railwayman, but an economist. We refer, of course, to the aforementioned Sir Josiah Stamp, later Lord Stamp of Shortlands, President of the LMS Executive. He brought to the LMS Railway a management style quite alien to the traditional British way of operating a railway and it owed not a little to contemporary American practice. Not surprisingly it paid scant respect to the traditional view of things and was, in some respects, at odds with many of the 'old guard' railway officers as typified by those of the former Midland Railway.

The MR was undoubtedly a well managed and well organised, if rather old fashioned railway in 1922. Thus, when men like Follows and Anderson found themselves in positions of power, they understandably applied to the 'Greater Midland' the principles they knew. Unfortunately for them, the Great War and the 1921 Railways Act had brought about profound changes to which they persisted in applying Midland solutions. Stamp's analytical mind made him realise that what the LMS needed was not the mixture as before but engines that worked longer hours, pulled bigger loads and cost less to maintain. By presenting these ideas to the LMS Board of Directors and, more importantly, backing them up with carefully and accurately compiled facts and figures rather than past experience, he was able to persuade the Board to agree to the many beneficial changes the LMS so badly needed, including the decision — much disliked by enthusiasts — to paint nearly all the engines black! Thus, although it was Stanier who produced the actual hardware, it was Sir Josiah Stamp who, by looking at the LMS motive power problems in a scientific and totally unsentimental manner, not only made it possible for Stanier to be appointed but also set up the conditions under which the policy could succeed.

Although such considerations are often felt to be outside the terms of reference of a book such as this, we have deliberately included them because, in our view, they give the background to so many developments in LMS motive power which would otherwise be less easy to understand.

Stanier's name will be for ever associated with the LMS 'scrap and build' policy but in fairness to his predecessors, one can argue that he merely developed a philosophy which had been LMS policy (in fact if not in name) since 1923. Controversy there may have been, projected designs may have been rejected without good cause, but the sheer volume of production of locomotives like the Compounds, '4Fs', '3F' tanks, '2Ps', Horwich 2—6—0s, '7Fs', 2—6—4Ts and 'Royal Scots' had already injected a considerable measure of rationalisation before the 1930s began. Furthermore, there were many good things for Stanier to inherit on the LMS. In the locomotive works offices there were very many capable men

Plate 21 0—4—4T No. 6408 heads a passenger train on the Harrow to Stanmore branch, leaving Belmont. 6408/9 were equipped to work motor trains; note the vacuum control gear by the side of the smokebox. Originally built with stovepipe chimneys as the picture shows, these were later replaced with rather more attractive design c1942, see Plate 228, page 140. These locomotives are often attributed to Stanier or Lemon but in reality they were designed by the Derby drawing office. Livery not clear, almost certainly B3.

Locomotive Club of Great Britain

whose talents were only waiting to be harnessed properly and in the works themselves there was a formidable potential for large scale new production. What was lacking was co-ordination of effort. The good things which had emerged seemed more accidental than planned and, sadly for the LMS, the pre-grouping loyalties had not yet been fused into one coherent philosophy. It was for this latter reason, more than any other, that the LMS Board decided upon a complete outsider for its new CME and to allow time for full consideration of choice, Ernest Lemon was appointed to serve in what turned out to be an interim capacity. During his term, only two classes of locomotive were initiated, small both in size and number. These two types (0—4—4Ts and 0—4—0STs) both actually emerged after Stanier assumed office. There was still much that was Midland about both types, particularly the 0—4—4T, but this was soon to change as nine years of 'Derby Dominance' came to an end.

Summing up this first phase of LMS locomotive history, it is all too easy to write it off as a period of mismanagement and lost opportunities — and to some extent it was. But the real tragedy was that at a time when the railways were having to fight for their very existence for the first time after almost a century of largely uninterrupted progress, Britain's largest system wasted the best part of a decade on petty rivalries completely at odds with the whole philosophy of the railway grouping idea. The supreme irony was that individually, the constituents of the LMS contained amongst their number all that was best in British railway operating. The Midland really was a magnificent railway, save perhaps in the all-important area of locomotive design, and one can find little with which to quarrel in many of its management methods. The LNWR was, in truth, the 'Premier Line' with a vast inherited tradition of service to the public. The LYR was well to the fore in locomotive matters and the Caledonian Railway had already gone well on the road to standardisation before 1923. If only all these individually excellent characteristics could have been brought together earlier, what a different story might have unfolded. It was, in the event, left to a man from Swindon to sort matters out and it is a matter of history that he succeeded right royally.

Plate 22 This class is also referred to as a 'Stanier' design but in reality it was designed by Kitsons who built them at their Leeds works. Originally numbered 1540-4 they were renumbered 7000-4 in 1934. In 1953 a further batch, slightly enlarged, were constructed, see Plate 226, page 139. Livery Code C14.

Real Photographs

Plate 23 'Princess Royal' Class 4—6—2 No. 6201 *Princess Elizabeth*, temporarily fitted with a double chimney, is shown coupled to the original tender. Livery Code A6.   *BR LMR*

On 1st January, 1932, William Arthur Stanier was appointed as Chief Mechanical Engineer to the LMS Railway and the well known and most comprehensive locomotive standardisation phase ever to be seen on a British railway began — a 'mighty re-stocking' as one writer has put it.* Stanier's entire working life had been spent on the GWR so it might seem surprising that he should go to another company. However, he was only five years junior in age to C. B. Collett who had occupied the top GWR post for less than ten years himself, so there was little chance of Stanier ever reaching the top at Swindon or of having a long term of office even if he did succeed. He came to the LMS full of Swindon practice, including Churchward's low-degree superheat — basically 'steam drying' — but as it turned out many of the Stanier ideas were adapted to, rather than adopted by, the LMS. He was eminently suited to Sir Josiah Stamp's purpose, having a long experience of a highly standardised locomotive fleet and he immediately set to work to produce a series of standard designs, some of which were totally new in concept, others being derived from earlier LMS standard types of the Fowler era.

His early locomotives in order of appearance were the 4—6—2, the 2—6—0 (actually designed ahead of the 4—6—2), the 2—6—4T Class 4P (3 cylinder), the 4—6—0 Class 5XP, the 4—6—0 Class 5, the 2—6—2T Class 3P and the 2—8—0 Class 7F (later 8F). All except the 2—8—0s originally suffered from the superheaters being too small. This resulted in some cases in uncertain steaming and heavy coal consumption, particularly the '5XPs' — or 'Jubilees' as they eventually became known. The early Class 5 4—6—0s suffered from light frame construction leading to severe wear on axleboxes, guides and the like, not to mention rough riding. These were all later alleviated by the introduction of heavier frames and horn blocks in place of axlebox guides. In the case of the 4—6—2s, since there were only two of them, alteration to the boilers to improve the steaming was relatively inexpensive and was carried out with marked success before the main production batch, embodying further improvements, was built. The two cylinder 4—6—0s and 2—8—0s were a pretty well instant success, even those Class 5s initially fitted with low degree superheat. When augmented by later batches with larger superheaters, they developed into amazingly versatile performers which between them eventually numbered almost 1,700 units. It was the '5XPs' which were the real trouble. According to one footplateman who drove them in their early days, they ran like a man 'with his trousers round his ankles' and the cure would cost vast sums of money since over 100 units had been ordered straight off the drawing board.

* H.A.V. Bulleid — *Master Builders of Steam* (Ian Allan 1963).

Plate 24 Stanier's first design was a taper boilered version of the Hughes 'Crab' 2—6—0, and No. 13265 is shown in its pre-1934 renumbering condition. The locomotives were coupled to the final style of Fowler 3,500 gallon tenders with snap head rivets and there were variations of the dome design, a point more fully discussed in *Volume II*. Livery Code probably B2.

Authors' Collection

Plate 25 We have selected a British Railways period picture to illustrate the 3 cylinder Stanier 2—6—4Ts. No. 42522 was photographed at Barking on 21st July, 1954, and this view clearly shows the exhaust injector and associated pipework below the cab. There were variations of cab design within this class and these points are further discussed in *Volume III*.

A.G. Ellis

Plate 26 Stanier 'Jubilee' 4—6—0 No. 5563 *Australia* in 1936 style livery. This class of locomotive ran with a variety of tenders and boiler arrangements, and this picture shows a domeless boiler locomotive with an early style Fowler tender. Livery Code A12.

Photomatic

Plate 27 Stanier Class 5P5F No. 5038 photographed at Bristol on 27th May, 1935. Livery Code B3 in original condition, clearly showing the close spaced 'LMS' on the tender, an arrangement peculiar to these locomotives. The reader's attention is drawn to the domeless boiler, short firebox arrangement of these early Class 5s (compare with No. 45305, Plate 236, page 144).

H.C. Casserley

Plate 28 (Above) Stanier produced a taper boiler version of the Fowler 2–6–2T but it must be recorded that these were probably the least effective of his designs. No. 185 was photographed at Grantown-on-Spey in 1938 hauling a 3rd brake. The early versions were domeless, however No. 185 has a domed boiler and is fitted with a small snowplough. Livery Code B10.   *G.L. Wilson*

Plate 29 Stanier Class 8F, originally Class 7F No. 8003, photographed at Derby on 11th July, 1937, showing the original arrangement of domeless boiler and short firebox. Note the smokebox door hinges. Livery, believed to be code C14.   *L. Hanson*

There used to be told in the Derby drawing office a story for the truth of which the writers cannot vouch. Suffice it to say that the source was normally reliable and the story has been confirmed by others. By late 1935, the performance of the '5XPs' was so bad that complete re-tubing of the boilers incorporating an increase from 14 to 24 superheater elements was necessary and, indeed, took place. It is said that Stanier was called before the Board to account for the poor performance and returned to Derby in very low spirits having been given six months to put the engines right — or else! It is at this point that another man comes onto the scene, Tom Coleman, Stanier's chief draughtsman. Stanier confided his problem to Coleman who opined that given a free hand he could cure the troublesome '5XPs'. He got his free hand and the engines were, very largely, cured of their troubles — but it must have been a close run thing.

Coleman's position in the Stanier team was crucial and, in many ways, indicative of Stanier the man. Stanier's chief strength was his extraordinary ability to inspire loyalty amongst his staff and to fuse together the talents of his team. Nowhere was this better exemplified in the early days than in the part played by Coleman. The previous chief draughtsman, Herbert Chambers, was very much a Midland man and, to be frank, did not take too kindly to the new order. Eventually, he was moved to another appointment at Euston and Stanier replaced him with Coleman who had originated on the North Staffordshire Railway and came to Stanier's team from, of all places, the Horwich drawing office. In passing, it is interesting to note that it was Tom Coleman who basically schemed out the characteristic visual lines of most Stanier designs which were to become increasingly associated with the LMS.

To revert to the troublesome Class 5XPs, the difficulty caused by the low superheater was compounded by the poor draughting of these engines. In fact, some experts aver that the draughting was the crucial issue, the blast pipe of a three cylinder engine needing to be different from that of a two cylinder machine in order to produce a similar amount of smokebox vacuum from six exhaust beats per revolution rather than four. Stanier had no three-cylinder experience on the GWR and this may have been part of the problem. Certainly, the story gained credence that Stanier did not really like three cylinder locomotives and he certainly did not build many others. There may also have been an element of unfamiliarity about the early Stanier engines which caused the footplate crews to take a little time to adjust to them. Designed very much in the Swindon tradition, they may conceivably have needed the experience of GWR footplatemen to give of their best — and the LMS of the 1930s was not that sort of railway, yet! Furthermore, there was an undoubted urgency to get new locomotives into service — so much so that Stanier himself authorised the building of the bulk of the 'Patriot' Class 5XPs between 1932 and 1934 to bridge the gap. Stanier himself cannot be blamed for the motive power crisis he inherited and one feels tolerably certain that he would have preferred to build just a few engines for evaluation purposes (as in the case of the 4—6—2s) before launching into volume production.

Whatever the precise reasons, all these ramifications during the early Stanier days were to result, eventually, in a beneficial way to both the LMS and its nationalised successor. The adaptation of Swindon practices rather than their wholesale adoption proved in the event to be the way forward and maybe the early difficulties with Stanier's first designs were instrumental in revealing this truth. Thus, in the classic Stanier locomotive, the tapered boiler shell remained but the heating surface proportions became largely of Horwich style. The intricate contours of the firebox remained since they had proved to increase the life of stays by avoiding areas of high stress but the dome type regulator valve was reinstated. The Swindon axleboxes with complete white metal bearing surfaces and underfed lubrication keeps were immeasurably superior to erstwhile LMS practice and all but eliminated the problem of 'hot boxes'. Improved upon still further by the addition of mechanical lubrication the 'Swindon' axlebox could also be applied retrospectively to such locomotives as the 'Royal Scots', thereby improving their performance from the maintenance aspect.

These alterations were applied as a matter of course to most Stanier engines of the early phase, although a number of Class 5 4—6—0s remained domeless (without any apparent ill effects!) until scrapping. The Stanier 2—6—2T version of the Fowler design could not be thus treated since the smokebox tubeplate was too small to permit a larger superheater and they shared many of the feeble characteristics of the earlier design. Later Stanier locomotives, of course, embodied all the improvements from new, not the least of which was the introduction of atomiser cylinder lubrication.

Amongst the ephemera of the Stanier order it is worth remarking that the cab design of his engines was almost pure 'Horwich' but the cab layout, including the extraordinary position of the blower valve right over the firehole door, owed much to Derby practice. To be fair, the Midland cab layout was in most other respects a good one. It also took Stanier some time to get the Derby drawing office totally away from the hallowed 8 ft plus 8 ft 6 in for the wheelbase of a six-coupled locomotive — a straight throw back to the days of Matthew Kirtley on the mid-Victorian Midland Railway!

The immediate problems of the first Stanier years having been overcome, the search for improvement in performance continued at the instigation of Coleman. In 1936, design work was proceeding on a new 4—6—2, principally with a new high-speed train in mind for introduction in 1937. Stanier was by now in India, conducting investigation into the riding characteristics of their various classes of 4—6—2 and he left the design of the new engines largely in the hands of the 'second team' as it were. Rarely can a locomotive chief have been so well served by his staff; for the outcome was the immortal 'Princess Coronation' or 'Duchess' which, in terms of power output measured scientifically, was to prove to be Britain's most powerful ever express passenger steam locomotive design, and it could run as well — 114 mph and still accelerating when it had to be slowed down on its first real outing!

In this design, several departures from the earlier 4—6—2 appeared, notably the use of two sets of motion to actuate four piston valves. Not only that, but the Swindon layout of the four cylinders on the earlier 'Princess' type Pacifics was replaced on the 'Duchesses' by an arrangement with the outside cylinders moved further forward using the bogie stretcher

Plate 30 The cab shown in this picture of No. 5714 has been included to illustrate the backhead arrangement of a Stanier class of locomotive and should be compared with the earlier Fowler design, see *Volume III*. *BR LMR*

Plate 31 This picture illustrates 'Coronation' Class 4—6—2 No. 6227 *Duchess of Devonshire* leaving Carlisle on the down 'Royal Scot' and the view has been chosen to show the boiler top of these locomotives. No. 6227 was one of the second series of streamlined Pacifics and showed slight detail differences from the first series (for more details see *Volume III*). The livery was crimson lake with gold stripes. *Authors' Collection*

Plate 32 This ex-works view of turbine driven 4—6—2 No. 6202 emphasises the handsome, clean lines achieved by Stanier in his experimental engine. The turbine was housed in the bulbous casings at the front of the engine. This side carried the reverse turbine, the left side of the engine carried the (somewhat larger) forward turbine. Livery Code A6.   *BR LMR*

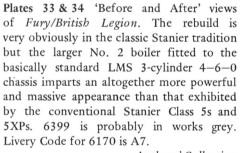

Plates 33 & 34 'Before and After' views of *Fury/British Legion*. The rebuild is very obviously in the classic Stanier tradition but the larger No. 2 boiler fitted to the basically standard LMS 3-cylinder 4—6—0 chassis imparts an altogether more powerful and massive appearance than that exhibited by the conventional Stanier Class 5s and 5XPs. 6399 is probably in works grey. Livery Code for 6170 is A7.

Authors' Collection

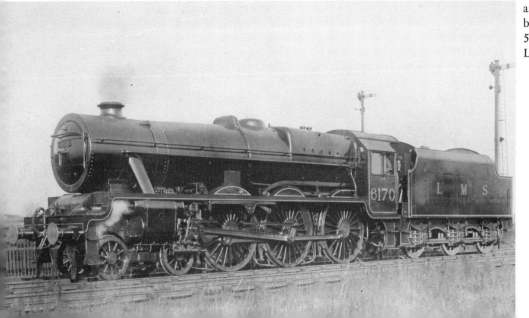

and the inside motion bracket to provide the necessary staying. On the 'Princess' type, the outside cylinders were over the trailing bogie wheels in a position where the frame was cut away too extensively to provide really adequate staying. It is probably not entirely insignificant that the frame and cylinder arrangement of the 'Duchess' 4—6—2 shows a remarkable similarity to that of the rebuilt Hughes LYR type 4—6—0, as does the valve motion arrangement.

The 'Duchesses' were true 'first time' engines and the only significant alteration was the fitting of double chimneys after the trials with *Duchess of Abercorn* in 1939.

At about the same time as the big 4—6—2s (both 'Princesses' and 'Duchesses') were being introduced to service, the LMS was also conducting successful experiments with a turbine driven 4—6—2 and a taper boilered rebuild of the experimental high pressure compound 4—6—0 *Fury* which had failed with disastrous results in the pre-Stanier period and did little of note after his arrival. The turbine engine remained a solitary experiment — albeit successful — but the rebuilt 4—6—0, now called *British Legion* was the harbinger of things to come in the three-cylinder field. Given a larger boiler than the '5XPs' and with large superheater, the engine proved highly successful and led to a shortened version of the boiler being used experimentally on two rebuilt '5XPs' (5735/6) in 1942. This boiler was then used for the complete rebuilding of the whole 'Royal Scot' Class and eventually, 18 of the 'Patriot' Class 5XPs. But for nationalisation, it is reasonably certain that all the LMS three cylinder 4—6—0s would have been rebuilt when due for boiler replacement. As it was, those that were rebuilt were to become what is generally regarded as Britain's finest express passenger 4—6—0 types, fully up to GWR 'King' standards although nominally some 20% less powerful in terms of tractive effort.

Experience with bigger superheaters on the 'Duchesses' (and on the turbine locomotive) led Coleman to incorporate a further increase in the superheaters in the final pre-war batches of Class 5 4—6—0s. Once again the performance improved. According to one experienced ex-LMS locomotive inspector, there was not a single poor engine amongst the last pre-war batch of Class 5s (5452—71) — or amongst the rebuilt 'Patriots' either when they emerged after the war.

Thus, at the outbreak of war, the LMS was in a very different position from that which had existed only eight years earlier. It possessed large numbers of engines which were highly successful from a technical standpoint and, with the benefit of hindsight, it can be seen that, alone of the British railway companies in the inter-war period, in our opinion, the LMS had in embryo, all the essential ingredients necessary to cope with the very changed conditions which were to occur during and after the war in the field of steam locomotive operating. It was a truly remarkable transformation and almost entirely to Stanier's credit. One has only to look at some of the names of his senior staff in those days to realise how significant his work was in depth: George Ivatt (son of the famous H. A. Ivatt of the GNR) who was to carry Stanier's work forward on the post-war LMS; Coleman himself, of course; Robin Riddles and Roland Bond, both of whom were to become CMEs in their own right for the whole of British Railways and Stuart Cox who worked for all of them and whose latter day writings about his experiences form such a vital element of any study of locomotive affairs. A fine legacy indeed and one which few could have imagined stemming from the LMS of the early 1930s.

Much of the success of the LMS team of the 1930s and 1940s, stems from the attention given to those less glamorous aspects of locomotive affairs which rarely receive mention in the enthusiast press, so it is perhaps appropriate at this time to consider the other definition of the words 'Motive Power' given earlier in the chapter, i.e. the organisation whose purpose was to service and maintain locomotives while in traffic. This was largely a Midland organisation and, like most things Midland, was highly and successfully organised. Basically, methods were developed of examining and repairing locomotives in traffic, culminating in the document known to all LMS locomotive men as 'M.P.11', or the schedule of standard examinations. Commencing with the daily examination for all passenger engines and weekly for freight engines (with certain exceptions) through the 'X' examination, which coincided with washing out the boiler, it carried through progressively more comprehensive examinations at 6,000 mile intervals up to a Number 8 examination at 48,000 miles, the most comprehensive done at a depot. Depending on the class of locomotive concerned, the Number 6 (36,000) or Number 8 examination included valves and pistons.

As the latter two examinations involved equipment which it would not have been financially sound to provide at every depot, these examinations were performed at a concentration depot. From this arrangement it is not difficult to see why it was that the depots themselves were organised into districts, each containing a concentration depot surrounded by a varying number of garage depots. From the records kept of the repair work carried out on each locomotive at each examination (each locomotive had its own individual 'history' record card), it could be seen if any individual units, or specific classes, called for more repairs than others and as such provided very useful feed back to the design staff. It was from this source that most of the improvements emanated after 1939 and it had a strong influence on the form taken by post-war designs. The more detailed story of this massive re-organisation is given in the next chapter.

Such innovations as self-cleaning smokeboxes, rocking grates and hopper ashpans played a large part in the time required for servicing locomotives. Another feature was the not infrequent introduction of minor detail modifications to improve maintenance. A few examples will serve to illustrate the point. The Stanier Class 8Fs built for the War Department had the crosshead moved back 5″ with consequent lengthening of the piston rod and shortening of the connecting rod. This meant that when the crosshead and connecting rod were parted and the crosshead moved fully forward, the piston head protruded from the front of the cylinder, thereby allowing piston rings to be changed without parting piston rod and crosshead — a tremendous time saving for one operation. Similarly, when the streamline 'Duchess' 4—6—2s had their casings removed after the war, the footplate was left with a 'break' ahead of the cylinders which materially eased the removal of the valves for examination and maintenance.

Plate 35 (Above) A labour saving device was the rocking grate fitted to a number of locomotives and in this picture we see a locoman operating the lever which dropped the fire. The rocking grate could be activated from the footplate and used while the locomotive was in motion but when disposing a locomotive at the end of its turn of duty the fire would be dropped from the grate to ashpan and then, as shown in this picture, the fire would be dropped into the ash pit. Class 8F 2—8—0 No. 8490 displays Livery Code C22. The reader's attention is drawn to the wartime blacked out side window.   *BR LMR*

Plate 36 (Below) 'Coronation' Class 4—6—2 locomotive No. 6224 *Princess Alexandra* in an early variation of the 1946 livery. Note the absence of boiler bands lining and the close spaced 'LMS' on the tender and the classification below the running number. The locomotive carried the bevelled top to the smokebox, later replaced by the cylindrical pattern by BR. Livery Code B13. This clearly illustrates the 'break' in the running plate ahead of the cylinders, to assist maintenance.   *Real Photographs*

Plate 37 Fairburn 2—6—4T No. 2238 was a member of the final design of LMS 2—6—4T which finally outnumbered the earlier Fowler/Stanier versions. Many of these locomotives entered traffic after nationalisation and the design formed the basis of the British Rail standard class of 2—6—4T. Note the 'SC', self cleaning smokebox sign on the smokebox door which meant that the smokebox need only be cleared of char when the locomotive boiler was washed out. Location and date unknown. Livery Code C23.

A.G. Ellis

Another feature adopted was to minimise damage if an engine was subject to priming. This took the form of a groove machined in the cylinder covers. If water became trapped between the piston head and a cylinder cover it could not be compressed and something had to give way. The machined groove ensured that the centre of the cylinder cover became the point of weakness, a much less expensive replacement than the whole of the cylinder casting.

This shift of emphasis to measures which would reduce maintenance costs and time out of traffic was brought about by increasing labour and material costs. In the case of self-cleaning smokeboxes one finds a strange parallel with the measures taken by J. F. McIntosh on the Caledonian in 1909-14. His arrangement was not meant to be self-cleaning but appears to have been effective in that role.

Sir William Stanier, as he had then become, retired from an active part in the locomotive scene at the end of 1942 and was succeeded by C. E. Fairburn whose background was in electrical engineering and whose short tenure of office saw but one new design — a short wheelbase version of the Stanier 2—6—4T. Significantly, one of the obvious visual differences was the break in the front footplate ahead of the cylinders for ease of access. These engines formed the basis of the BR standard derivative.

In 1945, Fairburn died and was succeeded by H. G. Ivatt who had, originally, come from the North Staffordshire Railway and was thus well acquainted with Coleman who remained at Derby as chief draughtsman. This régime continued the previous policy, including the rebuilding of the 'Royal Scots' and it was under Ivatt that the first of the 'Patriot' rebuilds with taper boilers entered service. Further Class 5 4—6—0s appeared, many with modifications, while the Fairburn version of the 2—6—4T eventually became the most numerous single variant of this, by now very considerable class of locomotives. In 1947-8, the final pair of 'Duchess' Pacifics was also completed with an even bigger superheater, roller bearings throughout and a redesigned trailing truck carrying the weight behind the axle instead of directly over it. These changes were intended to equip the two engines (6256 and 46257) to work the same duties single handed as the two new diesel-electric main line locomotives, 10000/1 working in tandem. There was also a desire to increase the annual mileage of the big 4—6—2s to the 100,000 mile figure — it was never quite achieved. The increased superheating surface and the roller bearing chassis undoubtedly contributed in a positive way but the trailing end alterations were not so successful and these two engines gained something of a reputation for rougher riding than the rest of the 4—6—2s which were exemplary machines in this respect.

Plates 38 & 39 (Left and Above) Caprotti valve gear Class 5 No. 4749 and modified 'Coronation' Class 4–6–2 No. 46256 *Sir William A. Stanier, F.R.S.* typify the post-war LMS developments in steam locomotive operating. No. 46256 was photographed in BR green livery in 1953 — No. 4749 when new. *Authors' Collection*

Plate 40 The only main line diesel locomotive to run prior to the nationalisation of Britain's railway companies. No. 10000 in service shortly after entering traffic. *Authors' Collection*

Plate 41 Photographed at Crewe South on 15th August, 1937, No. 7051, originally 7401, was one of the first diesel locomotives placed in service. No. 7051 was the Hunslet prototype of 1932, the first of four units from that works and was loaned to the WD during the war. After service with the Middleton Railway Trust in Leeds and being named *John Alcock* it is now preserved at the NRM, York. Non-standard livery, gold shaded black 'LMS', straw-coloured numbers. *L. Hanson*

The two main line diesels were Britain's first essay in this field and the LMS was, understandably, anxious to get at least one into service before 1948. This it achieved — just — and No. 10000 thus became the only main line diesel locomotive to run in this country wearing the insignia of a privately owned railway company. Whatever one's personal view of the diesel locomotive, it can only be regarded as unfortunate that No. 10000 was not preserved in the National collection. Its visual lines were somewhat similar to the BR Sulzer Type 4 (BR Classes, 44, 45, 46) and mechanically, the English Electric Class 37 owes much of its ancestry to the LMS design.

Although the main line diesel was something of a new departure in British terms, the LMS was no stranger to diesel propulsion for it started the move to diesel shunting locomotives well back in the 1930s and its standard locomotive in this category was the direct lineal ancestor of the ubiquitous BR Class 08 diesel shunter. Much of the credit for the pioneering work of the LMS in this field is attributable to Fairburn and it is worth back tracking a little to outline the story.

In an earlier part of this chapter we pointed out how Stamp had applied his analytical approach to motive power. The result was a series of locomotives which could do far more work in a year than the engines they superseded. But whilst this was going on Stamp also initiated a study which was to have far-reaching consequences, not just for the LMS but for their successors forty years later.

Stamp was very conscious that nearly 50% of all freight engine hours were spent on shunting work. His response was to set up a study group charged with finding a means of reducing shunting costs. From the work of this group emerged the most numerous and probably the most reliable class of locomotive owned by British Rail today, the Class 08 shunter. Furthermore, the very success of the group's recommendations caused the LMS to apply the diesel electric locomotive to main-line service, something which was to lead to the elimination of steam 20 years later.

Put like this it sounds simple but the diesel shunter did not arrive overnight and the LMS had its share of failures. In fact its first attempt, the conversion of 0—6—0T No. 1831 to a diesel-hydraulic shunter, apparently made the LMS steer clear of this form of transmission for good. Trials with a small Hunslet diesel shunter with mechanical transmission, however, were so successful that eight similar machines were ordered in January 1933. They were from various manufacturers and all were in the 150-200 hp range. For comparison a 250 hp diesel electric locomotive and a Sentinel-Doble oil-fired compound steam shunter were also purchased. This latter, No. 7192, was the last steam shunter built for the LMS.

Shortly afterwards, following trials with an English Electric 300 hp machine, some twenty 350 hp diesel-electric shunters were also ordered, the contracts being placed in June 1934. Trials with these larger machines proved the worth of the diesel locomotive and it was decided to standardise on the 350 hp design. The operating people were delighted with their new tools whilst drivers were equally enthusiastic. To give an example, the diesel turns at Crewe were manned largely by former passenger top-link drivers who preferred the comfortable cabs and regular shifts to the more taxing lodging turns associated with main-line duties.

The first production order was for forty 0—6—0 single motor diesel-electrics, numbered 7080-7119, placed on Derby in 1939. This arrangement, with the single motor driving through a jackshaft, produced a rather ungainly machine and although the locomotives were a tremendous improvement over the steam shunter the design was not perpetuated. It was followed by the twin-motor, outside framed version which became the BR standard.

Apparently the War Department also thought highly of the diesel shunter because many of the LMS locomotives were commandeered for military use, sometimes before seeing service on the parent company. Consequently, the history of the LMS diesel shunters is very complex with requisitionings, transfers and re-numberings and one is thankful that the company did not have so many shunters as it had 8F 2—8—0s. The reader wishing to cover the subject in more detail is referred to J.W.P. Rowledge's excellent book *Diesel Locomotives of the LMS* (Oakwood Press, 1975). It is fair to assume that it was because the LMS was so impressed with the performance of its diesels under wartime conditions that it decided to try out main-line diesel electrics and three locomotives were ordered.

Plate 42 (Above) Sentinel-Doble oil fired, four cylinder 0—4—0T No. 7192 was the last steam shunter built for the LMS, after which the diesel shunter policy was adopted.

BR LMR

Plate 43 (Below) Standard LMS 350 hp diesel electric 0—6—0 shunting locomotive (ex-LMS 7124) running as BR 12037 in 1955. This design was to lead to the ubiquitous BR Class 08 diesel shunter. *Authors' Collection*

Plate 44 An example of the light 2—6—0s designed by Ivatt is illustrated in this picture which shows No. 46401 in original condition still carrying the 1946 style 'LMS' on the tender. Burton 1950.

Authors' Collection

Plate 45 Ivatt 2—6—2T Class 2MT No. 41242 in service with the Southern Region April 1965. Only ten of this class were built before nationalisation but after 1948 this class was found on other regions and formed the basis for the BR standard class 2MT.

Authors' Collection

Nevertheless, until the advent of 10000 and 10001, the diesel locomotive was a non-proven quantity in all but the shunting category and in 1946, Ivatt introduced the first of three new class of steam locomotives to cater for secondary and light-weight duties and thus allow the elimination of further of the already heavily depleted pre-group types whose residual survivors were now becoming positively aged. The new designs were the Class 2 2—6—0 and 2—6—2Ts (originally Class 2F and 2P) and the Class 4 2—6—0s (originally Class 4F). These locomotives represented the new LMS operating philosophy applied right across the board. Hitherto, the secondary services of the LMS, as with all British railway companies, were generally entrusted to old life-expired designs, serving out their days before scrapping. Ivatt felt that even in this area, useful economies could be made by providing modern, easy to maintain locomotives, rather than use up superannuated and expensive to maintain older types. In consequence, all the features which had come to be regarded as modern were incorporated except for roller bearings, since it was not expected that their work would require any high speed running. How wrong this premise was can be judged from the nickname bestowed upon the little 2—6—0s by the Carlisle men — the 'Penrith Lizzies'; 'Penrith' from their home depot and 'Lizzie' from the fact that they could run — almost — like a 4—6—2. High praise indeed.

Plate 46 The Ivatt 2—6—0 4MT Class was introduced to fulfil the need for more 0—6—0s of the Class 4F design. Three only entered service before nationalisation and this picture shows one of the first batch in service. Note the double chimney, later replaced with a smaller version. This class was not a complete success when first introduced and these points are further discussed in *Volume III.*

Authors' Collection

All three classes positively bristled with Coleman features which had been developed in other locomotives but there was one feature of the Class 4 which was completely new and very visible — the high running plate some 7 ft 6 in above rail level. This was the result of Coleman attempting to produce flexible frames and thus reduce frame stresses when working in sharply curved sidings. Had we but known it at the time, the Class 4s were giving a fairly accurate preview of the soon to be introduced BR standard classes.

When introduced, these Ivatt locomotives were a little disappointing in their steaming capacity but alterations to chimney and blast pipes soon corrected the situation and they all became effective and popular machines. Mention of draughting problems suggests comparison with the Stanier '5XPs' and it is, even now, hard to realise that it was well into the BR period before British steam locomotive engineers were able to scientifically investigate the 'front-end' characteristics of steam locomotives — by which time it was almost too late. The surprising thing is how many designs managed to achieve a reasonable front end utilising little more than the empirical approach.

The final LMS designs also marked, at last, the end of the fitting to new designs of the particular type of Gresham and Craven live steam injector favoured by Derby, which had been used on all standard engines since 1923. A sigh of relief went up from all maintenance men (and drivers too) except, of course, the Midland men. One experienced observer has described this particular live steam injector as an atrocity which no locomotive man deserved having foisted upon him and which would kick off when running through a crossing! Unless a wary eye was kept upon it, the first intimation the crew may have got would be when the water level was well below where it should have been. Of course, the old type of injector remained in use on vast numbers of engines so the problem did not go away!

Thus it was that apart from introducing new visual lines to the locomotive stock, the LMS standardisation policy resulted in major improvements right across the board of locomotive operation. That the improvements may have gone unnoticed by many contemporary observers is because they rarely affected the outward appearance of the locomotives to any marked extent, save in the very last years. Evidence is now available to show that the LMS policy of massive new construction, far from being more extravagant than prolonging the life of older classes, showed considerable medium and long term benefit to the company. However, at the time, such matters were probably only obvious to those close to the centre of affairs. The soul of a pre-1948 privately owned railway company was never laid as bare to the public as its nationalised successor has been.

At nationalisation, the LMS possessed a large fleet of locomotives of modern design, many of which were capable of every type of work from express passenger to loose coupled coal with equal competence. They were light on maintenance (with one or two exceptions) and would achieve high mileages between repairs. Many of the up to date features had also been incorporated in the residual pre-group locomotives but these are too numerous to be mentioned here. Much of this work could justifiably be said to stem from Coleman — a first class 'back room boy' who rarely receives his due credit. But the major share of the credit must undoubtedly belong to Sir William Stanier for having the personality to still the conflicts of the early days and for recognising the talent which he inherited and encouraged to develop.

The LMS motive power department was not perfect, nothing ever is; but it is at least arguable that it had a better appreciation of the changing circumstances than was the case on any of the other British railways at the time of nationalisation and was unquestionably more fitted than the others to lead British locomotive development into the uncharted waters of the immediate post-war era. The key positions in the BR hierarchy to which many of Stanier's lieutenants succeeded was no more than their due.

Chapter 2   Motive Power Organisation

In the first chapter, mention was briefly made of some of the factors leading up to the large scale re-organisation of LMS motive power practices in the 1930s. It is now necessary to examine this particular subject in a little more detail; but it should be clearly understood from the outset that this was really a quite separate issue from the emotive and often controversial field of locomotive design, already discussed.

Although it took some little time to achieve a totally integrated company policy, there was no real doubt in anyone's mind that more efficient locomotive operating was a desirable ideal, no matter what particular locomotives were involved. The sheer size of the system and the complexity of the problem meant that it would inevitably take some time to work out a standard and coherent plan but there was no overriding reason why the attempt should not be made fairly quickly, as indeed it was by the simple expedient of building a great many Midland type locomotives. Ideally, a railway should be operated by the smallest possible number of locomotive classes (regardless of who designs them!) since standardisation achieves economies of scale, reduction in spares carried at sheds and so forth. Even before Stanier arrived, the number of engines on book stock had been reduced by some 2,000 from the more than 10,000 existing in 1923; and by 1936 the total was down to 7,691 units representing only 173 classes instead of 393 varieties. It was further planned to reduce totals to 136 classes with the completion of the 1937 programme and the ultimate aim was to run the railway with no more than about a dozen different types. This was never to be achieved, because of nationalisation, but nonetheless, the reduction in complexity actually attained was a considerable achievement over a span of little more than 20 years.

Thus it was that the infusion of large numbers of the early standard classes inevitably led to a reduction in maintenance costs even if for no other reason than that newer engines on the whole cost less to maintain than older ones. To further monitor maintenance, there was introduced in 1926 a standard 'engine history card' system whereby every locomotive on the railway had a record card raised on which was recorded not only details of mileages, allocations and the like but all repairs carried out on the locomotive from full heavy general repairs down to the most minor alterations. Each and every item was costed and quickly revealed which classes were proving excessively expensive. It was this sort of exercise which revealed, for example, that the apparently heavy cost of replacing LNWR 'Claughton' class 4–6–0s by new 'Patriot' types in the early 1930s would be recovered within six years or so by cheaper maintenance costs.

Largely as a result of these policies (many of which were enacted before the Stanier régime), quite a measure of 'streamlining' was achieved from an early stage; but the company clearly felt that locomotive standardisation and more cost conscious accounting was only a half way house. More still might be achieved by a thorough examination of the actual maintenance *procedures* as well as their costs. Thus it was that in 1933, the first modernisation scheme was approved and its success led to the major 'whole line' reorganisation of 1935 and afterwards. Essentially, the aim of the exercise was to achieve even more intensive utilisation of locomotives, thus enabling further significant reductions in stock to take place. It is with this major restructuring of LMS motive power organisation that the rest of this chapter will concern itself.

The grouping of 1923 obviously presented the British railways with a splendid opportunity of developing better methods of operating designed to meet the very different circumstances of the 1920s and 1930s. Previous practices varied considerably and the LMS inherited more of them than the other companies, so progress could not be achieved overnight. The problem required both investigation and rectification and the LMS tackled it by first identifying those aspects where improvement was required:

a) Greater operating efficiency with increased reliability and availability of locomotives.

b) Elimination of lost motion, wasteful energy and delay.

c) Increasing the number of locations where work can be brought to the man and not vice versa.

d) Reduction of physical effort by the work force.

The first need, therefore, was to analyse all operations, following upon which, remedies could be implemented, and at this point it is well to remind the reader that the LMS of the 1930s was a bigger railway in terms of employees and locomotives than the whole of BR today, so a reorganisation of this magnitude was no small task. In the event it was carried out progressively and carefully with much attention given to fact gathering before changing any procedures already in being.

Starting from the point when a locomotive was turned off shed ready for duty, the questions which naturally arose were related to how much work it could do during the next 24 hours. Past experience suggested that the engine rosters themselves constituted the final word so any improvement here would have immediate effect. A detailed study was made of the results from six sheds — unfortunately the actual locations and the reasons for their choice have not survived. The results were, however, published at the time and are repeated at *Table 3*. Clearly they revealed several areas of operation where there were potential time savings to be achieved both on and off shed. Detailed analysis of the situation suggested the following lines of approach:

a) Improvement of yard and shed layouts to enable a planned sequence of operations to take place in correct order in the minimum of time as follows:

    i)   Coal and water (simultaneously if feasible) } All by mechanical appliances where possible

    ii) Ash pit work

    iii) Turning

    iv) Stable on shed or return to preparation pit for next duty

TABLE 3. RESULTS OF SURVEYS TAKEN AT SIX SHEDS FOR WEEK ENDING FEBRUARY 25, 1933.

Shed	(1) Working trains or assisting (required) H. M.	(2) Shunting H. M.	(3) Marginal time between shed and station or depot H. M.	(4) Margins between trips in traffic — Known loco. requirements H. M.	(5) Margins between trips in traffic — Traffic H. M.	(6) Time running light (other than col. 7 eng. and bk.) or assisting (not required) H. M.	(7) Preparation time H. M.	(8) Disposal time H. M.	(9) Available time — Steam being raised H. M.	(10) Available time — Other H. M.	(11) Washing out — Waiting period H. M.	(12) Washing out — Time from emptying to refilling boiler H. M.	(13) Running repairs — Waiting — Staff not available H. M.	(14) Running repairs — Waiting — For material H. M.	(15) Running repairs — Time occupied H. M.	(16) Periodical examination — Waiting period H. M.	(17) Periodical examination — Time occupied H. M.	(18) At or waiting loco. repair shops — Waiting shops or waiting CME decision H. M.	(19) At or waiting loco. repair shops — At shops H. M.	(20) Waiting CME boiler inspection H. M.
'A' (freight), 84 engines	4 2	4 6	0 34	0 3	0 57	0 37	0 53	1 15	2 32	2 38	0 35	0 11	2 13	0 14	0 48	0 26	0 10	—	1 46	—
'B' (passenger), 76 engines	4 24	3 28	0 42	0 7	1 6	0 10	0 44	1 7	2 47	5 14	0 19	0 12	1 14	0 16	0 48	0 21	0 15	—	0 37	0 9
'C' (passenger and freight), 35 engines	4 25	1 39	0 30	0 2	2 18	0 13	0 49	1 26	1 59	3 41	0 3	0 9	2 3	1 27	1 29	0 1	0 8	0 50	0 48	—
'D' (passenger and freight), 60 engines	4 10	4 6	0 54	0 5	0 11	0 17	0 48	1 45	2 34	3 21	0 21	0 16	1 23	0 13	1 4	0 15	0 10	0 48	1 19	—
'E' (passenger and freight), 44 engines	4 18	2 43	0 27	0 5	1 39	0 11	0 43	0 47	2 19	4 12	0 13	0 14	3 14	0 24	1 0	0 26	0 5	—	1 0	—
'F' (freight), 128 engines	4 44	4 55	0 36	—	0 13	0 16	0 42	0 52	2 33	3 5	0 6	0 23	1 43	0 56	0 43	0 20	0 23	0 14	1 11	0 5
Average of six sheds	4 23	3 54	0 38	0 3	0 50	0 18	0 46	1 9	2 31	3 35	0 17	0 16	1 52	0 33	0 54	0 20	0 14	0 15	1 10	0 2

Column groups: columns (1)–(8) are **Engine hours on other than shed duties**; columns (9)–(20) are **Engine hours on shed duties**.

Plate 47 Stafford in 1964. A tank was only considered full when it overflowed and this picture, showing a 3F 0–6–0T taking water, has been included to illustrate this point. *Authors' Collection*

Plate 48 Workington, June 1964. This picture shows No. 43963, an ex-Midland Class 4F 0–6–0 taking water. Note that it is now paired with an LMS standard tender. *Authors' Collection*

Plate 49 This picture shows an LYR shed with a newly installed ash plant in use. The ash from the ashpan was raked out while the locomotive stood over the pit and the ash dropped through into a skip which was then raised and tipped into the wagon standing on the line running between the two disposal tracks. *NRM*

    b) Obtain greater technical efficiency to reduce casualties
    c) Provide modern machinery for running repairs at sheds
    d) Equip as many turntables as possible for mechanical operation
    e) Introduce a completely new organisation and maintenance structure for the whole of the company motive power department which would be designed from the outset to meet the new criteria.

Some of the above points are reasonably self-evident but the matter of shed layouts merits amplification. It was quickly discovered that the layout of the yard had an enormous effect upon the amount of time spent on shed by an engine between spells in traffic. Indeed, at one shed six hours were required in which to complete the disposal duties for an individual locomotive. However, merely to state the ideal order in which operations should take place did not solve the problem of the unsuitable shed layout. The company therefore devised its theoretical 'ideal' layout for a reorganised shed — *Fig 1*. Wherever possible, shed layouts were to be altered to conform as nearly as feasible to this model, allowing, of course, for any unavoidable site constraints. Merely achieving this degree of rationalisation frequently reduced disposal time from the previously acceptable two to three hours down to about one hour — and with less physical effort for the men as an additional bonus.

The first schemes for modernisation were approved in 1933 and within three years, 47 had been authorised at a total expenditure of £75,000. The improvements were immediate and, added to those already achieved by locomotive standardisation caused the miles per day per engine in use to rise from 94.6 in 1929 to 118.14 in 1936 and the hours per day per engine to climb from 11.37 to 13.74 over the same period. Interestingly, the mileage figure climbed steadily throughout

29

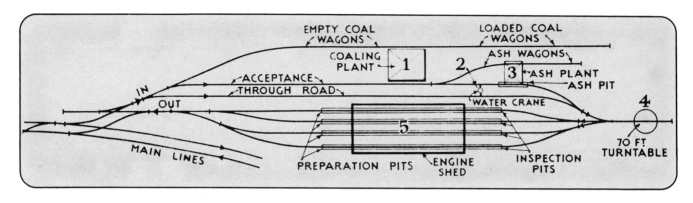

Fig. 1 Basic plan of reorganised motive power depot, showing locations of plant and sequence of disposal operations.

TABLE 4. LMSR OPERATING UNITS IN RELATION TO THE YEAR 1929 CONSIDERED AS 100

—	1929	1930	1931	1932	1933	1934	1935	1936	Percentage improvement in 1936 compared with 1929
1. Steam locomotives —									
Train-miles per train-hour									
Coaching	14.13	14.30	14.41	14.53	14.48	14.51	14.46	14.33	
	100	101.20	101.98	102.83	102.48	102.69	102.34	101.42	1.42
Freight	8.43	8.89	9.13	9.66	9.53	9.21	9.09	8.43	
	100	105.46	108.30	114.59	113.05	109.25	107.83	100.00	—
2. Assisting required mileage per									
100 train-miles —									
Coaching	1.72	1.45	1.26	1.29	1.33	1.73	1.32	1.29	
	100	84.30	73.26	75.00	77.33	100.58	76.74	75.00	25.0
Freight	6.04	4.78	3.45	2.91	2.93	2.96	2.78	2.80	
	100	79.14	57.12	48.18	48.51	49.01	46.03	46.36	53.64
3. Shunting per 100 train-miles —									
Coaching	8.99	8.91	8.89	8.89	8.60	8.30	8.10	7.98	
	100	99.11	98.99	98.89	95.66	92.32	90.10	88.77	11.23
Freight	71.16	70.04	68.89	68.33	68.63	68.72	68.40	69.25	
	100	98.43	96.81	96.02	96.44	96.57	96.12	97.32	2,68
4. Wagon-miles per train-engine-hour									
(including assisting and light) . .	238.38	252.14	262.16	274.96	275.18	268.26	267.20	250.03	
	100	105.77	109.98	115.35	115.44	112.53	112.09	104.89	4.89
Per total engine hour	119.15	123.06	126.78	129.52	130.15	129.03	129.44	124.50	
	100	103.28	106.40	108.70	109.23	108.29	108.64	104.49	4.49
5. Engine-miles per day per locomotive									
in use —									
Weekdays	94.60	95.18	99.54	102.76	106.77	110.48	115.58	118.14	
	100	100.61	105.22	108.63	112.86	116.79	122.18	124.88	24.88
6. Coal consumed in lb. per									
engine-mile —									
Steam locomotives									
Coaching	53.02	51.61	51.32	51.22	51.48	51.50	51.49	52.10	
	100	97.34	96.79	96.61	97.10	97.13	97.11	98.26	1.74
Freight	61.82	61.17	61.68	61.16	61.21	60.92	60.45	60.65	
	100	98.95	99.77	98.93	99.01	98.54	97.78	98.11	1.89
7. Oil consumed in pints per 100									
engine-miles —									
Steam locomotives	6.42	6.08	5.85	5.73	5.69	5.73	5.74	5.78	
	100	94.70	91.12	89.25	88.63	89.25	89.41	90.03	9.97

The figures relating to coal and oil consumption have been revised for each year, to bring them into line with new method adopted by Ministry of Transport from 1936, whereby coal consumed by purely shunting engines is not recorded separately, and oil consumed is not divided between coaching and freight.

NOTE. — The unfavourable results from 1936 under items 1 and 4 were due to abnormal climatic conditions during January-February, and November-December.

Plate 50 Cricklewood in May 1934 showing a Garratt 2—6—6—2T No. 4977 taking coal under the new mechanical coaling stage. Livery Code C15. *BR LMR*

the whole seven year period, partly explained by faster schedules, but the improvement in hours available was mostly confined to the 1933-6 period. *Table 4* gives additional details under more specific categories and it can be readily seen that certain improvements were more spectacular than others. At all events, the modernisation programme enabled the LMS to achieve yet another substantial reduction in locomotive stock numbers from 8,226 at the end of 1933 to 7,691 three years later and an overall reduction of some 25% compared with 1923.

It would be too simplistic to assume that improved shed layouts and a more standardised fleet represented the whole of the story in the LMS quest for more economical working. A close study of both *Tables 3* and *4* will indicate that other factors were also at work to effect an improvement. A particularly important factor affecting the time an engine was available for traffic purposes was the extent to which it was 'stopped' for repairs both at shops and running depots. To improve this aspect was the objective of the rather grandiosely titled 'Motive Power Area locomotive supply, repair, concentration and garage scheme', introduced generally in 1935 after a 'pilot' scheme trial in the Wellingborough district in 1934. The full 1935 scheme divided the system into 29 areas, three of which were in Scotland. Each was under the charge of a District Locomotive Superintendent and comprised one main or 'concentration' depot and a number of sub or 'garage' depots. The map (*Fig. 2*) shows the original scheme but the number of districts was later raised to 32. The 1935 scheme set the boundaries of the areas to coincide generally with traffic flow, to obviate light engine mileage as far as possible to and from main depots for repairs and to coincide with District Traffic Control areas as far as possible. This meant that in the majority of cases a District Controller dealt with only one District Locomotive Superintendent.

Prior to this reorganisation, the various LMS motive power depots had operated largely on the pre-group pattern of administration, even though the 'all-line' modernisation schemes had been started; but after 1935 the policy became to allocate locomotives on an area rather than a depot basis and, increasingly, the areas could be considered for working purposes as one large depot. Thus, for example, if a number of special trains had to be worked from a particular shed, engines were drafted there by the main depot in the area and it was no longer necessary to keep as many spare engines as

31

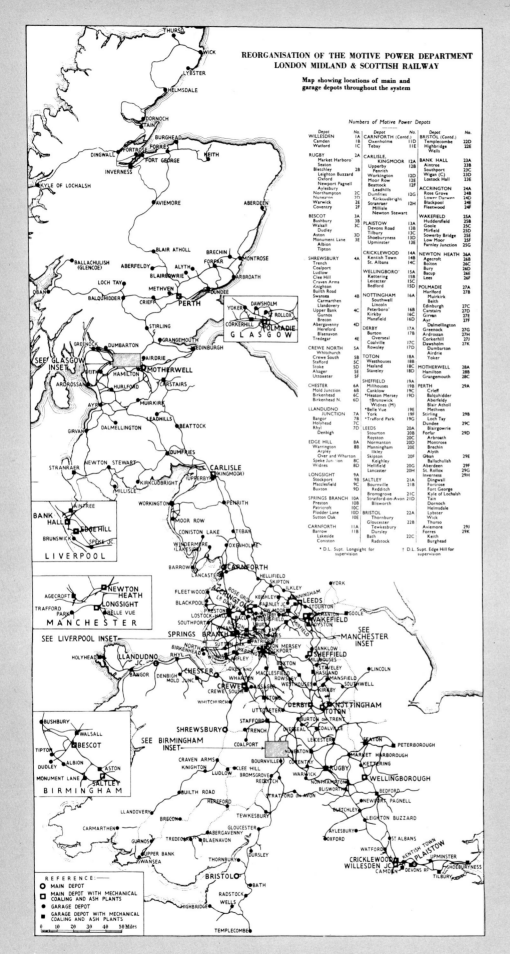

REORGANISATION OF THE MOTIVE POWER DEPARTMENT
LONDON MIDLAND & SCOTTISH RAILWAY

Map showing locations of main and
garage depots throughout the system

Numbers of Motive Power Depots

Depot	No.	Depot	No.	Depot	No.
WILLESDEN	1A	CARNFORTH (Contd.)		BRISTOL (Contd.)	
Camden	1B	Oxenholme	11D	Templecombe	22D
Watford	1C	Tebay	11E	Highbridge	22E
				Wells	
RUGBY	2A	CARLISLE,			
Market Harboro'		KINGMOOR	12A	BANK HALL	23A
Seaton		Upperby	12B	Aintree	23B
Bletchley	2B	Penrith		Southport	23C
Leighton Buzzard		Workington	12D	Wigan (C)	23D
Oxford		Moor Row	12E	Lostock Hall	23E
Newport Pagnell		Beattock	12F		
Aylesbury		Leadhills		ACCRINGTON	24A
Northampton	2C	Dumfries	12G	Rose Grove	24B
Nuneaton	2D	Kirkcudbright		Lower Darwen	24D
Warwick	2E	Stranraer	12H	Blackpool	24E
Coventry	2F	Millisle		Fleetwood	24F
		Newton Stewart			
BESCOT	3A			WAKEFIELD	25A
Bushbury	3B	PLAISTOW	13A	Huddersfield	25B
Walsall	3C	Devons Road	13B	Goole	25C
Dudley		Tilbury	13C	Mirfield	25D
Aston	3D	Shoeburyness	13D	Sowerby Bridge	25E
Monument Lane	3E	Upminster	13E	Low Moor	25F
Albion				Farnley Junction	25G
Tipton		CRICKLEWOOD	14A		
		Kentish Town	14B	NEWTON HEATH	26A
SHREWSBURY	4A	St. Albans	14C	Agecroft	26B
Trench				Bolton	26C
Coalport		WELLINGBORO'	15A	Bury	26D
Ludlow		Kettering	15B	Bacup	26E
Clee Hill		Leicester	15C	Lees	26F
Craven Arms		Bedford	15D		
Knighton				POLMADIE	27A
Builth Road		NOTTINGHAM	16A	Hurlford	27B
Swansea	4B	Southwell		Muirkirk	
Carmarthen		Lincoln		Beith	
Llandovery		Peterboro'	16B	Edinburgh	27C
Upper Bank	4C	Kirkby	16C	Carstairs	27D
Gurnos		Mansfield	16D	Girvan	27E
Brecon				Ayr	27F
Abergavenny	4D	DERBY	17A	Dalmellington	
Hereford		Burton	17B	Greenock	27G
Blaenavon		Overseal		Ardrossan	27H
Tredegar	4E	Coalville	17C	Corkerhill	27J
		Rowsley	17D	Dawsholm	27K
CREWE NORTH	5A			Dumbarton	
Whitchurch		TOTON	18A	Airdrie	
Crewe South	5B	Westhouses	18B	Yoker	
Stafford	5C	Hasland	18C		
Stoke	5D	Staveley	18D	MOTHERWELL	28A
Alsager	5E			Hamilton	28B
Uttoxeter	5F	SHEFFIELD	19A	Grangemouth	28C
		Millhouses	19B		
CHESTER	6A	Canklow	19C	PERTH	29A
Mold Junction	6B	*Heaton Mersey	19D	Crieff	
Birkenhead	6C	†Brunswick		Balquhidder	
Birkenhead N.	6D	Widnes (M)		Aberfeldy	
		*Belle Vue	19E	Blair Atholl	
LLANDUDNO		York	19F	Methven	
JUNCTION	7A	*Trafford Park	19G	Stirling	29B
Bangor	7B			Loch Tay	
Holyhead	7C	LEEDS	20A	Dundee	29C
Rhyl	7D	Stourton	20B	Blairgowrie	
Denbigh		Royston	20C	Forfar	29D
		Normanton	20D	Arbroath	
EDGE HILL	8A	Manningham	20E	Montrose	
Warrington	8B	Ilkley		Brechin	
Arpley		Skipton	20F	Alyth	
Speke Junction	8C	Keighley		Oban	29E
Widnes	8D	Hellifield	20G	Ballachulish	
		Lancaster	20H	Aberdeen	29F
LONGSIGHT	9A			St. Rollox	29G
Stockport	9B	SALTLEY	21A	Inverness	29H
Macclesfield	9C	Bournville	21B	Dingwall	
Buxton	9D	Redditch		Fortrose	
		Bromsgrove		Fort George	
SPRINGS BRANCH	10A	Stratford-on-Avon	21D	Kyle of Lochalsh	
Preston	10B	Blisworth		Tain	
Patricroft	10C			Dornoch	
Plodder Lane	10D	BRISTOL	22A	Helmsdale	
Sutton Oak	10E	Thornbury		Lybster	
		Gloucester		Wick	
CARNFORTH	11A	Tewkesbury		Thurso	
Barrow	11B	Dursley		Aviemore	29J
Lakeside		Bath	22C	Forres	29K
Coniston		Radstock		Keith	
				Burghead	

*D.L. Supt. Longsight for
supervision

†D.L. Supt. Edge Hill for
supervision

REFERENCE:—

- ○ MAIN DEPOT
- □ MAIN DEPOT WITH MECHANICAL COALING AND ASH PLANTS
- ● GARAGE DEPOT
- ■ GARAGE DEPOT WITH MECHANICAL COALING AND ASH PLANTS

0 10 20 30 40 50 Miles

Figure 2 This map is a photo-reduction of the original official LMS map issued at the time of reorganisation. In order to fit the page it is depicted only half full size and apologies are offered for any consequent loss of legibility.

Plate 51 (Opposite) Although the majority of turntables were revolved by human muscle power some vacuum operated turntables were installed and this picture, taken at Camden MPD, shows an unrebuilt 'Royal Scot' No. 46142 being turned using its vacuum to provide the power.

BR LMR

hitherto at each individual depot. Similarly, when engines became due for major examination, heavy running repairs or shopping, the complement at the 'garages' was maintained by the main depot. Thus on the one hand the locomotive stock of a particular area could be used to better advantage, thus needing fewer units, and most of the major examination and running repairs could be concentrated at the main depot — bringing the work to the men as it were.

To facilitate this operation, main depots were equipped with suitable machinery and the repair staff was augmented, where necessary, by the transfer of men from the sub depots. Engines were worked to the main depots in such planned sequence as to ensure the minimum amount of time standing before being taken in hand by the repair staff. One of the advantages of this system was that repairs could be carried out continuously through 24 hours if need be and it also allowed particular classes of work to be allocated to specified men with a consequent increase in efficiency.

In order to operate the new scheme it was necessary to devise regular locomotive inspections. The garage depots only undertook minor examinations and repairs which could be completed in less than 24 hours. Ideally these should all have been planned as routine operations under the 'Locomotive Maintenance and Mechanical Efficiency Scheme', better known to all LMS men as the 'X' scheme. The object of this scheme was to prevent the development of defects and maintain high mechanical efficiency by carrying out thorough and detailed examinations and repairs at predetermined intervals. This has been briefly alluded to in the previous chapter but essentially the aim was to try and synchronise minor examinations and repairs with the routine wash-out day. In this way, repetition repairs could be reduced or eliminated and most engines could be expected to run their predetermined periods between 'X' days without any other attention apart from routine inspection, preparation and disposal.

Plate 52 Edge Hill, August 1934. This view shows an old LNWR running shed with two 'Coal Tanks' and a 'Patriot' in the foreground.

V. Forster Collection

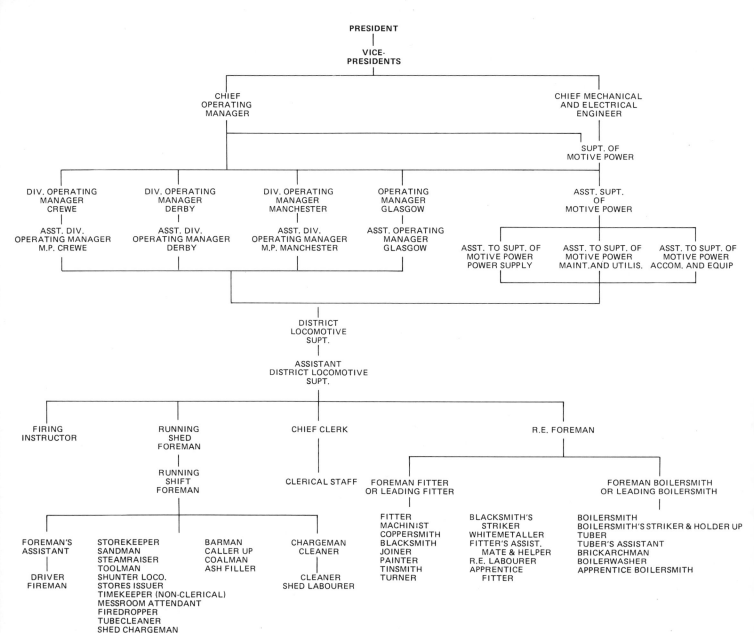

PRESIDENT

VICE-PRESIDENTS

CHIEF OPERATING MANAGER

CHIEF MECHANICAL AND ELECTRICAL ENGINEER

SUPT. OF MOTIVE POWER

DIV. OPERATING MANAGER CREWE

DIV. OPERATING MANAGER DERBY

DIV. OPERATING MANAGER MANCHESTER

OPERATING MANAGER GLASGOW

ASST. SUPT. OF MOTIVE POWER

ASST. DIV. OPERATING MANAGER M.P. CREWE

ASST. DIV. OPERATING MANAGER DERBY

ASST. DIV. OPERATING MANAGER M.P. MANCHESTER

ASST. OPERATING MANAGER GLASGOW

ASST. TO SUPT. OF MOTIVE POWER POWER SUPPLY

ASST. TO SUPT. OF MOTIVE POWER MAINT. AND UTILIS.

ASST. TO SUPT. OF MOTIVE POWER ACCOM. AND EQUIP

DISTRICT LOCOMOTIVE SUPT.

ASSISTANT DISTRICT LOCOMOTIVE SUPT.

FIRING INSTRUCTOR

RUNNING SHED FOREMAN

CHIEF CLERK

R.E. FOREMAN

RUNNING SHIFT FOREMAN

CLERICAL STAFF

FOREMAN FITTER OR LEADING FITTER

FOREMAN BOILERSMITH OR LEADING BOILERSMITH

FOREMAN'S ASSISTANT

STOREKEEPER
SANDMAN
STEAMRAISER
TOOLMAN
SHUNTER LOCO.
STORES ISSUER
TIMEKEEPER (NON-CLERICAL)
MESSROOM ATTENDANT
FIREDROPPER
TUBECLEANER
SHED CHARGEMAN

BARMAN
CALLER UP
COALMAN
ASH FILLER

CHARGEMAN CLEANER

CLEANER
SHED LABOURER

FITTER
MACHINIST
COPPERSMITH
BLACKSMITH
JOINER
PAINTER
TINSMITH
TURNER

BLACKSMITH'S STRIKER
WHITEMETALLER
FITTER'S ASSIST.
MATE & HELPER
R.E. LABOURER
APPRENTICE FITTER

BOILERSMITH
BOILERSMITH'S STRIKER & HOLDER UP
TUBER
TUBER'S ASSISTANT
BRICKARCHMAN
BOILERWASHER
APPRENTICE BOILERSMITH

DRIVER
FIREMAN

34

Locomotives were called forward by the main depot for the progressively more comprehensive examinations as their mileages since works attention built up, until finally, a given area would release certain of its locomotives for main works attention, after which the whole cycle would commence again.

Naturally, the intervals between periodic examination varied according to the type of locomotive and the duties performed. In general, engines with boiler pressure above 200 psi had the boilers washed out every 12-16 working days and those below 200 psi were attended to every 24-32 working days. These two intervals coincided with the 'X' day periods for passenger and freight tender engines respectively. The only major exception was the case of express passenger locomotives which were given 'X' day examinations every 6—8 working days — i.e. two per boiler washout period in general.

This careful attention to routine examination and maintenance paid good dividends both in reducing the number of casualties (i.e. unscheduled stoppages of engines) and in extending locomotive mileages between heavy works attention. For example, as early as 1936 casualties showed a better than 30% decrease from the 1934 figure and during the same period, engine miles per casualty had improved by over 50%. These were considerable achievements and were aided by the establishment of a motive power area league to foster friendly rivalry between areas on a competitive basis to try and improve the miles per engine casualty.

On the more ephemeral side, the new organisation was visually indicated by a new type of shed plate fixed to the smokeboxes of all engines. This was of oval shape carrying a number followed by a letter. The number indicated the area to which the locomotive was allocated while the letter indicated which specific shed within that area was its 'home' base as it were. The letter 'A' was usually reserved for the main concentration depot in any area.

For those who are uncertain about the exact place of this scheme in the general LMS management structure, the appended diagram (Fig. 3) may help. From this it can be clearly seen that the District Locomotive Superintendent occupied a key position in the LMS hierarchy. His own area organisation was a well defined structure but the Superintendent himself had a dual responsibility. On the one hand he had a direct link to the operating manager in dealing with the day to day running of services while on the other he had an equal responsibility to the CME's department when it came to the purely engineering aspects of locomotive management. To further amplify the diagram it should, perhaps, be pointed out that the post of running shed foreman was established at all depots including the main depot but that the R.E. Foreman was found *only* at the main depot, along with the bulk of the specialised maintenance staff.

Plate 53 (Right) Rowsley, ex-Midland Railway, in 1927. Two locomotives, one probably a Class 4F 0—6—0 and the other an old Kirtley 0—6—0 No. 2510, are shown being coaled. Note how the coal is transferred from the coal wagon in the skip up into the hopper before being dropped into the tenders. This method was much quicker than the incline ramp more usually employed by the Midland Railway. In the foreground is an ash pit and the locomotive runs over the pit, the damper doors are opened and the fireman goes into the pit to rake out the ashes using a long rake. Note fire irons lying by the side of the pit and the pile of ash from smokeboxes on the right of the picture. *BR LMR*

◀ **Figure 3 (Left)** Organisational diagram of the LMS Motive Power Department after reorganisation.

Plate 54 St. Rollox, September 1936, showing the Caledonian Railway coaling stage with an 0—6—0 on the line along which coal wagons were propelled to the point where they were unloaded into tubs. These were then tipped into the tenders of locomotives standing on the lower track.

V. Forster Collection

Plate 55 Windermere shed with an ex-LNWR 4—6—0 No. 8848 on the turntable. Unlike the table shown in *Plate 51* this is a hand operated unit. Livery Code C1.

Authors' Collection

Plate 56 Perth shed in 1930, showing 2—6—0 No. 13183 and Compound 4—4—0s Nos. 1144 and 921. Note that No 1144 has shields fitted to protect the locomotive from water splashed up from a leading locomotive when taking water double-headed. It will be seen that these shields are not fitted to No. 921.

G. Coltas

Plate 57 Willesden in July 1964. This picture has been included to give the reader some idea of the conditions under which locomotives were prepared for service right to the end of steam days. It shows a driver oiling and examining a BR standard 'Britannia' Class locomotive prior to leaving the shed, the latter having hardly changed since LMS days. The sun was shining on this occasion but it would have made no difference had there been a thunderstorm.

Authors' Collection

Plate 58 Camden in January 1937, showing 'Royal Scot' 4—6—0 No. 6167 *The Hertfordshire Regiment* under the coaling stage with another 'Royal Scot', No. 6101, in view. Livery Code for 6167 is A12.   *BR LMR*

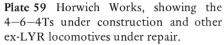

Plate 59 Horwich Works, showing the 4–6–4Ts under construction and other ex-LYR locomotives under repair.

NRM

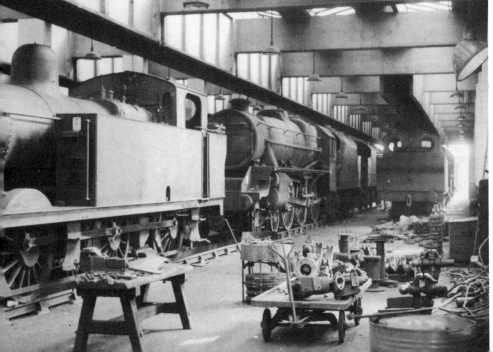

Plate 60 Stafford on 27th September, 1964. The view was typical of that seen inside running sheds and this picture, taken on a Sunday, shows workbenches for fitters and various parts, spares, etc. *Authors' Collection*

Plate 61 Class 5P5F No. 5016 being lifted from its wheels. Note that the outside valve gear has to be removed for this operation to take place. *A.G. Ellis*

There can be no real doubt that this formidable reorganisation paid handsome dividends to the LMS system and it also withstood the test of the Second World War very well. In spite of the acutely difficult conditions, quite outside those for which the structure had been devised, the LMS in 1947 could claim a locomotive availability as high as 15 hours out of 24 with only some 4% of the stock out of service for examination and/or repair. It is not really surprising that the newly formed BR organisation in 1948 adopted what was to all intents and purposes the old LMS system and it lasted substantially unaltered until 1973, long after the total demise of the steam locomotives for which it was designed.

The reorganisation of maintenance and other procedures at the depots was, however, only half of a two pronged attack which the company made on its motive power costs with the object of using very expensive assets (locomotive) more intensively. In the same way that locomotives queueing up for coal on shed are not earning revenue, so engines being repaired in the main company shops are costing the company money because they are not available for traffic — especially so if they are in shops for longer than necessary. Thus, the depot reorganisation went hand in hand with an equally formidable reorganisation of the main workshops which was actually the first of the two areas to be tackled.

The London and North Western Railway had set in motion the re-organisation of Crewe Works in 1921 but with the upheavals of grouping, it was several years before the scheme was completed. Put at its simplest, the aim was to introduce work-flow techniques by moving materials rather than men. In practice, the whole works was reorganised, even to the extent of building a whole new erecting shop. The results were dramatic. Whereas previously an engine could be under repair for up to 50 days, this figure was reduced to a maximum of twelve days with the smaller engines at times taking only eight days.

On the basis of a locomotive going into shops somewhere between once a year for the express passenger locomotives to once every 30 months for the smallest tank engines, the scope for saving was enormous. As an example, let us take the 130 engines of the 'Claughton' class. In 1928, the CME ruled that they, like all Class 5 4—6—0s, should be shopped every twelve months. Where this might have taken 40 days it now took about one third of the time so that each 'Claughton' was available for traffic on an additional 25—30 days per year. This was equivalent to having an extra ten engines — or having to build them.

When the ideas were later applied to Derby Works, the scope for savings was even greater. Midland practice decreed that an engine kept the same boiler and tender whilst under repair and on this basis the company worked on the assumption that no less than ten per cent of its locomotive stock would be under repair at any one time. At the cost of building a few spare boilers and the abandonment of some cherished shibboleths, the LMS was able to reduce the figure to two per cent. Since at that time, Derby was responsible for some 3,000 locomotives, this re-organisation was equivalent to putting another 240 into traffic.

It is against this background of systematic analysis followed by logical re-organisation that LMS motive power should be considered. It must, of course, be admitted that, compared with accounts of footplate wizardry (not infrequently written by people with more journalistic than engineering knowledge), details of workshop and shed re-organisation do not make riveting reading for enthusiasts. Consequently, aspects such as these have received but little attention in the popular railway press. This is singularly unfortunate since the availability of published work is one of the prime sources for making valid comparisons. After all, it would have served the LMS little purpose if all this re-organisation had shown no noticeable improvement over its rival companies.

Plate 62 Perth MPD, c1938. This is a not uncharacteristic summation of the Scottish scene during the 1930s — a combination of new standard types and almost exclusively Drummond-derived pre-group designs. *BR LMR*

It therefore seemed natural to turn to the records of the other three of the 'Big Four' grouped companies to see what their comparative unit and maintenance costs were like and how their performance improved over the same period of time. Much to our surprise, we could find no data at all which was in any way comparable to that which exists for the running cost of LMS locomotives. Could it be that Swindon, Doncaster and Eastleigh did not really know what their engines were costing them to operate? It rather seemed to point that way so we enquired further of a very senior railway engineer indeed (now retired) and discovered that while the other railways could certainly produce costings for motive power on an 'all line' basis at the time of nationalisation, it was difficult, if not impossible for them to isolate which classes were costing a disproportionate amount of money. Neither had there been many investigations as to costs which may have prompted overdue re-organisation. Again it is hardly surprising that the LMS influence was so strong after 1947 in motive power matters.

Nevertheless, by dint of not a little searching we have come up with one comparable statistic which we are prepared to offer, tongue slightly in cheek, to sum up this chapter; and it concerns the relative revenue mileages of those two eminent designs, the Gresley 'A4' and the Stanier 'Duchess' 4—6—2s. Setting prejudices aside, there was little to choose between them as locomotives. They were not identical, nor designed for precisely the same criteria, but they were contemporary with each other and broadly comparable in thermodynamic efficiency and performance on the road. They also ran in service for approximately the same number of years and the total built of each type was nearly enough the same (35 'A4s', 38 'Duchesses'). The 'A4s' averaged some 56,000 miles per year in revenue service, the 'Duchesses' some 64,000 per year. Put another way one would need eight 'A4s' to do the same mileage as seven 'Duchesses' and as far as the LMS was concerned, that one fact was a great deal more significant than the colour it was painted or even whether the machine was kept clean!

Chapter 3   Locomotive Numbering and Renumbering

THE 1923 RENUMBERING OF PRE-GROUP LOCOMOTIVES

For recording purposes, the locomotive stock in 1923 was divided into four main operating Divisions viz Midland, Western 'A', Western 'B' and Northern. These divisions broadly coincided with old company boundaries, smaller railways being incorporated into the appropriate major division. The Western 'A' and 'B' later became Western and Central respectively and we shall use the latter terminology.

The first visible effect of this early divisional standardisation was reflected in the comprehensive locomotive renumbering which the LMS instituted, the basis of which was the complete renumbering system which the Midland Railway had successfully adopted in 1907. The LMS version of the scheme was fairly simple. Each division was allocated a complete number series within which the engines were renumbered in the following order, passenger tender engines carrying the lowest numbers in any series: Passenger Tender; Passenger Tank; Freight Tank; Freight Tender. Within each fourfold subdivision of the main series, the least powerful machines (frequently amongst the oldest) were given the lowest numbers. This, in turn, involved the categorisation of all locomotives into some standardised power classification system. Again, the old Midland Railway system was adopted (see *Chapter 9*).

The result of this renumbering/power classifying operation was to bring together the pre-group locomotives in the following series:

a. Midland Division — LMS number series 1-4999

This division included the ex-MR locomotives, the ex-LT & SR locomotives (which had been incorporated into the MR lists in 1912), the ex-NSR locomotives and the ex-S & MJR locomotives. The Midland Division was allocated the first block of LMS numbers because the MR locomotives could, thereby, largely maintain their 1907 numbers, already allocated on the same basis, thus reducing by some considerable proportion the total amount of renumbering after grouping. In fact, only a few MR locomotives had to be renumbered in order to clear complete series for the NSR and S & MJR locomotives. There were, of course, gaps in the MR series arising from withdrawals between 1907 and 1923.

At a later date, some of the surviving NSR locomotives were renumbered into the Western Division series to clear blocks of numbers for new standard locomotives. It should finally be noted that on the absorption of the S & DJR locomotive stock in 1930, many of the engines concerned were given numbers in the Midland Division series, often taking numbers of MR locomotives withdrawn prior to 1930.

b. Western Division — LMS number series 5000-9999 (originally Western 'A')

The Western Division series was reserved for ex-LNWR classes plus those few locomotives which came from the Wirral Railway. At a later stage, many of the 5000-9999 series numbers were used again for new standard classes (see page 52). Although the 1923 re-numbering destroyed the 'number identity' of the old LNWR locomotives it did bring them together in complete classes for the first time ever.

c. Central Division — LMS number series 10000-12999

The Central Division, originally known as Western Division — 'B', included locomotives from the Cumbrian region (FR, M & CR, C & WR) and the KER as well as those from the LYR which was the principal contributor. The LYR engines were considerably in the majority in the division, but because of the numbering by *power class,* the other companies' engines occasionally interrupted the LYR series, especially in the 4—4—0 and 0—6—0 groups.

d. Northern Division — LMS number series 14000-17999

This series of numbers was used for all locomotives absorbed from the Scottish elements of the LMS. The Caledonian Railway contribution was numerically the largest but did not predominate in the sense that the LNWR did in the Western Division or even the LYR in the Central Division. Because of the over-riding power classification philosophy, many series of consecutive locomotive numbers had all three Scottish constituents represented in them. However, the individual locomotive *classes* were kept together by pre-group company.

Some numbers in the Northern Division 16XXX range were used for some 10-12 years on standard Class 3 0—6—0Ts. This necessitated some minor renumbering of pre-group classes.

This first renumbering policy, although not completed until the absorption of the S & DJR stock in 1930, catered adequately and logically for the 10,000-odd locomotives acquired by the LMS in 1923. There were also close on 8,000 vacant numbers available for allocation to new standard classes. However, although in many respects the new locomotives could be fitted logically into the pre-group series, there were anomalies and difficulties and these are considered below.

A full list of the 1923 LMS numbers by locomotive class is given at *Table 5.*

Main text continues on page 46.

TABLE 5. LMS 1923 NUMBER ALLOCATIONS —
PRE-GROUP AND NON-STANDARD POST-GROUP LOCOMOTIVES

NOTE: This table includes all pre-group locomotives which were allocated LMS Capital stock running numbers. It should, however, be appreciated that a considerable number of engines were scrapped too soon after the grouping to receive their allotted LMS series numbers, while some engines were scrapped before the new LMS numbers were even allocated.

LMS NUMBER SERIES	PRE-GROUP COMPANY	WHEEL ARRANGEMENT	LOCOMOTIVE TYPE/CLASS	POWER CLASS 1923	1928
1-22	MR	2–4–0	Kirtley '156' Class } double frame	1	1P
23-67	MR	2–4–0	Kirtley '800' Class	1	1P
68-126	MR	2–4–0	Kirtley '890' Class } inside frame	1	1P
127-146	MR	2–4–0	Kirtley '1070' Class	1	1P
147-156	MR	2–4–0	Johnson 6' 3" design	1	1P
157-191	MR	2–4–0	Johnson 6' 6½" design	1	1P
192-196	MR	2–4–0	Johnson 6' 9" design ('1400' Class)	1	1P
197-206	MR	2–4–0	Johnson 7' 0½" design	1	1P
207-216	MR	2–4–0	Johnson 6' 9" design (as per 192-6)	1	1P
217-221	MR	2–4–0	Johnson 6' 6½" design (as per 157-91)	1	1P
222-271	MR	2–4–0	Johnson 6' 9" design (as per 192-6)	1	1P
272-281	MR	2–4–0	Johnson 7' 0" design (as per 197-206)	1	1P
290	SMJR	2–4–0	Beyer Peacock design	1	—
300-309	MR	4–4–0	Johnson 6' 6½" design (unrebuilt)	1	1P
310-327	MR	4–4–0	Johnson 7' 0½" design (unrebuilt)	1	1P
328-562	MR	4–4–0	Rebuilt Johnson designs and Fowler superheated design	2	2P
595-598	NSR	4–4–0	Adams 'G' Class	3	3P
599	NSR	4–4–0	Adams 'KT' Class	3	—
600-683	MR	4–2–2	Johnson designs	1	—
700-779	MR	4–4–0	Johnson 'Belpaire' Class	3	3P
990-999	MR	4–4–0	Deeley 2-cylinder simple design	4	—
1000-1004	MR	4–4–0	Johnson (rebuilt Fowler) 3-cylinder compound	4	4P
1005-1044	MR	4–4–0	Deeley 3-cylinder compound	4	4P
1200-1225	MR	0–4–4T	Kirtley design (double frame)	1	1P
1226-1430	MR	0–4–4T	Johnson designs	1	1P
1431-1439	NSR	0–4–4T	Adams 'M' Class	3	3P
1440-1451	NSR	2–4–0T	Clare 'B' Class	1	1P
1454-1459	NSR	2–4–2T	Longbottom 'A' and 'B' Class (converted)	1	1P
1500-1527	MR	0–4–0ST	Johnson designs	—	0F
1528-1537	MR	0–4–0T	Deeley design	—	0F
1550-1598	NSR	0–6–0T	Longbottom 'D' Class	2	2F
1599	NSR	0–6–0T	Hookham experimental 4-cylinder design, rebuilt in 1924 to 0–6–0 tender type	—	—
1600-1601	NSR	0–6–0ST	Hudswell-Clarke design (rebuilt)	1	1F
1602-1603	NSR	0–6–0T	Kerr-Stuart design	1	1F
1605/1607	MR	0–6–0T	Kirtley design (double frame)	1	—
1606/1608	MR	0–6–0T	ex-Severn and Wye and Severn Bridge	1	—
1610-1619	MR	0–6–0T	Kirtley design (inside frame)	1	—
1620-1899	MR	0–6–0T	Johnson designs	1	1F
1900-1959	MR	0–6–0T	Rebuilt Johnson 'heavy' freight tank	3	3F
2000-2039	MR	0–6–4T	Deeley design	3	3P
2040-2047	NSR	0–6–4T	Adams 'C' Class	5	5F
2048-2055	NSR	0–6–4T	Adams/Hookham 'F' Class	4	4P
2100-2107	MR(LT&SR)	4–6–4T	R.H. Whitelegg design	3	3P
2110-2145	MR(LT&SR)	4–4–2T	Designed by W. Adams of LSWR	1	1P
2146-2157	MR(LT&SR)	4–4–2T	T. Whitelegg design (rebuilt from Class 2)	3	3P
2158-2175	MR(LT&SR)	4–4–2T	T. Whitelegg design	2	2P
2176-2179	MR(LT&SR)	4–4–2T	T. Whitelegg design (built new as Class 3)	3	3P
2110-2134) 2151-2160) (second numbers)	MR(LT&SR)	4–4–2T	LMS built version of final LT&SR type	3	3P
2180-2186	NSR	4–4–2T	Adams 'K' Class	3	3P
2220-2233	MR(LT&SR)	0–6–2T	T. Whitelegg design	3	3F
2234-2239	NSR	0–6–2T	Longbottom 'DX' Class	2	2F
2240-2273	NSR	0–6–2T	Adams 'L'/'New L' Class	3	3F
2290	MR	0–10–0	Fowler Banking engine	Unclassified	
2300-2302	SMJR	0–6–0	Beyer-Peacock design (double frame)	2	2F
2303	SMJR	0–6–0	Stroudley (ex-LB&SCR) design	2	—
2304-2311	SMJR	0–6–0	Beyer-Peacock design (double frame)	1&2	1F
2320-2331	NSR	0–6–0	Dodds 'E' Class	1	1F
2334-2342	NSR	0–6–0	Dodds 'E' Class	1	1F
2332-2333	NSR	0–6–0	Sharp Stewart	1	1F
2343-2350	NSR	0–6–0	Longbottom '100' Class	2	2F
2351-2356	NSR	0–6–0	Pettigrew (Furness Rly) design	2	2F

LMS NUMBER SERIES	PRE-GROUP COMPANY	WHEEL ARRANGEMENT	LOCOMOTIVE TYPE/CLASS	POWER CLASS 1923	POWER CLASS 1928
2357-2358	NSR	0—6—0	Adams 'New 100' Class	2	2F
2359-2366	NSR	0—6—0	Adams 'H' and 'HI' Class	3	3F
2367	NSR	0—6—0	Hookham 4-cylinder type (ex-No. 1599)	3	—
2369 2382-2398	MR	0—6—0	Kirtley 'straight frame' engines whose ex-MR numbers in the lower 23xx series were required for NSR locomotives. Double frame type	1	—
2399-2867	MR	0—6—0	Kirtley design (curved top double frame type)	1&2	1F&2F
2898-2899	MR(LT&SR)	0—6—0	Engines originally built for the Ottoman Railway	2	2F
2900-3129	MR	0—6—0	Johnson designs	2	2F
3130-3764	MR	0—6—0	Johnson designs generally as per 2900-3129 plus rebuilds to Class 3 (numbers intermixed)	2&3	2F&3F
3765-3834	MR	0—6—0	Johnson/Deeley designs	3	3F
3835-4026	MR	0—6—0	Fowler design (superheated)	4	4F
5000-5079	LNWR	2—4—0	Webb 'Precedent' Class	1	1P
5080-5109	LNWR	2—4—0	Webb 'Waterloo' Class	1	1P
5110-5117	LNWR	4—4—0	Webb 'Jubilee' Class (Compound)	2	—
5118-5130	LNWR	4—4—0	Webb 'Alfred the Great' Class (Compound)	2	—
5131-5186	LNWR	4—4—0	Webb 'Renown' Class (Simple)	2	2P
5187-5266	LNWR	4—4—0	Whale 'Precursor' Class (saturated)	2	2P
5270-5319	LNWR	4—4—0	Whale 'Precursor' Class (superheated)	3	3P
5320-5409	LNWR	4—4—0	Bowen-Cooke 'George the Fifth' Class	3	3P
5450-5554	LNWR	4—6—0	Whale 'Experiment' Class	3	3P
5600-5845	LNWR	4—6—0	Bowen-Cooke 'Prince of Wales' Class	4	4P
5900-6029	LNWR	4—6—0	Bowen-Cooke 'Sir Gilbert Claughton' Class	5	5P
6400-6419	LNWR	0—4—2ST	Webb design (wrongly classified as passenger tanks and later numbered more logically as 7850-69 in the freight tank series)	1	1F
6420-6434	LNWR	2—4—0T	Webb design	1	1P
6435-6438	LNWR(NLR)	4—4—0T	Adams design	1	—
6439-6512	LNWR(NLR)	4—4—0T	Adams and Park designs	1	1P
6515-6600	LNWR	2—4—2T	Webb 4' 6" design	1	1P
6601-6757	LNWR	2—4—2T	Webb 5' 6" design	1	1P
6758-6761	WIRRAL	2—4—2T	Webb (ex-LNWR) 4' 6" design	1	1P
6762	WIRRAL	2—4—2T	Aspinall (ex-LYR) design	2	2P
6770-6775	WIRRAL	0—4—4T	Beyer-Peacock design	1	—
6776	WIRRAL	0—4—4T	Hunter design	2	2P
6780-6829	LNWR	4—4—2T	Whale 'Precursor' Tank	3	3P
6830	WIRRAL	4—4—2T	Beyer-Peacock design	1	—
6850-6851	WIRRAL	4—4—4T	Hunter design	1	—
6860-6936	LNWR	0—6—2T	Webb 'Watford' Tank	2	2P
6948-6949	WIRRAL	0—6—4T	Beyer-Peacock design	2	—
6950-6996	LNWR	4—6—2T	Bowen-Cooke 'Prince of Wales' Tank	4	4P
7200-7205	LNWR	0—4—0T	Webb design well tanks for works use	—	—
7206-7216	LNWR	0—4—0ST	Ramsbottom design	—	0F
7217	LNWR(NLR)	0—4—2ST	Sharp Stewart Crane engine	—	—
7220-7457	LNWR	0—6—0ST	Ramsbottom 'Special' tank	2	2F
7458-7502	LNWR	0—6—0ST	Webb design with 'square' saddle	2	2F
7503-7532	LNWR(NLR)	0—6—0T	Park design	2	2F
7550-7841	LNWR	0—6—2T	Webb 'Coal' tank	2	2F
7870-7899	LNWR	0—8—2T	Bowen-Cooke design	6	6F
7930-7959	LNWR	0—8—4T	Beames design (built by LMS)	7	7F
8000-8087	LNWR	0—6—0	Ramsbottom 'DX' Class	1	1F
8088-8314	LNWR	0—6—0	Webb 'Coal' engines	2	2F
8315-8624	LNWR	0—6—0	Webb 'Cauliflowers' (not 8328-9 which were blank numbers)	2	2F
8700-8869	LNWR	4—6—0	Whale '19" Goods'	4	4F
8900-8952	LNWR	0—8—0	Webb 'B' Class (compound)	3	3F
8953-8967	LNWR	0—8—0	Whale 'C' Class	4	4F
8968-9001	LNWR	0—8—0	Whale 'C1' Class	3	3F
9002-9064	LNWR	0—8—0	Whale 'D' Class	5	5F
9065-9154	LNWR	0—8—0	Whale 'G' Class	5	5F
9155-9394	LNWR	0—8—0	Bowen-Cooke 'G1' Class	6	6F
9395-9454	LNWR	0—8—0	Bowen-Cooke 'G2' Class	7	7F
9600-9609	LNWR	2—8—0	Webb 'E' Class (compound)	3	—
9610-9615	LNWR	2—8—0	Webb 'F' Class (compound)	3	—
9616-9665	ex-ROD	2—8—0	Robinson GCR design	7	7F
10000	LYR	2—4—0	Ramsbottom (ex-LNWR) design modified as CME's personal coupé	—	—
10002	FR	2—4—0	Sharp Stewart design	—	—
10005-10007	M&CR	2—4—0	Smellie design	—	—
10010-10013	M&CR	0—4—2	Smellie design	1	—
10100-10101	LYR	4—4—0	Barton-Wright Class 2	2	2P

LMS NUMBER SERIES	PRE-GROUP COMPANY	WHEEL ARRANGEMENT	LOCOMOTIVE TYPE/CLASS	POWER CLASS 1923	1928
10102-10130	LYR	4—4—0	Aspinall Class 2	2	2P
10131-10134	FR	4—4—0	5' 7½" design	1	1P
10135-10142	FR	4—4—0	Pettigrew 6' 0" design	1	1P
10143-10146	FR	4—4—0	Pettigrew 6' 6" design	1	1P
10150-10183	LYR	4—4—0	Aspinall Class 3	2	2P
10185-10188	FR	4—4—0	Pettigrew 6' 0" design	2	2P
10190-10195	LYR	4—4—0	Aspinall Class 4 (superheated)	2	2P
10300-10339	LYR	4—4—2	Aspinall Class 7 (1400 Class)	2	2P
10400-10404	LYR	4—6—0	Hughes Class 8 (saturated)	—	—
10405-10474	LYR	4—6—0	Hughes Class 8 (superheated) — some LMS built	5	5P
10600-10617	LYR	0—4—0T	Hughes Railmotor	—	—
10618	M&CR	0—4—4T	Robinson design	—	—
10619-10620	FR	2—4—2T	Sharp Stewart design	—	—
10621-10821	LYR	2—4—2T	Aspinall design (short bunker)	2	2P
10822-10899	LYR	2—4—2T	Aspinall/Hughes design (long bunker)	2	2P
10900-10954	LYR	2—4—2T	Hughes design (superheated)	3	3P
11080-11085	FR	4—4—2T	Pettigrew design	1	1P
11100-11104	FR	4—6—4T	Rutherford design	4	4P
11110-11119	LYR	4—6—4T	Hughes design (built by LMS)	5	5P
11200	LYR	0—4—0ST	Vulcan Foundry design	—	0F
11201-11257	LYR	0—4—0ST	Aspinall design	—	0F
11258	FR	0—4—0ST	Sharp Stewart design	—	—
11259-11260	M&CR	0—4—0T	Neilson design	—	—
11300-11301	KER	0—6—0ST	Hudswell-Clarke design	—	—
11302	KER	0—6—0T	Manning-Wardle design	—	—
11303-11532	LYR	0—6—0ST	Barton-Wright/Aspinall design	2	2F
11533-11546	LYR	0—6—0T	Aspinall Dock tank	2	2F
11547-11548	FR	0—6—0T	Ex-Whitehaven, Cleator & Egremont Railway design	—	—
11549-11552	FR	0—6—0T	Sharp Stewart design	1	—
11553-11562	FR	0—6—0T	Pettigrew design	2	2F
11563	M&CR	0—6—0T		1	—
11564-11568	C&WR	0—6—0ST		1&2	—
11600-11601	LYR	0—6—2T	Barton Wright '22A' Class	1	1F
11602-11621	LYR	0—6—2T	Barton Wright '22' Class	1	1F
11622-11624	FR	0—6—2T	Pettigrew 4' 8" design	3	—
11625-11640	FR	0—6—2T	Pettigrew 5' 1" design	3	3F
11641-11644	FR	0—6—2T	Pettigrew 4' 7½" design	3	3F
11680	KER	2—6—0T	Manning-Wardle design	1	—
11700-11716	LYR	2—6—2T	Hoy '26' Class	3	—
11800-11804	LYR	0—8—2T	Hughes '32' Class	6	6F
12000-12014	FR	0—6—0	Sharp Stewart design	1	—
12015-12064	LYR	0—6—0	Barton Wright '25' Class	2	2F
12065-12076	FR	0—6—0	Sharp Stewart/Pettigrew design	1	1F
12077-12082	M&CR	0—6—0		1	—
12083-12467	LYR	0—6—0	Aspinall '27' Class	2	3F
12468-12479	FR	0—6—0	Pettigrew 4' 8" design	2	2F
12480-12483	FR	0—6—0	Pettigrew 5' 1" design	2	2F
12484-12493	M&CR	0—6—0		2	2F
12494-12512	FR	0—6—0	Pettigrew 4' 7½" design	3	3F
12513-12514	M&CR	0—6—0	Adamson design	3	3F
12515-12619	LYR	0—6—0	Aspinall/Hughes '28' Class	3	3F
12700-12759	LYR	0—8—0	Aspinall '30' Class (small boiler)	6	6F
12760-12770	LYR	0—8—0	Hughes '30' Class (compound)	6	—
12771-12839	LYR	0—8—0	Hughes '30' Class (large boiler, saturated)	6	6F
12840-12994	LYR	0—8—0	Hughes '31' Class (large boiler, superheated)	7	7F
14000	GSWR	2—4—0	J. Stirling design	—	—
14001-14002	GSWR	2—4—0	Smellie design	—	—
14010	CR	4—2—2	Neilson design	1	1P
14100-14107	CR	4—4—0	Brittain design ('Oban Bogies')	1	1P
14108-14115	CR	4—4—0	D. Drummond design	1	1P
14116-14137	GSWR	4—4—0	Smellie 6' 1¼" design		
14138-14156	GSWR	4—4—0	Smellie 6' 9½" design		
14157-14202	GSWR	4—4—0	Manson 6' 9½" design		
14203-14212	GSWR	4—4—0	Manson 5' 9" design	1	1P&2P
14213-14227	GSWR	4—4—0	Manson 6' 1¼" design		
14228-14243	GSWR	4—4—0	J. Stirling 7' 1" design		
14244-14270	GSWR	4—4—0	Manson 6' 9½" designs (two types)		
14271-14276	HR	4—4—0	Jones 'Strath' Class	1	1P
14277	HR	4—4—0	Jones 'Skye Bogie'	1	1P
14278	HR	4—4—0	Jones 'Bruce' Class	1	1P

LMS NUMBER SERIES	PRE-GROUP COMPANY	WHEEL ARRANGEMENT	LOCOMOTIVE TYPE/CLASS		POWER CLASS 1923	1928
14279-14285	HR	4—4—0	Jones 'Skye Bogie'		1	1P
14290-14310	CR	4—4—0	D. Drummond/Lambie design		2	2P
14311-14325	CR	4—4—0	McIntosh 'Dunalastair I' Class		2	2P
14326-14336	CR	4—4—0	McIntosh 'Dunalastair II' Class	saturated	2	2P
14337-14348	CR	4—4—0	McIntosh 'Dunalastair III' Class		2	2P
14349-14365	CR	4—4—0	McIntosh 'Dunalastair IV' Class		2	2P
14366-14378	GSWR	4—4—0	Manson 6' 9½" design		2	2P
14379-14396	HR	4—4—0	Jones 'Loch' Class		2	2P
14397-14416	HR	4—4—0	P. Drummond 'Small Ben' Class		2	2P
14417-14422	HR	4—4—0	P. Drummond 'Large Ben' Class		2	2P
14430-14433	CR	4—4—0	McIntosh 'Dunalastair II' Class	superheated	3	3P
14434-14437	CR	4—4—0	McIntosh 'Dunalastair III' Class		3	3P
14438-14460	CR	4—4—0	McIntosh 'Dunalastair IV' Class		3	3P
14461-14508	CR	4—4—0	Pickersgill design		3	3P
14509	GSWR	4—4—0	Whitelegg rebuild of Manson 4-cylinder design		3	3P
14510-14521	GSWR	4—4—0	P. Drummond design		3	3P
14522-14523	HR	4—4—0	Cumming design		3	3P
14600-14608	CR	4—6—0	McIntosh '55' Class		3	3P
14609-14618	CR	4—6—0	McIntosh '908' Class		3	3P
14619-14626	CR	4—6—0	Pickersgill '191' Class		3	3P
14630-14655	CR	4—6—0	Pickersgill '60' Class (some built by LMS)		4	4P
14656-14674	GSWR	4—6—0	Manson design		3	3P
14675-14693	HR	4—6—0	P. Drummond 'Castle' Class		3	3P
14750-14751	CR	4—6—0	McIntosh '49' Class		4	4P
14752-14755	CR	4—6—0	McIntosh '903' Class		4	4P
14756-14761	CR	4—6—0	Smith 'River' Class (designed for HR)		4	4P
14762-14769	HR	4—6—0	Cumming 'Clan' Class		4	4P
14800-14803	CR	4—6—0	Pickersgill '956' Class		5	5P
15000-15001	CR	0—4—2ST	D. Drummond design for Killin Branch		—	—
15010-15012	HR	4—4—0T	Jones design		—	—
15013-15017	HR	4—4—0T	Dübs & Co design		—	—
15020-15031	CR	4—4—0T	Lambie design		1	1P
15050-15054	HR	0—4—4T	Jones/Drummond design		—	—
15100-15114	CR	0—4—4T	D. Drummond design		1	1P
15115-15124	CR	0—4—4T	McIntosh '19' Class		2	2P
15125-15146	CR	0—4—4T	McIntosh '92' Class		2	2P
15147-15158	CR	0—4—4T	McIntosh 'Balerno' Class		1	1P
15159-15240	CR	0—4—4T	McIntosh '439' Class		2	2P
15241-15244	GSWR	0—4—4T	Smellie design		1	—
15245-15254	GSWR	0—4—4T	Manson design		1	1P
15260-15269	GR	0—4—4T	McIntosh '439' Class (built by LMS)		2	2P
15300-15307	HR	0—6—4T	P. Drummond design		4	4P
15350-15361	CR	4—6—2T	Pickersgill design		4	4P
15400-15405	GSWR	4—6—4T	Whitelegg design		5	5P
16000	CR	0—4—0ST	Barclay design		—	—
16001-16002	CR	0—4—0ST	Dübs design		—	—
16003-16007	CR	0—4—0ST	Neilson design		—	0F
16008-16039	CR	0—4—0ST	D. Drummond/McIntosh design		—	0F
16040-16043	GSWR	0—4—0ST	Various designs		—	—
16044-16049	GSWR	0—4—0T	Manson design		—	—
16050-16051	G&PJt	0—4—0ST	Neilson design		—	—
16080-16085	GSWR	0—4—4T	Manson design		—	—
16100-16102	CR	0—6—0ST	D. Drummond design		—	—
16103-16117	GSWR	0—6—0T	Manson design		—	—
16118-16119	HR	0—6—0T	Stroudley design		—	—
16150	CR	0—6—0ST	Brittain design		1	—
16151-16173	CR	0—6—0T	McIntosh design		2	2F
16200-16224	CR	0—6—0ST	D. Drummond design		3	3F
16225-16229	CR	0—6—0ST	Lambie design		3	3F
16230-16376	CR	0—6—0T	McIntosh design		3	3F
16377-16379	GSWR	0—6—0T	P. Drummond design		2	2F
16380-16382	HR	0—6—0T	P. Drummond design		2	2F
16383	HR	0—6—0T	Stroudley design (as per 16118-19) — wrongly numbered after 16380-2 and the mistake never rectified		—	—
16400-16409	GSWR	0—6—2T	Whitelegg design		3	3F
16410-16427	GSWR	0—6—2T	P. Drummond design		3	3F
16500-16505	CR	0—8—0T	McIntosh '492' Class		4	4F
17000-17020	CR	0—4—2	Brittain design		1	1F
17021-17075	GSWR	0—4—2	P. Stirling and J. Stirling designs		1	1F
17100	GSWR	0—6—0	P. Stirling design		—	—

LMS NUMBER SERIES	PRE-GROUP COMPANY	WHEEL ARRANGEMENT	LOCOMOTIVE TYPE/CLASS	POWER CLASS 1923	1928
17101-17102	CR	0—6—0	Ex-Solway Junction Railway engines	—	—
17103-17111	GSWR	0—6—0	J. Stirling design	1	—
17112-17164	GSWR	0—6—0	Smellie designs	2	2F
17165-17202	GSWR	0—6—0	Manson design	2	2F
17203-17212	GSWR	0—6—0	Smellie design rebuilt by Manson	2	2F
17230-17392	CR	0—6—0	D. Drummond 'Jumbo' design	2	2F
17393-17473	CR	0—6—0	McIntosh design	2	2F
17474-17522	GSWR	0—6—0	Manson designs	2&3	2F&3F
17523-17524	GSWR	0—6—0	Whitelegg design	3	3F
17550-17628	CR	0—6—0	McIntosh '812' Class	3	3F
17629-17645	CR	0—6—0	McIntosh '652' Class	3	3F
17646-17649	CR	0—6—0	McIntosh '30' Class	3	3F
17650-17692	CR	0—6—0	Pickersgill design	3	3F
17693-17704	HR	0—6—0	P. Drummond design	3	3F
17750-17764	GSWR	0—6—0	P. Drummond design	4	4F
17800-17804	CR	2—6—0	McIntosh '34' Class	3	3F
17820-17830	GSWR	2—6—0	P. Drummond design	4	4F
17900-17904	CR	4—6—0	McIntosh '918' Class	3	3F
17905-17915	CR	4—6—0	McIntosh '179' Class	3	3F
17916-17930	HR	4—6—0	Jones 'Goods'	4	4F
17950-17957	HR	4—6—0	Cumming 'Clan Goods'	4	4F
17990-17997	CR	0—8—0	McIntosh '600' Class	6	—

INITIAL NUMBERING OF 'NON-STANDARD' NEW LOCOMOTIVES

Unlike the LNER, the LMS did not build many non-standard engines. In most cases, the engines which were built represented outstanding orders for already existing pre-group designs although, in two cases, new types did emerge (the Beames LNWR type 0—8—4T and the Hughes LYR type 4—6—4T). The non-standard locomotives were numbered logically with their pre-group 'relations' in the appropriate divisional lists. The full list of types was as follows:

Midland Division (apart from classes standardised by the LMS)
LT & SR type 4—4—2Ts   (LMS Numbers: 2110-34; 2151-60)
NSR type 0—6—2Ts   (LMS Numbers: 2270-3)
NSR design 0—6—0 (ex 0—6—0T)   (LMS Number: 2367 (ex-1st LMS 1599))

Western Division
One only 'Prince of Wales' Class 4—6—0   (LMS Number: 5845)
LNWR type 0—8—4Ts (new design)   (LMS Numbers: 7930-59)

Central Division
LYR type 4—6—0s   (LMS Numbers: 10434-74)
LYR type 4—6—4Ts (new design derived from
the 4—6—0 locomotives)   (LMS Numbers: 11110-19)

Northern Division
CR '60' Class 4—6—0s   (LMS Numbers: 14630-49)
CR modified '439' Class 0—4—4Ts   (LMS Numbers: 15260-9)

The detailed coverage of these locomotives will be found in the appropriate pre-group sections and their running numbers are incorporated in *Table 5*.

One further non-standard class remains to be considered. In 1928, the LMS rebuilt 20 of the ex-LNWR 'Claughton' Class 4—6—0 engines with large boilers. In most respects, these properly fall into the LNWR section and have been included there. It should, however, be mentioned that their boiler design formed the basis of that used on the LMS standard 'Patriot' 4—6—0 class.

Plate 63 (Opposite) LMS built *Prince of Wales* No. 5845 ▶ at Crewe in crimson lake, Livery Code A1. This picture provides the reader with a good impression of the outside Walschaerts valve gear locomotives known as 'Tishies'. This was one of relatively few LNW locos to be given the full version of the first LMS crimson lake livery. The reader's attention is drawn to the lining on these locomotives and the fact that on the original print there does not appear to be any lining next to the cab front.   *NRM*

Plate 64 The final design of LNWR locomotive was an 0—8—4T which began to enter traffic after the grouping, at first with LNWR numbers and livery, then a batch in crimson lake and finally in plain black as illustrated. Livery Code C3.   *Real Photographs*

Plate 65 Ten 0—4—4Ts of Caledonian design were constructed after the grouping, and this picture of No. 15269 illustrates an example in service being prepared for a turn of duty. Livery Code probably B1, lining detail not clear.   *Authors' Collection*

Plate 66 Twenty CR '60' Class were constructed by the LMS and this picture of No. 14643 has been selected to represent the type. Photographed at Kingmoor on 7th August, 1938, the smokebox door numberplate has been removed and the locomotive carries Livery Code B3 or B9, probably the former.   *L. Hanson*

Plate 67 (Above) A number of LYR 4—6—0s were built after 1923 and this picture of No. 10447 illustrates a locomotive in crimson lake livery but prior to the introduction of the crest on the cabside (see Plate 289). Livery Code A2.

NRM

Plate 68 (Below) The large 4—6—4Ts of LYR design all entered service after grouping and this ex-works grey livery picture has been selected to illustrate the lining details when painted crimson lake. Livery Code A1.

NRM

Plate 69 (Above) This illustrates the experimental Hookham four-cylinder 0—6—0T of 1922 as rebuilt in 1924 and carrying its allocated LMS number. Livery Code C1. *Real Photographs*

Plate 70 (Below) No. 2125 was an example of an ex-LTSR design ordered by the Midland Railway but which entered service after the grouping in 1923. This ex-works picture has been selected to illustrate the lining details when running in crimson lake livery. Livery Code A1.
BR LMR

INITIAL NUMBERING OF LMS STANDARD CLASSES

The first standard classes were the perpetuated MR designs. In the case of the Class 4 Compound 4—4—0s, the Class 2 4—4—0s and the Class 4 0—6—0s, the LMS built examples were numbered immediately following their MR ancestors starting at 1045 (Compounds), 563 (Class 2 4—4—0s) and 4027 (Class 4 0—6—0). The new Class 2 engines involved one minor renumbering of five ex-NSR 4—4—0s which initially carried LMS numbers 595-9. The Class 2s eventually ran up to No. 700 but by the time this number was reached, the ex-MR Class 3 4—4—0 No. 700 had been scrapped.

New Compound construction more than filled the original vacant number series (1045-1199) but, rather than involve an extensive renumbering of the ex-MR 12xx series 0—4—4Ts, the final batch of Compounds was numbered in the 900 upwards series. There were vacant numbers from 900 to 989 but the ex-MR Class 4 simple 4—4—0s (990-9) were, additionally, renumbered to clear the whole 9xx series. This may have been to cope with projected new Compound construction but it may also have been to avoid confusion with the Class 4 simple engines. In fact, the Compound series stopped at 939.

The new 0—6—0s presented no real problem, there being the whole 4027-4999 range available. In 1930, the five ex-S & DJR Class 4s were numbered at the end of the then completed LMS examples. This placed a batch of pre-1923 locomotives (4557-4561) amongst the LMS built examples but was, presumably, preferable to renumbering the whole of the LMS series.

It was the new Class 3 0—6—0Ts which saw the first departure from pure 'divisional' numbering. The MR locomotives from which the class was derived were numbered 1900-59 with but 40 vacant numbers before the Class 3 0—6—4Ts started at No. 2000. The planned construction of new 0—6—0Ts was well in excess of the vacant numbers available in the 19xx series so the initial 50 new locomotives were given 71xx numbers (at the head of the ex-LNWR freight tank engine list). To these 50 were added the seven ex-S & DJR 0—6—0Ts of the same design in 1930. The remaining Class 3 tanks were allocated the 16400-16764 series in the Northern Division freight tank series. This involved a certain amount of renumbering of Scottish locomotives.

The Class 3 0—6—0Ts were, therefore, the first large class of LMS standard engines to carry numbers which did not reflect the division of origin of the design. At the same time they were at least numbered among pre-group locomotives of the same generic type and this policy was to continue to some extent.

The next standard design — the so-called Horwich 2—6—0 tender type — was numbered in the vacant 13xxx series between the Central and Northern Division series. Following as they did the predominantly ex-LYR number allocation, the 13xxx series had a certain amount of logic since the engines were of much more LYR than MR inspiration. The series terminated at 13244 and was later continued without a number break with the Stanier 2—6—0 derivative of the Horwich design.

The 2—6—6—2Ts (Garratts) were employed almost exclusively on the Midland Division and received appropriate Midland Division numbers in the 49xx series until the later Stanier Class 5s invaded this number block. The Fowler 2—6—2Ts, like the Class 3 0—6—0Ts, were placed in the Northern Division series while the 0—6—0 Class 2 dock tanks were given Central Division numbers. In each case, the number series chosen for the new locomotives, although in the middle of pre-group designs, was related to the generic type of locomotive concerned (155xx for the 2—6—2Ts and 1127x for the 0—6—0Ts).

It cannot be denied, however, that the policy of intruding standard types into the pre-group lists was beginning to cause confusion. True, it retained classes in consecutive number series, but it very quickly corrupted the power classification philosophy which formed the basis of the 1923 numbering system.

For example, the 'Royal Scot' Class came, logically enough, at the end of the LNWR 4—6—0 series and, being mainly used on the Western Division, the locomotives were comfortably 'at home' in the 61xx series — as indeed were the standard Class 7F 0—8—0s in the 95xx series at the end of the ex-LNWR 0—8—0 classes. However, the Fowler standard Class 4 2—6—4Ts in the 23xx series were somewhat uncomfortably inserted ahead of the vast army of superannuated ex-MR 0—6—0 goods engines and, *inter alia*, necessitated the renumbering of many ex-NSR 0—6—0s.

Finally, the running numbers of the first 42 Class 5XP 'Patriot' 4—6—0s were, when first built, very bewildering. They were nominally rebuilds/replacements of some of the ex-LNWR 'Claughtons' and, for accountancy reasons, they took the running numbers of the locomotives 'rebuilt'. As a result, their running numbers were indiscriminately scattered throughout the 59xx and 60xx series.

A summary of the first and second generation of standard class numbering is given at *Table 6*.

TABLE 6. LMS STANDARD STEAM LOCOMOTIVE CLASSES — PRE-1934 NUMBER ALLOCATIONS

RUNNING NUMBERS	WHEEL ARRANGEMENT	LOCOMOTIVE CLASS	TOTAL IN SERVICE
563-700	4—4—0	Fowler Class 2P	138
900-939 } 1045-1199	4—4—0++	Fowler Class 4P Compound	195
1540-1544	0—4—0ST	'Stanier' Class 0F	5
2300-2424	2—6—4T	Fowler Class 4P	125
4027-4556	0—6—0	Fowler Class 4F	530
4967-4999	2—6—0 + 0—6—2T†	Garratt Class	33
Various: 5901-6026*	4—6—0++	Fowler 'Patriot' Class 5XP	42
6100-6169	4—6—0++	Fowler 'Royal Scot' Class 6P	70
6200-6201	4—6—2†	Stanier 'Princess Royal' Class	2
6400-6409	0—4—4T	'Stanier' Class 2P	10
7100-7156	0—6—0T	Fowler Class 3F	57
7160-7164	0—4—0T	Sentinel type engines (two variants)	5
9500-9674	0—8—0	Fowler Class 7F	175
11270-11279	0—6—0T	Fowler Class 2F	10
13000-13244	2—6—0	Hughes/Fowler Class 5P/4F	245
13245-13284	2—6—0	Stanier Class 5P/4F	40
15500-15569	2—6—2T	Fowler Class 3P	70
16400-16764	0—6—0T	Fowler Class 3F	365
		Total	2117

++   three cylinder locomotives
†   four cylinder locomotives
*   These engines took the running numbers of the ex-LNWR 'Claughton' Class 4—6—0s which they had, nominally, replaced. The complete details are contained in the class article.

THE 1934 RENUMBERING POLICY

By 1934, the tidy pattern of the 1923 renumbering had been considerably disrupted by the construction of new types and with the large scale building of Stanier classes now imminent, the need was felt for a partial renumbering to clear complete series for the projected Stanier engines.

It was decided, as a matter of policy, that all *standard* locomotive types should carry running numbers below 10000. In time, this would mean that no locomotives would carry five figure numbers but, as an interim measure, provision had to be made for the renumbering of sizeable batches of locomotives still extant in the wanted four figure series. The principal areas which were to be wholly or partially cleared were as follows:

1—299	This series to be used for 2—6—2Ts.
2400—2999	This series to be used for 2—6—4Ts and renumbered 13xxx 2—6—0 tender locomotives.
5000—5899	This series to be used for renumbered 'Patriots' and new Stanier 4—6—0 types.
7000—7999	This series to be used for standard freight tank classes — including diesel shunting engines.
8000—8999	This series to be used for heavy freight tender engines.

The 61xx and 62xx series for 'Royal Scots' and the 4—6—2 tender engines fitted nicely into this breakdown as did the residual 'Claughtons' in the 59xx and 60xx series. It will be seen that, all told, a surprising degree of consistency with the original 1923 concept was maintained. Some of the passenger tanks now came ahead of passenger tender engines but, if one allows that the renumbered 13xxx series 2—6—0s and the forthcoming Stanier Class 5 4—6—0s were legitimate passenger classes, rather than pure freight types, then the standard passenger tender engine classes from Class 2Ps through to Pacifics were in ascending power class and number order — albeit interrupted by such other types as 2—6—4Ts and Class 4 0—6—0s.

The selection of number blocks to be cleared was possibly governed partly by the need to maintain some consistency with the 1923 policy and partly by the desire to renumber as few locomotives as possible. Thus the 1—299 series was an obvious choice as was the 2400 upwards series — both being all but clear of engines, the numbers having previously been carried by elderly MR types.

The 5000 upwards series was an obvious place for new Stanier 4—6—0s of both Class 5 and 5X and there were many gaps in the series caused by withdrawal of old LNWR engines. The same could be said of the 7000 and 8000 upwards series (originally mainly occupied by older and less powerful LNWR freight types). Thus, the renumbering was not as formidable as at first glance might appear to be the case.

The method adopted for the renumbering of the pre-group classes was, in general, to introduce a post-grouping version of the much loved pre-group 'duplicate' list. This was done by the simple expedient of adding 20000 to the original LMS number when the original was needed for a new standard locomotive. This, of course, maintained the LMS 'number identity' of the old locomotives. In most cases, only the conflicting engines were renumbered into the 2xxxx series but for some reason, the ex-LNWR 'Prince of Wales' Class was renumbered completely and well beyond the series required for the Stanier 'Jubilee' Class 5XPs.

One or two pre-group engines were placed on the duplicate list when there was no necessity to do so, but the number of such cases was surprisingly small.

In general, the 1934 renumbering stood the test for the remainder of the LMS period. Most new construction was fitted into the planned blocks and when new classes emerged — e.g. the Ivatt post-war standard designs — further scrapping of pre-group classes had, in most cases, already vacated suitable series of numbers in the 'below 10000' range. There were, however, one or two miscalculations. The 1934 plan must have envisaged only 500 Stanier Class 5 4—6—0s (5000—5499). Construction actually rose to 842 units and the last 342 of these had to be inserted between the Class 4Fs and the first of

Plate 71 Ex-LNWR 0—8—0 No. 29281 placed upon the duplicate list in error.

Real Photographs

the Class 5s, all but filling the available gap and also involving the renumbering of the Garratts into the 79xx series. Similarly with the Class 4P 2−6−4Ts: the Stanier versions of this wheel arrangement almost filled the gap between the Fowler series and the first of the Horwich 2−6−0s. In consequence, the post-war Fairburn development overflowed into the 21xx and 22xx series ahead of the Fowler 2−6−4Ts. This, in turn, involved further renumbering of ex-LT & SR type locomotives which had already been subjected to some quite bewildering exercises of this nature some years earlier.

In 1945, some thought seems to have been given to placing more engines on the duplicate list — even though their numbers were not needed for new construction. However, little seems to have come of it and only a handful of locomotives were actually renumbered.

A summary of all LMS standard classes with their 1934 series numbers is given at *Table 7*. This table includes locomotives built after 1947 to LMS design but, for consistency, these latter are shown without the BR 40000 added — see below.

TABLE 7. LMS STANDARD STEAM LOCOMOTIVE CLASSES — FINAL NUMBER ALLOCATIONS (INCLUDING BR BUILT LOCOMOTIVES TO LMS STANDARD DESIGN)

Note: Those classes which continued building after Nationalisation are marked thus*. Most of the engines which entered service after 1947 did so with their full BR 4xxxx numbers but for consistency, this table merely shows the LMS number series.

LMS RUNNING NUMBERS	WHEEL ARRANGEMENT	LOCOMOTIVE CLASS	TOTAL BUILT
1-70	2−6−2T	Fowler Class 3P	70
71-209	2−6−2T	Stanier Class 3P	139
563-700	4−4−0	Fowler Class 2P	138
900-939 1045-1199	4−4−0++	Fowler Class 4P Compound	195
1200-1329*	2−6−2T	Ivatt Class 2P	130
1900-1909	0−4−4T	'Stanier' Class 2P (renumbered in 1946)	10
2050-2299*	2−6−4T	Fairburn Class 4P	250
2300-2424	2−6−4T	Fowler Class 4P	125
2425-2494	2−6−4T	Stanier Class 4P	70
2500-2536	2−6−4T++	Stanier Class 4P	37
2537-2672	2−6−4T	Stanier Class 4P	136
2673-2699	2−6−4T	Fairburn Class 4P	27
2700-2944	2−6−0	Hughes/Fowler Class 5F	245
2945-2984	2−6−0	Stanier Class 5F	40
3000-3161*	2−6−0	Ivatt Class 4F	162
4027-4556 4562-4606	0−6−0	Fowler Class 4F	575
4658-5499*	4−6−0	Stanier Class 5	842
5500-5551	4−6−0++	Fowler 'Patriot' Class 5XP — } including rebuilds to Class 6P	52
5552-5742	4−6−0++	Stanier 'Jubilee' Class 5XP — } including rebuilds to Class 6P	191
6100-6169	4−6−0++	Fowler 'Royal Scot' Class 6P — including rebuilds with taper boiler	70
6170	4−6−0++	Stanier 'Royal Scot (Taper Boiler)' Class 6P	1
6200-6201	4−6−2†	Stanier 'Princess Royal' Class 7P	2
6202	4−6−2	Stanier Experimental Turbine Locomotive Class 7P	1
6203-6212	4−6−2†	Modified Stanier 'Princess Royal' Class 7P	10
6220-6257*	4−6−2†	Stanier 'Princess Coronation' Class 7P	38
6400-6527*	2−6−0	Ivatt Class 2P	128
7000-7009*	0−4−0ST	'Stanier' Class 0F	10
7160-7169	0−6−0T	Fowler Class 2F (ran as 7100-9 from 1934-9)	10
7180-7184	0−4−0T	Sentinel locomotives (renumbered in 1939)	5
7192	0−4−0T	Sentinel-Doble (unclassified)	1
7260-7681	0−6−0T	Fowler Class 3F	422
7967-7999	2−6−0 + 0−6−2T†	Garratt Class (renumbered in 1938-9)	33
8000-8399	2−8−0	Stanier Class 8F	400
8400-8479	2−8−0	Stanier Class 8F (GWR built) } These engines all classed as LMS stock — some later to WD use	80
8490-8495	2−8−0	Stanier Class 8F } These engines all classed as LMS stock — some later to WD use	6
8500-8559	2−8−0	Stanier Class 8F (LNER built) } These engines all classed as LMS stock — some later to WD use	60
8600-8704	2−8−0	Stanier Class 8F (SR built) } These engines all classed as LMS stock — some later to WD use	105
8705-8729	2−8−0	Stanier Class 8F (SR built) } ex-LNER locomotives *loaned* to LMS in 1947	25
8730-8772	2−8−0	Stanier Class 8F (LNER built) } ex-LNER locomotives *loaned* to LMS in 1947	43
	2−8−0	Stanier Class 8F — WD locomotives never allocated LMS series numbers although some returned to BR after 1947 and were given vacant 48xxx numbers	133
9500-9674	0−8−0	Fowler Class 7F	175

++   three cylinder locomotives } Remainder were two cylinder machines
†   four cylinder locomotives }

Footnote: Stanier Class 8F 2−8−0 A total of 852 locomotives were built of which 719 were either owned by the LMS or carried LMS running numbers at some time. Fuller details will be found in *Volume III*.

BRITISH RAILWAYS RENUMBERING OF LMS LOCOMOTIVES

After a very short interim period of adding an 'M' prefix to the old LMS number, the BR complete renumbering system finally adopted in 1948 was relatively straightforward. It took the form of the addition of 40000 to the previous LMS number *except* for the case of engines on the 2xxxx list which, along with a few other exceptions — see below— were completely renumbered after the 1923 pattern.

Other than the duplicate list engines, the LMS locomotives remaining at Nationalisation fell into the 1—17956 range so the BR number block became 40001—57956. This left a completely empty range of numbers before the ex-LNER engines started at 60001. Opportunity was, therefore, taken to renumber the surviving 2xxxx LMS engines (now heavily depleted) into the BR 58000—59999 series. New consecutive blocks of numbers were allocated to the surviving locomotives but many were withdrawn before getting them. Those that were renumbered lost their LMS 'number identity' and, in the case of the ex-MR engines, with the 1907 Midland list too. One or two groups of engines not on the duplicate list were also renumbered into the BR 58xxx series. These included the ex-MR 0—4—4Ts (to clear the original series for new construction of Ivatt 2—6—2Ts) and *all* the ex-MR Class 2F 0—6—0s. Some of these latter engines were already on the duplicate list to make room for the various LMS standard 2—6—0 tender classes but the remainder of the Class 2Fs were intermixed with the ex-MR Class 3F 0—6—0s in the 3xxx series. This was largely a legacy from the frequent rebuilding of ex-MR 0—6—0s (generally from Class 2 to Class 3 but sometimes the other way!) most of which had taken place subsequent to the 1907 renumbering. The BR renumbering separated Class 2 from Class 3 engines for the first time in some 40 years. With but one exception (3137—43750), the Class 3Fs retained their 3xxx numbers with 40000 added.

Finally, the original BR renumbering policy allocated a separate series altogether for diesel locomotives. These were numbered between 10000 and 19999 irrespective of company of origin and the LMS examples were, accordingly, placed in the appropriate parts of the series. Curiously enough, this resulted in the first LMS main line diesel (No. 10000) becoming the only 'pure' LMS locomotive to retain its number at Nationalisation — together, of course, with 10001 which did not enter service until 1948.

A full list of LMS steam locomotives which were renumbered in 1948, other than by addition of 40000, is given at *Table 8*.

Plate 72 The British Railways renumbering scheme saw the introduction of an entirely new sequence for some old locomotives many of which previously carried numbers in the 20xxx series. This scheme effectively made it difficult to recall the old LMS number without a reference book and this picture shows ex-LNWR 0—6—0 2F No. 28492 running as BR No. 58389.
A.G. Ellis

TABLE 8. LMS STEAM LOCOMOTIVES RENUMBERED BY BR
(OTHER THAN BY ADDING 40000 TO THE OLD LMS RUNNING NUMBER)

Note: Many of the locomotives concerned in this summary did not survive for long enough after 1947 to receive their allotted BR numbers.

FINAL LMS NUMBER(S)	WHEEL ARRANGEMENT	LOCOMOTIVE CLASS	BR NUMBER/ SERIES
Between 2092-2160	4—4—2T	LMS and LTSR designs	41910-41926 (Class 2P) 41928-41978 (Class 3P)
2180-2193	0—6—2T	ex-LTSR design	41980-41993
25648/73 25752/87	4—6—0	Bowen-Cooke ex-LNWR 'Prince of Wales' Class (none received BR numbers)	58000-58003
25297	4—4—0	Whale ex-LNWR 'Precursor' Class — did not receive BR number	58010
25350/73	4—4—0	Bowen-Cooke ex-LNWR 'George the Fifth' Class (neither received its BR number)	58011-58012
20155/85 20216	2—4—0	Johnson ex-MR designs — none renumbered by BR	58020-58022
Various: 1239-1430	0—4—4T	Johnson ex-MR design	58030-58091
26428	2—4—0T	Webb ex-LNWR design	58092
22290	0—10—0	Fowler ex-MR Banking Engine	58100
22630/846 22853/63	0—6—0	Kirtley ex-MR design — one only (22630) renumbered by BR	58110-58113
Various: 22900-23018	0—6—0	Johnson ex-MR Class 2F*	58114-58187
Various: 3023-3764	0—6—0	Johnson ex-MR Class 2F†	58188-58310
Various: 28088-28313	0—6—0	Webb ex-LNWR 'Coal' engines	58320-58361
Various: 28318-28622	0—6—0	Webb ex-LNWR 'Cauliflowers'	58362-58430
Various: 27505-27532	0—6—0T	Park ex-NLR design	58850-58863
27217	0—4—2ST	ex-NLR Crane Engine	58865
27480	0—6—0ST	Webb ex-LNWR 'Square' Saddle tank	58870
Various: 27553-27681	0—6—2T	Webb ex-LNWR 'Coal' tank	58880-58898
Various: 7692-7840	0—6—2T	Webb ex-LNWR 'Coal' tank	58899-58937

† The ex-MR Class 3F 0—6—0s in this same number series retained their LMS numbers (plus 40000) except for LMS 3137 which became BR 43750 to clear the 431xx series for new construction of Ivatt Class 4F 2—6—0s.

* Note that Nos 22987-99 were never employed by the LMS in the 2xxxx series. The engines concerned always carried their original 4-figure numbers but went into the BR 58xxx series none the less.

Plate 73 A Caledonian Railway 0—6—0 2F of Drummond design as first renumbered by British Railways, photographed at Balornock on 14th February, 1950. During the period after Nationalisation and before the overall renumbering scheme was introduced the running numbers of several locomotives were prefixed 'M' as illustrated. The LMS series of numbers on the cabside are to a regular pattern but to no known LMS or BR standard design. *A.G. Ellis*

Plate 74 Rebuilt 'Patriot' 4—6—0 No. 45529 *Stephenson* carrying its former LMS number with the BR standard addition of 40000. The livery of LNWR style of lined black became a BR standard, but not for this particular class of locomotive.

BR LMR

CONCLUSION

Few significant changes took place after the initial BR renumbering scheme was devised. The 4xxxx lists grew numerically larger with the addition of post-1947 building as did the diesel series. There were also odd renumberings of pre-1948 locomotives but these will be considered with the separate class articles.

The 1923, 1934 and 1948 renumbering operations all took some time to complete and this tends to confuse the picture when referring to periods of changeover. Moreover there were other less comprehensive renumbering operations at other times. To maintain consistency, it will be the policy in this work, unless stated otherwise, to refer to the number which the locomotive *should have carried* at the time concerned — regardless of whether or not the actual renumbering had been carried out. Thus, references to the 1923—34 period will use the first LMS numbers; the 1934—47 period will use the new 1934 numbers (where applicable) and post-1947 references will use the BR number. References to locomotives affected by other renumbering operations will also follow this broad principle.

Given an understanding of the LMS locomotive numbering system, it is now possible to turn to a broad survey of the LMS locomotive fleet. We must confess that we thought very hard before deciding to include a basic review of the whole fleet in this introductory volume. In *Volumes II and III*, the locomotives and, in particular, their outward appearance, are considered comprehensively class by class but without overdue reference to LMS locomotive philosophy. In these introductory chapters, therefore, we thought it would be useful to summarise the basic outlines of pre-group locomotive policy, company by company. Obviously space permits only the broadest treatment, but it is our hope that by dividing the coverage of the various locomotive types in this way, the reader will, at an early stage, gain a basic understanding of the LMS locomotive situation as a whole, before embarking upon the more detailed information incorporated in the later volumes.

For completeness, we have also included a separate chapter summarising all the new locomotives built after the grouping either by the LMS or to LMS design.

Finally, the general principle of these surveys will be to concentrate on capital stock, using LMS numbers and regarding engines built after 1922 to pre-group designs (other than ex-MR designs) as non-standard types.

Chapter 4   Pre-Group Locomotives — Midland Division

The Midland Division locomotive list took running numbers below 5000. In fact, the highest number allocated at the grouping was that of the final MR Class 4 0—6—0 No. 4026, but later construction of this type by the LMS (and the building of other classes) eventually all but filled the 4xxx list.

The bulk of the locomotives involved in this series were the ex-Midland classes which, with a few exceptions (noted below), retained their original Midland numbers. Setting aside pre-group loyalties, this policy made a great deal of sense. The engines were already carrying numbers allocated from 1907 onwards in accordance with principles now applicable to the whole LMS system and there was no logical need to renumber them. This would obviously save time and money — a not inconsiderable thought when it is realised that the ex-MR locomotives represented some 30% of the total LMS stock. It will, of course, be readily appreciated that there were some gaps in the ex-MR lists caused by pre-1923 withdrawals but the LMS rarely regarded 'gap filling' as anything more than a temporary expedient for the odd few locomotives, so the gaps in the lists in 1923 were simply accepted as a natural consequence of the numbering system.

The Midland Division series also included the ex-NSR and ex-SMJR locomotives which are listed separately and this chapter also includes, for convenience, a separate summary of the ex-LT & SR locomotives (already incorporated in the MR system) and the S & DJR locomotives absorbed in 1930.

THE MIDLAND RAILWAY

Locomotive superintendents:

Matthew Kirtley	1844—1873
Samuel Waite Johnson	1873—1903
Richard Mountford Deeley	1904—1909
Henry Fowler	1909—1922

Passenger Tender Engines

The Midland was, basically, a 'small engine' line and at the time of the grouping, its main passenger services were mostly handled by a large series of 4—4—0s. The majority of these were of power class 2 but they were supplemented by a number of Class 3 and Class 4 engines for the heavier work. Nevertheless, double heading was common. Lighter passenger duties were in the hands of 2—4—0s and 4—2—2s, together with a few older 4—4—0s, all these latter engines being in power class 1.

The oldest MR engines were the 2—4—0 Class 1 locomotives of Kirtley design, with double frames and other Kirtley features (LMS 1—67). Some of them dated back to 1866 and the first 22 had 6 ft 3 in driving wheels, the remainder having 6 ft 9 in driving wheels. They were followed in numerical sequence by further 2—4—0 locomotives of Kirtley origin (LMS 68—146). These started life with inside frames so once they had received the Johnson treatment they were visually very similar to the pure Johnson designs. All but the final 20 had 6 ft 9 in driving wheels, the last ones having 6 ft 3 in drivers.

The balance of the 2—4—0 Class 1 engines were all of genuine Johnson design (LMS 147—281) derived from the final Kirtley designs. Several variants were involved, generally differing only in driving wheel size and minor details:

147—156	6 ft 3 in driving wheels
157—191 157—191 } 217—221	6 ft 6½ in driving wheels
192—196 207—216 } 222—271	6 ft 9 in driving wheels
197—206 272—281 }	7 ft 0½ in driving wheels

The ex-MR 4—4—0 classes dated well back into the nineteenth century with the 17 survivors of the beautifully proportioned and unrebuilt Class 1 locomotives to Johnson's 1876 and 1877 designs (numbered between 300 and 327). They were largely in original condition at the grouping. The engines numbered 310 upwards had 7 ft 0½ in driving wheels, the earlier ones having 6 ft 6½ in wheels. These engines only lasted until the early 1930s, the last one (311) going in 1934.

The main batch of Midland 4—4—0s was the somewhat bewildering array of Class 2 locomotives (LMS 328—562). Many of these came to the LMS as first stage Deeley rebuilds of older Johnson engines with saturated boilers and often with Belpaire fireboxes. Many more were second stage Fowler rebuilds with superheated Belpaire boilers and high running plates. Most of the long term survivors were of the superheated Fowler variety. Some rebuilding continued into LMS days and more details will be given in *Volume III*. Most of the Class 2s had 7 ft 0½ in driving wheels but quite a number of the non-superheated engines had 6 ft 6½ in or 6 ft 9 in drivers — these being generally the first to be scrapped. Unlike the Class 1 tender engines, the Class 2 series was intact at the grouping and the Fowler superheated version formed the basis for the LMS standard Class 2P 4—4—0. The ex-MR engines finally became extinct in 1963.

Sandwiched in the MR number series between the Class 2 and Class 3 4—4—0s were the 43 survivors of Johnson's celebrated bogie 'singles' (numbered between 600 and 683). Examples of four of the five main classes of 4—2—2 survived grouping, the missing variety being the final version — the 'Princess of Wales' type. The fact that they carried numbers higher than the Class 2 4—4—0s is possibly explained by the fact that at the MR 1907 renumbering, many of these 4—4—0s were still Class 1 engines — i.e. unrebuilt. The singles were all withdrawn by 1928.

In a sense, although totalling but 80 members, the Class 3 Johnson 'Belpaire' 4—4—0s (LMS 700—779) were the mainstay of the MR's more arduous passenger workings for many years. Although all came to the LMS, none were in their original Johnson condition. Indeed the last 20 were built new to Deeley's modified design and the Johnson series were subsequently rebuilt. They thus exhibited a somewhat more austere appearance than in their early days. Most were superheated before the grouping and a few were given superheaters afterwards but some early withdrawals were in saturated state. Gradual inroads were made in the class during the LMS period from 1925 onwards but 22 survived to BR and the last survivor was scrapped in 1953.

The remaining 55 ex-MR 4—4—0s were all placed in power class 4. Ten of them (LMS 990—999) were the simple expansion two-cylinder Deeley engines with 6 ft 6 in wheels, generally assumed to have been built for comparison with the more well known Compounds. The '990s' became especially noted for their work on the Settle and Carlisle line and rarely came south of Leeds save for their regular visits to Derby works. They did not long survive grouping although 991/3/5—9 did last long enough to be renumbered 801/3/5—9 by the LMS in 1926/7 and 992 ran until 1928 with its original number.

The final Class 4 engines were, of course, the famous Midland three-cylinder Compounds. The first five (LMS 1000—4) were the original Johnson engines as modified and superheated by Fowler while 1005—44 were the pure Deeley machines, later superheated by Fowler. The superheating of these engines was not completed until after the grouping and the class was adopted, almost unchanged, as an LMS standard.

Total ex-MR passenger tender engines at grouping:

2—4—0 types	245
4—2—2 types	43
4—4—0 types	386
Total	674

Plate 75 The oldest 2—4—0s to come into LMS ownership were some 6′ 3″ locomotives numbered between 1-22. This picture illustrates No. 4 and is particularly interesting since it was taken at Inverness in May 1928, the locomotive having been transferred to the Highland Section, far from its native Midland haunt. It is shown in crimson lake livery, Code A1.

Authors' Collection

Plate 76 This picture of an unidentified member of the batch of Kirtley 2—4—0s numbered 68-125 with 6′ 9″ wheels, has been selected to provide a direct comparison with the 6′ 3″ wheel locomotive in *Plate 75*. This locomotive is in crimson lake, Livery Code A1.　　*Authors' Collection*

Plate 77 The final 20 Kirtley 2—4—0s were built with 6′ 3″ driving wheels and this picture shows No. 132 at Northampton Castle on 14th April, 1931, with a stopping passenger train. Livery Code B3.　　*L. Hanson*

Plate 78 A Johnson 6′ 9″ 2—4—0 No. 193 in crimson lake livery but rebuilt with a Belpaire firebox is shown on Bedford shed. Livery Code A1.　　*A.G. Ellis*

Plate 79 There was a batch of 7' 0" driving wheel 2—4—0s constructed and this picture of No. 280 at Derby shows a locomotive in crimson lake livery, Code A1. The locomotive has been rebuilt with a Belpaire boiler and examples of both round-top and rebuilt locomotives are to be found in *Volume III*.

Real Photographs

Plate 80 This picture of No. 306 illustrates an example of one of the elegant 4—4—0s which came into LMS ownership in virtually their original condition. No. 306 was a 6' 6½" driving wheel locomotive and examples of the 7' 0½" locomotives are to be found in *Volume III*. Livery Code A1.

Authors' Collection

Plates 81-4 Midland 4—4—0s came in a variety of styles and it is not possible to illustrate every type in this volume; the matter is dealt with in greater depth in *Volume III*. However, these four plates have been selected to give readers a look at three 'non-standard' locomotives and the pioneer standard locomotive No. 483.

Plate 81 This picture is No. 355 a Johnson 6' 9" driving wheel locomotive as rebuilt by Deeley. The last 4—4—0s in this condition were withdrawn in 1937. Livery Code A1.

Real Photograph

Plate 82 No. 476, rebuilt by Deeley, was a 6′ 6″ driving wheel Johnson locomotive and this picture, taken c1925, shows it carrying crimson lake livery, Code A1. This particular batch depicted a variety of guises, more completely discussed in *Volume III.* *Real Photographs*

Plate 83 Fifteen 4—4—0s with 6′ 6″ driving wheels, Nos. 378-392, were never superheated and they lasted until 1952. This picture of No. 378, Livery Code probably B4, shows a locomotive fitted with a replacement Stanier chimney.

Authors' Collection

Plate 84 The final rebuilding of the Johnson 4—4—0s produced the 483 Class, so called after the first locomotive so treated in 1912. These Fowler superheated locomotives formed the basis of an LMS standard design carrying running Nos. 563-700 (see Plate 11, page 7). This locomotive has been fitted with an exhaust steam injector — see the pipe emerging from the smokebox. It also has a replacement Stanier chimney. Livery Code B4. *Authors' Collection*

Plate 85 (Above) Apart from the cab-side crest and MR on the buffer beam this locomotive is carrying the first LMS style and this picture shows the method employed when lining these locomotives. Note the line along the bottom of the side framing, buffer body, cab front under the roof, front of the tender, footsteps and tender side frames. *BR LMR*

Plate 86 This picture of Nos. 672 and 1042 has been selected to show a member of the batch 670-684 in traffic. In their final years they were often used as pilots and the last of the 4—2—2s was withdrawn in 1928. *Real Photographs*

Plate 87 The Johnson Class 3 4—4—0s (known as 'Belpaires') came into the LMS in both superheated and saturated form and the saturated locomotives, not rebuilt, were withdrawn by 1926, whereas the final survivors of the rebuilt locomotives lasted until 1953. This picture of superheated No. 700, Livery Code A1, shows its condition in c1925. *Authors' Collection*

Plate 88 The ten Deeley 4—4—0 Class 4 locomotives, originally numbered 990-9, were allocated 801-9. In 1927 No. 990 had already been scrapped and this picture of No. 803, Livery Code A1, shows the locomotive at Derby in 1927.

Real Photographs

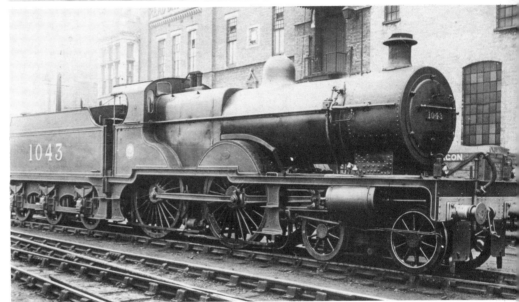

Plate 89 (Right) Not all the Compounds were superheated by 1923 and this picture of No. 1043 in LMS Livery Code A1 illustrates an example in saturated condition. It should be compared with *Plate 90* which shows No. 1000 in superheated form.

Real Photographs

Plate 90 (Below) Photographed at Derby in 1930 this picture of No. 1000 shows the locomotive, ex-works, in Livery Code A6. The Ross pop safety valves have replaced the original Ramsbottom version but the locomotive still carries the original Midland chimney and dome. *A.G. Ellis*

Passenger Tank Engines

Most ex-MR passenger tank engines were locomotives of 0—4—4 wheel arrangement, the vast bulk of which still existed in 1923. The remaining engines were 0—6—4Ts to Deeley design. These were allocated running numbers after the freight tank series.

The first 25 of the 0—4—4Ts (LMS 1200—25), were double framed Kirtley well tanks dating from 1869. These old veterans managed to survive the initial onslaught of post-group scrapping quite well, but by 1935 all had gone. The remaining 0—4—4Ts (LMS 1226—1430) were all variants of the basic Johnson design of 1875. Although scrapping had started just prior to the grouping, 62 survived to be allocated BR 580xx series numbers and the class only became extinct in 1960. As with most MR classes there were some external variations apparent in this large class of engines (e.g. many had Belpaire boilers fitted by the LMS).

The final ex-MR passenger tanks were the distinctive 'hole in the wall' Deeley 0—6—4Ts of 1907 (LMS 2000—39). They were built with round topped boilers and the subsequent rebuilding with superheated Belpaire boilers overlapped the grouping. These engines were satisfactory if not brilliant and, like many others, fell victim to the ever accelerating spread of Stanier designs in the 1930s. The whole class was scrapped during the period 1935—8.

Total ex-MR passenger tank engines at grouping:

0—4—4 type	226
0—6—4 type	40
Total	266

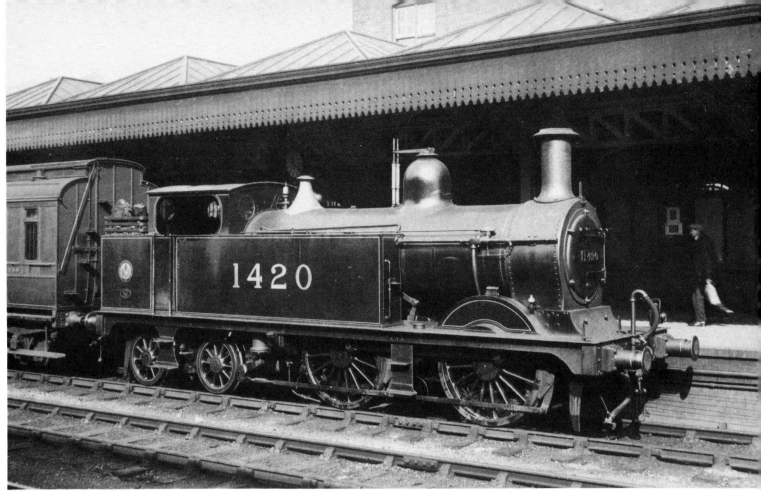

Plate 93 (Above) The smaller wheel locomotives are represented by No. 1420. The final batch (which included No. 1420) carried higher pitched boilers than the earlier series and the variations of these locomotives are further discussed in *Volume III*. Many were rebuilt with Belpaire boilers and examples lasted until 1960. Livery Code A3.

Stephen Collection — NRM

Plate 94 (Below) The Midland built only 40 large passenger tank locomotives, and they retained their original Midland numbers 2000-39 for their entire life. Built in 1907 in saturated form with round top boilers, the engines were given superheated Belpaire boilers from 1920. It was 1926 before they were all rebuilt. The majority did not carry LMS livery until rebuilding but this picture of No. 2034 shows an engine in its saturated form carrying Livery Code A1.

Real Photographs

Plate 95 The Midland built a numb[er] of 0—4—0STs and this picture of N[o.] 1506 is an example of the smaller versio[n.] The locomotive was renumbered 150[0] in 1930 and carries Livery Code C1[ ] Note the bell on the top of the tank.
Authors' Collectio[n]

Plate 96 The Midland built ten 0—4—0[T] for shunting, numbered between 1528-[3] and two of these locomotives remaine[d] in service until 1966. This picture of N[o.] 1528, taken 1936, is in Livery Code C15[ ] *Authors' Collectio[n]*

Plate 97 The Midland 0—6—0Ts [ ] Class 1 came in a variety of forms a[nd] they are all illustrated in *Volume I.* To record these locomotives in th[is] section we have chosen No. 1661 wi[th] an open cab but rebuilt with a Belpa[ire] boiler. The lettering appears to be r[ed] shaded but this is almost certainly [an] optical effect of light on the bla[ck] shaded transfers. Livery Code C13.
Authors' Collectio[n]

Plate 98 The large 3F tanks were built in the form as depicted by No. 1943 which is in Midland livery and rebuilding with Belpaire boilers with a new cab began in 1919 but it was 1942 before the sixty locomotives were all rebuilt.

Authors' Collection

Freight Tank Engines

Most ex-MR freight tank engines were of the 0—6—0 wheel arrangement in several variations. However, there were in addition some 33 0—4—0Ts of which the oldest were the 23 surviving Johnson 0—4—0STs numbered between 1500 and 1527, the last ten being much bigger than 1500—17. These engines, first introduced in 1883, were not classified for power at the grouping but later became LMS Class OF. The other 0—4—0Ts (LMS 1528—37) were Deeley side tank engines dating from 1907.

Both varieties enjoyed a long life in the limited industrial environments in which they generally operated. Although only four of the Johnson engines outlasted the LMS, the final survivor did not go until 1958. The Deeley tanks were intact at nationalisation and lasted until 1965.

The oldest of the 0—6—0Ts were numbered between 1605 and 1619. The last ten (1610—19) were Kirtley engines dating from 1871 but the earlier ones (1605—8) were four survivors of a motley collection of old timers, one of which had ancestry dating back to 1848! None of these 14 engines lasted out the 1920s, by contrast with the main batch of Class 1 0—6—0Ts (1620—1899) which survived with but one withdrawal (1628) before the grouping and a relatively slow rate of attrition afterwards. Indeed, the last of them outlived almost all the ex-MR locomotives, not finally being withdrawn until 1966.

These long-lived engines were the standard Johnson Class 1 shunting tanks, first built in 1874. All were originally built to the basic round-topped boiler design but by 1923, many had acquired Belpaire boilers. Another characteristic feature of this class was the open-backed cab which many of them sported, even after rebuilding with Belpaire boilers in LMS days. One of these engines (1831), provided the frame and wheels for the experimental LMS heavy oil engine of 1932.

The newest of the MR freight tanks were the 18″ cylindered engines of Johnson design dating from 1899 (LMS 1900—59). These engines were the standard MR 'heavy' shunting tanks and by the time of the grouping, a few had been fitted with replacement Belpaire boilers. In this form to which all eventually conformed, the design became the basis of the LMS standard Class 3F 0—6—0T. The MR locomotives were renumbered 7200—59 during 1934—7 and the class became extinct as late as 1966, withdrawals not having commenced until 1954.

Total ex-MR freight tank engines at grouping:

0—4—0 type	33
0—6—0 type	353
Total	386

Freight Tender Engines

The Midland was an 0—6—0 line as far as freight traffic was concerned and, with the solitary exception of the 0—10—0 Lickey banking engine, all the freight tender engines handed over to the LMS were of 0—6—0 type. By 1923, a remarkable degree of variety existed in what had once (c1891—1903) been a very homogeneous series of engines all carrying the same class of boiler. All MR 0—6—0 tender classes shared a common 8 ft 0 in + 8 ft 6 in coupled wheelbase, first used by Kirtley in his double framed engines. Johnson opted for inside frames but the cylinder and motion layout he adopted was carried on, virtually unchanged, right through the LMS period until the final LMS Class 4F engines were built in 1941. This must surely have established some sort of record!

Modification and rebuilding commenced in 1903 and by twenty years later had produced much variety, particularly from the external viewpoint. Some changes were of an ephemeral kind (e.g. chimney and cab design) while others were occasioned by the gradual increase in boiler size and type, together with increased cylinder dimensions. The basic progression through the types is summarised below but it should be noted that the various rebuilding activities which took place over a period of many years resulted in the Class 2 and Class 3 engines becoming hopelessly mixed up in the number lists which, although dating from 1907, were based on the 1903 state of affairs. The LMS made no attempt to sort them out but in 1948, BR did renumber the Class 2 engines separately from the Class 3 machines.

Running Numbers	Description
2369, 2382—98	This series of numbers was allocated by the LMS to the surviving Kirtley Class 1 0—6—0s with 'straight topped' double frames. Most of the engines had, in fact, carried MR numbers in the 2300—68 series but this block was wanted for ex-SMJR and ex-NSR locomotives so the ex-MR engines were allocated new numbers in a block vacated by withdrawn Kirtley engines. Some of the engines concerned were, in fact, withdrawn before even getting their new LMS numbers. Total in stock (1923) 18
2399—867	These were the Kirtley 0—6—0s with 'curved top' double frames. Most were Class 1 engines in the Johnson rebuilt state but there were 31 engines carrying a variety of boilers which put them in Class 2. A few examples carried Belpaire boilers and Deeley cabs. Considering their great age, very few inroads had been made into the class at grouping, all but 18 reaching the LMS. One survived long enough to be renumbered 58110 by BR (LMS 2630, later 22630). It was finally scrapped in 1951, no less than 88 years after the first of the type had been built. Total in stock (1923) 453
2900—3129	This series of 230 Class 2 locomotives remained Class 2 until scrapping, although many were considerably rebuilt before final withdrawal (Belpaire boilers, Deeley cabs, etc). They were Johnson engines with 17½ in cylinders, first introduced in 1875 and all reached the LMS, many going onto the LMS duplicate list from 1934 onwards. The survivors in 1948 were numbered into the 58xxx series by BR. Approximately half of them (2900—3019) had 4 ft 11 in driving wheels, the remainder having the more common MR standard 5 ft 3 in driving wheels. Total in stock (1923) 230

Plate 100 The majority of Midland Class 2 goods engines were 5′ 3″ wheel engines but some ran with 4′ 11″ wheels as depicted by No. 2916. Almost all the 2900 Class, 2900-3019, were rebuilt with Belpaire boilers and Deeley cabs. This picture of No. 2916 in Livery Code C15 shows a locomotive in original condition with an old tender; note the axlebox springs above the running plate.

Real Photographs

Plate 101 In 1934 when the 2−6−0s were renumbered into the 27xx-29xx series, those 2Fs carrying the allocated numbers were renumbered by the addition of 20000 and this picture shows 2955 so renumbered. Photographed at Derby on 11th October, 1936, in Livery Code C14, No. 22955 is in ex-works condition. Note the absence of vacuum pipes and smokebox door numberplate: this was a steam brake only engine and has three-link, not screw, couplings.

L. Hanson

3130−764	This series of engines started life as Class 2 engines to Johnson design with 18 in cylinders. 3130−89 had 4 ft 11 in driving wheels, the remainder, 5 ft 3 in driving wheels. Apart from cylinder size, another reason for separating them from the earlier series is that by 1923, many of the 3130−764 series had been rebuilt with larger boilers and upgraded from Class 2 to Class 3. They retained their original Class 2 running numbers and some, indeed, were later rebuilt back to Class 2! In 1948, BR renumbered the Class 2 survivors into the 58xxx series.

Total in stock (1923)   635

3765−834	These locomotives were built new as Class 3 engines and most carried Belpaire boilers by 1923. In their original state they were basically an enlargement of the standard Johnson type carrying larger round topped boilers than the Class 2s. Later engines had Deeley modifications.

Total in stock (1923)   70

3835−4026	The final MR 0−6−0s were the standard Class 4 'big' goods locomotives first introduced by Henry Fowler in 1911 as a progressive enlargement of the basic Johnson/Deeley type. This was the design adopted, virtually unchanged, as an LMS standard and built until 1941.

Total in stock (1923)   192

The well known 0−10−0 Lickey banking engine (LMS 2290) was built in 1919. It was unclassified for power and was renumbered 58100 by BR after running for a year or so as LMS 22290. It was scrapped in 1956.

Total ex-MR freight tender engines at grouping:

0−6−0 type	1598
0−10−0 type	1
Total	1599

Plate 102 (Above) The 5' 3" engines came in a variety of forms, carrying either Belpaire or round top boilers — the round top boilered locomotives always retaining small cabs whereas those with the Belpaire boilers sometimes had new large Deeley cabs or still retained their original cabs, but examination of photographs will reveal variations in the side sheet design. This picture of No. 3543 in 1936 black livery, Code C19, is a rare example of a 2F in this livery.

Authors' Collection

Plate 103 (Below) The Midland Class 3 goods engines entered the LMS in both original and rebuilt form and this picture of No. 3268 in Livery Code C21 illustrates one in their most common LMS condition. Photographed at Derby in August 1937, this locomotive is just ex works in immaculate black paint. Readers will note that this locomotive has a 2,250 gallon tender with a small coal bulkhead. These low bulkhead tenders were less suitable for work over long distances than tenders of the type coupled to No. 3543, *Plate 102.*

A.G. Ellis

THE LONDON TILBURY AND SOUTHEND RAILWAY

Locomotive Superintendents:

Thomas Whitelegg	1880—1910
Robert Harben Whitelegg	1910—1912

The LT & SR became part of the Midland Railway in 1912 but its locomotives were distinctly different. The nature of its services, mainly of residential passenger nature augmented by seaside traffic, meant that most of its classes were passenger tanks. The LT & SR had no passenger tender engines and only one class each of freight tank and freight tender locomotives — moreover, the tender engines were but two in number and acquired more by accident than by design. In all, therefore, it seems reasonable to refer to the Tilbury as a tank engine railway.

Its locomotives were not added to the Midland stock until five years after the great 1907 renumbering and there was no room in the lists for them always to be inserted adjacent to the MR locomotives of similar design. They were, therefore, all given numbers in the considerable gap between the end of the Midland tank engines (2039) and the start of the freight tender series at 2290. This further confused the passenger and freight tank lists which had already been modified by the insertion of the Deeley 0—6—4Ts (page 64 — above). The situation became even more bewildering with the early LMS renumbering of the Tilbury engines together with the insertion of ex-North Staffordshire engines which took place in 1923. The following summary is given in order of the original numbers carried at the time of the grouping and before the LMS renumbering commenced.

Running Numbers	Description	Number in stock (1/1/23)
2100—2107	4—6—4Ts (LMS Class 3) designed by R. H. Whitelegg. These engines did not enter service until after the Midland had assumed control. 2101—7 were renumbered 2193—9 in 1928 to allow for the renumbering of 4—4—2Ts (below).	8
2110—2145	Small 4—4—2Ts (LMS Class 1) with 6 ft 0 in wheels. These were the oldest Tilbury tanks and were soon to be renumbered in rather bewildering fashion — see below.	36
2146—2157	Large 4—4—2Ts (LMS Class 3) with 6 ft 6 in wheels which had been rebuilt from older engines of lower power. They were later renumbered 2135—46 (below).	12
2158—2175	4—4—2Ts (LMS Class 2) with 6 ft 6 in wheels, later renumbered 2092—2109 (below).	18
2176—2179	Large 4—4—2Ts (LMS Class 3) built as such (of which *Thundersley* is preserved). They were later renumbered 2147—50 — see below.	4
	Total Passenger Tank Engines at Grouping	78
2180—2193	Class 3 0—6—2 freight tanks. They were immediately renumbered 2220—33 by the LMS, reverting to 2180—93 in 1939 and becoming 41980—93 in BR days. 2190—3 were delivered new to the MR.	14
2898—2899	0—6—0 freight tender engines built for the Ottoman Railway but never delivered and sold to the LT & SR instead.	2
	Total ex-LT & SR Engines at Grouping	94

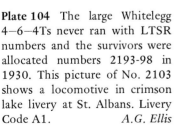

Plate 104 The large Whitelegg 4—6—4Ts never ran with LTSR numbers and the survivors were allocated numbers 2193-98 in 1930. This picture of No. 2103 shows a locomotive in crimson lake livery at St. Albans. Livery Code A1. *A.G. Ellis*

Plate 105 (Above) The LTSR 4—4—2Ts underwent a succession of confusing renumberings during their lifetimes. This picture of No. 2136 in crimson lake livery, Code A1, shows a locomotive approaching the end of its career, having started as No. 27 *Whitechapel* and ending as No. 2057 in 1932. Note the distinctive splashers over the bogies and pony wheels, a feature of LTSR locomotives (see Plate 106). *Real Photographs*

Plate 106 (Below) Ex-LTSR 4—4—2T No. 2099 was a member of the first 6′ 6″ driving wheel series, which were later developed into the series built by the LMS as late as 1930. *BR LMR*

Plate 107 The majority of LTSR tank engines were for passenger working but 14 were built for freight work. No. 2231 was taken direct into MR stock in 1912 and did not carry a LTSR number or name. In due course, No. 2231 reverted to its Midland number, 2191, and was later renumbered 41991 by British Railways. Livery Code C14.

Authors' Collection

The above engines were not the only ones built to LT & SR design. In 1922, the Midland decided to perpetuate the Class 3 4—4—2T type but the new examples did not enter service until 1923. Eventually, 35 more engines entered service, the last examples not being completed until 1930. During the building of these engines, it was decided to reorganise the numbering of all the 4—4—2Ts in ascending power class order. This renumbering was rather baffling, it involved the 4—6—4Ts as well and it was spread over the 1923—7 period. It is summarised below, this time using the *final* LMS numbers.

Running Numbers	Remarks
2056—2066	LT & S built Class 1 engines, originally 2135—45.
2067—2076	LT & S built Class 1 engines, originally 2125—34 but which ran as 2190—9 during 1927.
2077—2091	LT & S built Class 1 engines, originally 2110—24 but which ran as 2200—14 during 1923—7.
2092—2109	LT & S built Class 2 engines, originally 2158—75.
2110—2134	LMS built Class 3 engines placed in service during 1923—7.
2135—2146	LT & S built Class 3 engines (rebuilt from Class 2), originally 2146—57.
2147—2150	LT & S built Class 3 engines, originally 2176—9.
2151—2160	LMS built Class 3 engines placed in service during 1930.

At nationalisation, the surviving 4—4—2Ts (all in the 2092—2160 range) were renumbered again as BR 41910—26 (Class 2 engines) and 41928—78 (Class 3 engines). This was to make room for further Fairburn 2—6—4Ts.

Plate 108 The LTSR only owned two tender locomotives and these had originally been built for the Ottoman Railway but were never delivered, being purchased by the LTSR. No. 2899 was renumbered 22899 in 1935 and was withdrawn the following year. The combination of a 'Midland front end' looks somewhat unusual with the 'Eastern cab'. Livery Code C14.

Authors' Collection

THE SOMERSET AND DORSET JOINT RAILWAY

In 1930, the LMS absorbed the locomotive stock of the S & DJR. Since 1875, the Midland Railway had acted for the S & D in the locomotive field so the locomotives taken over in 1930 bore a distinctly Midland look. Some, in fact, were pure Midland designs. In most cases, the ex-S & D locomotives took running numbers vacated by similar Midland engines which had been withdrawn during the 1923—30 period. A summary list is given below:

Running Numbers	Description	Number Taken Over
300—303	Class 2P 4—4—0s with small wheels (5 ft 9 in).	4
320—321	Class 2P 4—4—0s with small wheels (6 ft 0 in).	2
322—326	Class 2P 4—4—0s of standard Midland pattern (the Fowler superheated version with 7 ft 0½ in wheels).	5
633—635	LMS standard Class 2P 4—4—0s built in 1928 as LMS 575/6 and 580. They were sold to the S & D and on return to the LMS were numbered at the end of the latest batch of standard 2Ps to be built.	3
	Total Passenger Tender	14
1200—1207 1230—1232 1305	Class 1P Johnson 0—4—4Ts very similar to the MR version. 1305 was, in fact, an ex-MR locomotive which was given back its original MR number.	12
	Total Passenger Tank	12
1500—1507	Fox-Walker Class 2F 0—6—0STs of non-Midland style.	8
7150—7156	LMS standard Class 3F 0—6—0Ts built for the S & D in 1928—9. They were renumbered 7310—16 after 1934.	7
7190—7191	Single speed geared Sentinel locomotives built in 1929 for the S & D. They were 0—4—0Ts.	2
	Total Freight Tank	17
2880—2890	Johnson Class 1F 0—6—0s. Unlike the pure Midland examples, the ex-S & D locomotives had 4 ft 6 in wheels and were noticeably smaller than the contemporary MR Class 2 0—6—0s.	11
Various: 3194—260	Apart from minor variations, these were standard Midland pattern Class 3F 0—6—0s all with Belpaire boilers. They were given numbers vacated by ex-MR locomotives as follows: 3194/8/201/4/11/16/18/28/48/60.	10
4557—61	Class 4F 0—6—0s of standard Midland type. They were given LMS numbers at the end of the latest batch of LMS standard 4Fs to have been built at the time of absorption of the S & DJR engines.	5
9670—80	These were Class 7F 2—8—0 locomotives designed at Derby specially for the S & DJR. Six were built in 1914 and the last five in 1925 with larger boilers. In essence they were a Midland design which was never adopted by the Midland for its own use. In 1932, the LMS renumbered the engines 13800—10 to allow for further construction of standard Class 7F 0—8—0s.	11
	Total freight tender	37
	Total ex-S & DJR engines absorbed by the LMS	80

Plate 109 The sturdy S&DJR 0—6—0s did not survive long after becoming LMS stock. Their outward appearance was very similar to the Johnson 0—6—0s built during the same period (see Plate 100, page 69) but the S&D locomotives had smaller driving wheels. No. 2883, originally S&DJR No. 37, again displays non-standard lettering applied locally following the absorption of the S&DJR locomotive stock by the LMS in 1930. Livery Code basically C18.

Real Photographs

Plate 110 This ex-S&DJR locomotive is in blue livery with a non-standard hand painted insignia. No. 303 was one of four locomotives, all being withdrawn shortly after the S&DJR became part of the LMS.   *H.C. Casserley*

Plate 111 (Right) The Fox Walker 0—6—0STs numbered nine in total and eight were taken over by the LMS, the last locomotive being withdrawn in 1934. This locomotive, No. 1506, has also been relettered by a local signwriter and displays a non-standard style of livery.
Authors' Collection

Plate 112 (Below) A pair of 0—4—0T single-speed geared Sentinel locomotives were built in 1929 and their LMS numbers were 7190/1. This picture reveals the presence of 'LMS' on the cabside but the locomotive number is only present on the front numberplate.
BR LMR

Plate 113 The largest S&DJR locomotives were the 2—8—0s and this picture of No. 9680 was taken at Bath on 9th June, 1930. Six small boilered locomotives were built in 1914 and five more with larger boilers in 1925. In due course all received small boilers as shown on No. 9680 (originally S&DJR No. 90). Later, in 1932 they were renumbered Nos.13800- 10 before becoming BR Nos. 53800-10. Livery Code C14.   *H.C. Casserley*

STRATFORD ON AVON AND MIDLAND JUNCTION RAILWAY

The SMJR contributed 13 locomotives to the LMS lists. There was one Beyer-Peacock 2—4—0 passenger tender engine, allocated LMS No. 290 but the engine was scrapped in 1924 before receiving it. The other 12 engines were a motley collection of 0—6—0 tender designs, all but one of Beyer-Peacock construction. They were allocated LMS numbers 2300—11 and most received them. The Beyer-Peacock 0—6—0 engines were double framed types, somewhat reminiscent of the Kirtley ex-MR locomotives; while the odd man out (2303) was an ex-LB & SCR locomotive of characteristic Stroudley lineaments.

Three SMJR engines lasted long enough to be in the way of new Fowler 2—6—4Ts (2302/5/6). They were renumbered 2397—9 in order but were all gone before 1931.

Plate 114 SMJR No. 14 was renumbered 2307 by the LMS and was one of the most modern locomotives owned by that company. This photograph was taken for the benefit of its new owners, the London Midland & Scottish Railway Company, on 21st May, 1923.   *BR LMR*

THE NORTH STAFFORDSHIRE RAILWAY

Locomotive Superintendents:

J. Johnson	1865—1870
T. W. Dodds	1870—1874
R. N. Angus	1874—1875
C. Clare	1875—1882
L. Longbottom	1882—1902
J. H. Adams	1902—1915
J. A. Hookham	1915—1922

The NSR locomotives were originally allocated numbers in the Midland Division series, since the NSR was at first part of this Division. The area was later transferred to the Western Division and many ex-NSR locomotives were ultimately renumbered into the Western Division lists to make way for new construction. Nevertheless, many more retained their Midland Division numbers until scrapping. Like the LT & SR, the NSR was predominantly a tank engine line, though not as markedly so as the Tilbury system. The engines added to the LMS lists were, for the most part, neat and unfussy machines. However, they contained many small classes of but a few engines each and they were destined during LMS days to be swept aside by the new standard classes.

It has already been remarked (page 71) how the insertion of the Tilbury engines and the Deeley 0—6—4Ts into the 1907 MR numbering scheme had slightly altered the normal principles of MR/LMS numbering policy (Passenger Tender; Passenger Tank; Freight Tank; Freight Tender); and at the grouping, the ex-NSR engines were numbered adjacent to their nearest MR or LT & SR equivalents rather than in strict order of types. In the summary which follows, the ex-NSR engines are given by generic types to maintain consistency with the rest of the pre-group chapters but because of the considerable number of small classes, semi-tabular presentation has been preferred to narrative description.

Running Numbers	Description
595—9	595—8 were Adams Class 'G' 4—4—0s dating from 1910 (599 was Class 'KT'). They were allocated 5410—14 in 1928 and extinct by 1933.
	Total Passenger Tender 5
1431—9	These nine engines were Adams Class 'M' 0—4—4Ts built 1907—20. They were withdrawn between 1931 and 1939.
1440—51	The surviving examples of the Longbottom Class 'B' 2—4—0Ts, introduced in 1882. The class became extinct in 1933.
1454—9	These six engines, Longbottom Class 'A' and 'B' 2—4—2Ts, were survivors of a group of eight engines rebuilt from 2—4—0Ts of 1878—95. They were all withdrawn by 1934.

Plate 115 Although the NSR owned but five 4—4—0s, these comprised four of Class G and a single representative of Class KT. The latter (illustrated here) was NSR No. 38, later LMS No. 599 and was renumbered 5414 when its first LMS number was required for new Class 2P 4—4—0 construction. Photographed at Llandudno in early grouping days (note LNWR coaches in the background still in LNWR livery), the locomotive is in crimson lake livery. Code A1.   *A.G. Ellis*

Plate 116 LMS No. 1436 was originally NSR Class M and is shown here in black lined livery, Code B4. Photographed at Stoke, date unknown, and the reader's attention is drawn to the white on the boiler top and coal, which is a layer of snow.

Authors' Collection

Plate 117 Clare 2—4—2T, LMS No. 1457, was originally NSR No. 21, and started life as a 2—4—0T. It is seen here in crimson lake livery, Code A3. *A.G. Ellis*

Plate 118 This shows an Adams Class C No. 2041 in crimson lake livery, Code A1. *A.G. Ellis*

Plate 119 Adams Class K 4—4—2T No. 2180 in crimson lake livery, Code A1, double-heads a stopping passenger train with an ex-LNWR 0—6—0 'Cauliflower' still in LNWR livery. This combination of post- and pre-group livery would have been commonplace during the first few years of the LMS.   *A.G. Ellis*

2040—7	Adams Class 'C' 0—6—4Ts.
2048—55	Adams and Hookham Class 'F' 0—6—4Ts.

(Note: The above two 0—6—4T classes were built during and after the First World War and are recorded as freight tanks in some sources. However, the LMS listed them as passenger tanks and gave them the fully lined pre-1928 crimson lake livery. They suffered the same fate as the similar Deeley 0—6—4Ts, succumbing to LMS standard designs between 1934 and 1937).

2180—6   Adams Class 'K' 4—4—2Ts, built during 1911—12 and extinct during 1935.

Total Passenger Tank   50

1550—98   These engines formed the largest single class of ex-NSR engines. They were Longbottom Class 'D' 0—6—0Ts introduced in 1883. Intact at grouping, the whole class was withdrawn between 1927 and 1937.

1599   This engine was the experimental Hookham four-cylinder 0—6—0T of 1922. It was rebuilt in tender form during 1924 without ever receiving the number 1599. After rebuilding it became LMS 2367.

1600—1   This pair of somewhat elderly Hudswell Clarke 0—6—0STs dated from 1866 but had been rebuilt in 1880—1. They were quite resilient engines, one going in 1927 and the other in 1930.

1602—3   These engines were much newer Kerr-Stuart 0—6—0Ts of 1919 and did not find much favour with the LMS. They were withdrawn in 1932/3.

2234—9   These Longbottom Class 'DX' 0—6—2Ts of 1899—1902 were yet further early casualties of the standardisation programme, most being scrapped by 1931, the last in 1935.

2240—73   The Adams Class 'L' and 'New L' 0—6—2Ts were built over a 20 year period between 1903 and 1923, the last four engines actually entering service after grouping. Nevertheless, they fared no better than many older engines, the last being withdrawn in 1937.

Total Freight Tank   90 + 4 (LMS Built)

2320—31	The Clare Class 'E' 0—6—0s were the oldest NSR tender engines. Yet, although in the region of 50 years old
2334—42	at grouping, the last was not withdrawn until 1934.

2332—3   Sharp Stewart engines built 1873—4.

2343—50	The Longbottom '100' Class 0—6—0s were much newer engines (1896) and lasted intact until 1928. Nos.
2357—8	2357—8 were the 'New 100' Class of 1907. All were withdrawn by 1931.

2351—6   These six 0—6—0 engines, to a Pettigrew Furness Railway design of 1900, were gradually withdrawn from service during 1929—36.

2359—66   The Adams Class 'H' 0—6—0 was a short lived design. They were built between 1909 and 1911 but although the most modern and powerful of the ex-NSR 0—6—0 engines, they were scrapped during 1929 and 1930. The last four had Belpaire fireboxes.

2367   This engine was the 0—6—0 tender rebuild of engine No. 1599 (above). Being experimental, it only ran for a few years and was scrapped in 1928.

Total Freight Tender[1]   47 + 1

Total ex-NSR engines absorbed by the LMS[2]   194 + 4 (LMS Built)

Note:

1 The surviving ex-NSR 0—6—0s in 1927 were numbered into the 8650—89 series to allow for construction of new Fowler 2—6—4Ts. The pre-1928 withdrawals were all from NSR Class 'E' plus 2332—3.

2 Total also includes two narrow gauge Leek and Manifold engines.

Plate 120 In resplendent condition, No. 1572, a Longbottom Class D 0—6—0T, shows the first LMS style for this class, Livery Code C4.
Authors' Collection

Plate 121 No. 1601 was one of two Hudswell Clarke 0—6—0Ts dating from 1866, this example lasting until 1930. Livery Code appears to be C16. *Real Photographs*

Plate 122 No. 2331 was an example of the Clare Class E 0—6—0s built by Vulcan in 1872. It was later re-numbered 8658 by the LMS before withdrawal. Livery Code C1.
Real Photographs

Chapter 5   Pre-Group Locomotives - Western Division

The Western Division locomotive number series (5000–9999), originally Western 'A', was almost entirely allocated to ex-LNWR engines. However, there were a few ex-Wirral Railway locomotives and, of course, the LNWR list itself contained engines of North London Railway origin. These two small companies will be treated separately in this chapter.

THE LONDON AND NORTH WESTERN RAILWAY

Locomotive Superintendents:

Southern Division
J. E. McConnell	1846–1862

Northern Division
F. Trevithick	1846–1857
J. Ramsbottom	1857–1862
John Ramsbottom	1862–1871
Francis William Webb	1871–1903
George Whale	1903–1909
Charles John Bowen-Cooke	1909–1920
Hewitt Pearson Montague Beames	1920–1921
George Hughes	1922

(after amalgamation with the LYR)

The LNWR contribution of some 3,360 engines to LMS capital stock (excluding NLR) represented the largest single total from any of the pre-group constituents and accounted for almost one third of the new company's engines at the time of the grouping. However, fate was to decree that, numerical superiority notwithstanding, the products of Crewe had little influence on LMS locomotive development compared with those from Derby. Moreover, as E. S. Cox has pointed out elsewhere*, the LNWR classes did not show up very well in terms of maintenance costs either when placed alongside those built by the Midland.

It is outside the scope of this account to analyse the reasons for this state of affairs but the fact remains that the LNWR engines (especially the passenger types) were scrapped in large quantities almost from the start of the LMS period. It is, of course, probably true to say that the LNWR engines had been worked harder during their pre-1923 existence than had those of the other constituents. In consequence many LNWR engines were worn out beyond economical repair. Whatever the reasons, the general state of the LNWR stock at the time of the grouping must have given the LMS management cause for concern. One must therefore conclude that the generally critical state on the Western Division was one of the major factors which led to the LMS 'scrap and build' policy of the later 1920s and throughout the 1930s.

* *Chronicles of Steam* – E. S. Cox (Ian Allan 1967)

Plate 123 No. 5005 *Pitt*, ex-LNWR No. 1522, has been chosen to represent the LNWR 2–4–0s, and this example was one of the larger wheeled 'Precedent' Class. The livery is interesting, original LNWR lining is clearly visible on the tender and cabside but the LMS emblem and 'Midland style' numbers are in evidence. Livery Code C8 (plus LNWR lining remaining).
Real Photographs

Plate 124 'Renown' Class 4—4—0 No. 5186 *Victorious* was originally an 'Alfred the Great' Class 4-cylinder compound which ran as LNWR No. 1950. Photographed in its final years its livery is Code C7 (plus LNWR lining).

Authors' Collection

Passenger Tender Engines

By 1923, the memories of F. W. Webb and his semi-obsession with compounding were beginning to fade and a major portion of LNWR passenger services was handled by the large family of two-cylinder, simple expansion 4—4—0 and 4—6—0 locomotives initiated by George Whale during the Edwardian period and later developed by Bowen-Cooke from 1910 onwards. These engines had swept away Webb's compounds almost as ruthlessly as they themselves were to be replaced by Fowler and Stanier engines during the next two decades. Augmenting these locomotives were well over 100 residual survivors of the Webb régime (mostly 2—4—0s but with a few 4—4—0s) and about the same number of the latest of all the Crewe products, the four-cylinder 'Claughton' Class 4—6—0s, the latter being in charge of the heaviest workings.

The 2—4—0 designs (LMS 5000—109), dating back to 1874, were, perhaps, the most successful of Webb's passenger engines. They were, of course, the celebrated two-cylinder simple expansion 'Jumbos' of which LNWR No. 790 *Hardwicke* is preserved, happily still in working order. After the grouping, 110 of the 112 surviving engines were allotted LMS numbers, the largest quota being the 80 machines with 6 ft 9 in wheels (LNWR 'Precedent' Class — LMS 5000—79). These were augmented by 30 of the 'Waterloo' Class (LMS 5080—109) which had 6 ft 3 in wheels. A few further 2—4—0s were also retained in the engineering departmental stock.

These veterans, complete with their splendid names, were to see barely ten years service before all were consigned to the scrap heap. A few managed to sport the new LMS crimson lake livery but most did not even manage to get renumbered until the later 1920s, by which time there was little future left for them; and they served out their days on minor workings — a far cry indeed from Shap Fell and the 'Corridor'. Only one lasted long enough for its number to conflict with the Stanier Class 5 4—6—0s and then only for a few months in 1934 (LMS 5001, later 25001; ex-LNWR 2191 *Snowdon*).

Of the 297 engines of 4—4—0 wheel arrangement given LMS numbers (5110—266/70—409), 220 were of the celebrated 'Precursor' and 'George the Fifth' types designed by Whale and Bowen-Cooke respectively. The remaining engines, mostly of the two-cylinder simple expansion 'Renown' Class, had started life as Webb four-cylinder compounds at the turn of the century. Rebuilding had taken place during the 1908—23 period and at the grouping, the 'Renowns' were allocated LMS numbers 5131—86. The remaining Webb engines (5110—30) were still in compound form at the end of 1922 but those that were not almost immediately scrapped were rebuilt as 'Renowns' during the first few post-grouping years. The compound classes from which the 'Renowns' were rebuilt were the 'Jubilee' Class (residual survivors LMS 5110—17) and the 'Alfred the Great' Class (residual survivors LMS 5118—30). The last 'Renown' was scrapped in 1931 and the class was of minor importance in LMS days.

It is a matter of history that the 'Precursor' and 'George the Fifth' Class 4—4—0s all but revolutionised LNWR locomotive affairs. However, by the time of the grouping, the earliest 'Precursors' were almost 20 years old and even the newest 'Georges' were half that age. Furthermore, for most of their life they had been flogged unmercifully in front of loads which would have made the majority of Midland 4—4—0 drivers turn pale! Not surprisingly, the LNWR 4—4—0s wore out quite rapidly and were steadily withdrawn during the 1927—49 period. A basic policy decision to build no more new boilers sounded their death knell.

The engines fell into three groups. LMS 5187—266 were the original saturated 'Precursors', several of which were superheated after the grouping. Most, however, were destined to become the first of the type to be withdrawn, still in saturated condition. The second group (LMS 5270—319) were those 'Precursors' which had been superheated before 1923 and the final group (LMS 5320—409) were the 'George the Fifth' series, all of which were superheated.

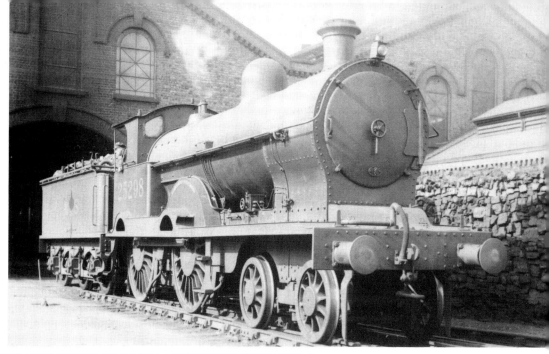

Plate 125 'Precursor' Class 4—4—0 No. 25298 *Dragon* after being added to the duplicate list. Note the round top boiler. Livery Code, probably B10.
A.G. Ellis

Plate 126 'George the Fifth' Class 4—4—0 No. 5345 *Foxhound* in early LMS livery, Code A1, with its number on the tender and carrying a smokebox numberplate, later to be removed. Ex-LNWR locomotives of the 'Precursor', 'George the Fifth' and 'Prince of Wales' classes ran with a variety of round top and Belpaire boilers and it is difficult to be certain just which variety of boiler was carried at any particular date and for how long on any locomotive.
A.G. Ellis

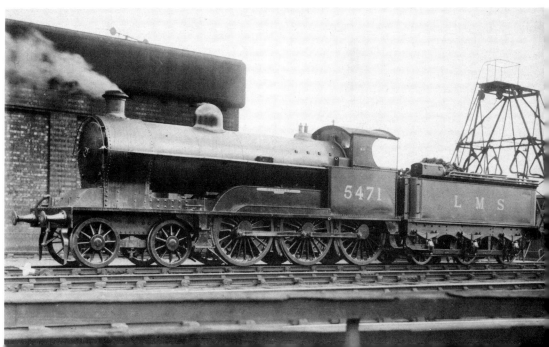

Plate 127 No. 5471 *President* was a member of the 'Experiment' Class, originally LNWR No. 1992. This picture can be considered typical for the class in the post-1928 period. Livery Code C18.

Authors' Collection

The LNWR 4—4—0s were slow to be renumbered during the early LMS period but a number did get repainted in the pre-1928 crimson lake livery. In later days, many of them sported unlined black as they served out time on lesser workings. Many survived long enough to be renumbered into the 25xxx series after the advent of the Stanier Class 5.

Over half the LNWR passenger tender engines were of the 4—6—0 wheel arrangement and three types were represented. The oldest were the 105 Whale 'Experiment' Class engines — essentially a 4—6—0 version of the 'Precursor' 4—4—0 which were allocated LMS numbers 5450—554. The last example (LMS 5554 *Prospero*) had been rebuilt in 1915 with four cylinders and Dendy-Marshall valve gear. Following on the 'Experiments' were the 245 Bowen-Cooke 'Prince of Wales' Class engines (LMS 5500—844). The first members of this class were contemporary with the 'George the Fifth' 4—4—0s and the class itself bore the same relationship to the 'Experiments' as the 'Georges' did to the 'Precursors'. Unlike the 'George', the 'Prince of Wales' engines continued to be built almost to the time of the grouping and the LMS itself added the 246th member to the class in 1924 (LMS 5845).

It should be noted that four of the 'Prince of Wales' type (5632/72/88/726) were fitted in 1923/4 with outside Walschaerts valve gear driving the inside cylinders and 5845 was built new to this design. The style received the unofficial nickname 'Tishy' — reputedly because the outside valve gear of these five engines resembled the legs of a racehorse of that name which apparently crossed them whilst running!

It is generally assumed that the 4—6—0 wheel arrangement on the 'Experiment' and 'Prince of Wales' engines was adopted (in preference to building more of the 4—4—0 type) in order to improve hill climbing — especially on the steeper gradients between Crewe and Carlisle. In fact, there did not seem to be a great deal to choose between the two arrangements but the 4—6—0s were, eventually, the more numerous. In many ways, the 'Prince of Wales' Class came to be to the LNWR what the Stanier Class 5 later became to the LMS — a general all-purpose maid of all work. In fact, it was not until Class 5 construction really began to get into its stride that serious inroads were made into the 'Prince of Wales' type. Most of them survived to reach the 25xxx duplicate list but, thereafter, scrapping became ever more rapid and only four lasted into BR days. The 'Experiments' were far less fortunate and all were scrapped by 1935.

The final LNWR passenger tender design was the Bowen-Cooke four-cylinder 'Claughton' Class which dated from 1913 (LMS 5900—6029). These engines were the mainstay of the most heavily loaded LNWR services in 1922, but were curiously patchy and disappointing in service. The LMS rebuilt 20 of them with larger boilers (half with Caprotti and half with conventional Walschaerts valve gear) and this effected something of an improvement. On the whole, however, the 'Claughtons' were no match, either in performance or serviceability, for the LMS standard Class 5XP and 6P classes which replaced them. Nevertheless, they formed an important element in the history and development of the three-cylinder 'Patriot' Class 5XP 4—6—0 and, as such, they will be considered in more detail in the 'Patriot' Class chapter in *Volume III*.

The original 'Claughtons' were swept aside in the 1930s, 42 of them being officially 'rebuilt' into 'Patriots' — not that much was left after the rebuilding! A few of the larger boilered engines fared rather better and lasted until the war years. One lone survivor of these (LMS 6004) reached BR but was scrapped before it received its BR number.

It should finally be pointed out that most of the ex-LNWR passenger tender engines which survived for more than a few years after the grouping had their cabs cut down to fit the LMS composite loading gauge and several of the 'Claughton' and 'Prince of Wales' engines were fitted with Robinson GCR type (ex-ROD) tenders.

Total ex-LNWR passenger tender engines at grouping:

2—4—0 type	112
4—4—0 type	299
4—6—0 type	481†
Total	892

† including one LMS built example.

Plate 128 'Prince of Wales' 4—6—0 No. 5607 *Defiance* equipped for oil burning. A number of locomotives were converted for oil burning in 1926 and many LNWR locomotives were renumbered by the simple expedient of removing the LNWR numberplate, in this instance No. 1721, and stencilling the new LMS number in its place. This picture has been selected to illustrate these points.   *A.G. Ellis*

Passenger Tank Engines

Webb's passenger tender engines may have been numerically well into decline at the grouping but the same cannot be said of his passenger tank classes which were very well represented on the LMS in its infancy. The Webb designs were supplemented by the larger and newer tank engine classes derived from Whale and Bowen-Cooke tender engines.

The oldest LNWR passenger tank engines were fifteen 2—4—0Ts dating back to 1876 (LMS 6420—34). Sometimes called 'Chopper' tanks, these engines were all but gone from the scene by 1936 except for one lone survivor (6428) which not only received its LMS duplicate number (26428) but also its BR number (58092) before being scrapped in 1952. It was retained in service to work on the Cromford and High Peak line.

Derived from both the 2—4—0Ts and the 2—4—0 tender engines were the much larger classes of 2—4—2Ts (LMS 6515—757) which saw widespread service throughout the LNWR system. Two classes were represented of which the older type, dating from 1882, had 4 ft 6 in driving wheels (LMS 6515—99) and the newer type, introduced in 1890, had 5 ft 6 in driving wheels. The older engines were decimated during the first few years after grouping and had all vanished by 1932, many neither being renumbered or repainted. However, in spite of continuous withdrawals throughout the whole LMS period, at least 20 of the large wheeled engines survived to BR and the class was not extinct until 1955.

The final Webb passenger tanks were the 0—6—2Ts of 1898—1902 vintage (LMS 6860—936). Known generally as 'Watford', or '18 in' tanks, thus indicating at least one important area of utilisation, these engines were not, strange to relate, quite as resilient as the 2—4—2Ts. Only a handful survived to BR and all were gone by the end of 1953.

It is interesting to contrast the relative longevity of the Webb passenger tanks with the much shorter life of the newer and larger Whale and Bowen-Cooke designs. In 1906, George Whale produced a 4—4—2T version of the 'Precursor' 4—4—0 but with 6 ft 3 in wheels. Fifty were built (LMS 6780—829) of which all were in existence as late as 1927; yet all had gone by 1941. The Bowen-Cooke 4—6—2Ts, derived from the 'Prince of Wales' type 4—6—0, had an even shorter life. Introduced in 1910, all were intact in 1936 but the last survivor was gone by 1942.

Essentially, the reason for this contrast is not hard to find. One of the most successful products of the LMS standardisation programme was the 2—6—4T in its various guises. This single type of engine proved a more than adequate replacement for most of the larger pre-group passenger tanks which were quickly scrapped. However, the smaller LMS standard tanks of the 1930s (Fowler and Stanier 2—6—2Ts) were neither as numerous or as successful as the 2—6—4Ts and it was not until the post-war Ivatt Class 2 designs made widespread appearance that the smaller and older pre-group machines could finally be pensioned off.

Total ex-LNWR passenger tank engines at grouping:

2—4—0 type	15
2—4—2 type	243
0—6—2 type	77
4—4—2 type	50
4—6—2 type	47
Total	432

Plate 129 No. 6422 is an example of one of the 15 2—4—0Ts, sometimes known as 'Choppers'. The bunker was not big enough for the normal size 'LMS' cab panel, a problem shared by a number of other classes.

Authors' Collection

Plate 130 (Above) The older LNWR 2–4–2Ts were numbered within the series 6515-6599 but many never carried LMS livery. This picture of No. 6597, Livery Code C18, is a good example of the class condition in their final LMS years when re-numbered. *Real Photographs*

Plate 131 (Left) The large wheel 0–6–2Ts were sometimes referred to as 'Watford Tanks' and this picture of No. 6883 at Birmingham New Street on 2nd October, 1937 carrying Livery Code C18 can be considered typical in both livery and external condition for this period of their life-time. *L. Hanson*

Plate 132 The 4–6–2Ts were some-times referred to as 'Prince of Wales' tanks and this picture of ex-LNWR No. 1184 shows a locomotive in LNWR livery which has just been renumbered by removing the LNWR numberplate and stencilling the new LMS number 6976 in its place. *Authors' Collection*

Freight Tank Engines

To say that the LNWR freight tanks were a varied collection is to put it mildly. The designs covered virtually all sizes from the smallest 0—4—0 well tanks for works use to the massive 0—8—4Ts which emerged immediately after the grouping. However, by far the majority of ex-LNWR freight tanks were six-coupled engines of either 0—6—0 or 0—6—2 wheel arrangement.

The smallest LNWR standard gauge engines were the Webb 0—4—0WTs of 1880. Ten were built but only six were numbered into LMS capital stock (LMS 7200—5), the others being listed in the departmental series. These diminutive little engines were confined to works use and were so small as to defy all attempts to give them LMS liveries or numbers — even the LNWR number plate had to be mounted on the side frames between the driving wheels! Nevertheless, they lasted very well and the last survivor (a departmental example) was not withdrawn until 1942.

Almost as small (and even older) were the quaint Ramsbottom 0—4—0STs whose design dated from 1864 (LMS 7206—16 plus five more in departmental stock). These engines enjoyed a very long twilight period and withdrawals (which had started prior to the grouping) were not complete until 1947, the survivor again being in departmental use. One is preserved in the National Collection.

Completing the tally of four-coupled freight tanks were 20 Webb 0—4—2STs with the well known 'Square' saddle feature. Dating from 1896, these engines were destined to last 60 years. In the early post-grouping years they were, for some reason, wrongly numbered in the passenger tank series as LMS 6400—19 but in 1927 they were renumbered more logically as 7850—69 after only five had received 64xx numbers.*

The basic LNWR freight tank was a six-coupled engine and these fell neatly into two groups; 0—6—0 saddle tanks and 0—6—2 side tanks.

The saddle tanks were of two classes. The most numerous and oldest were the Ramsbottom 'Special' 0—6—0STs (LMS 7220—457 plus a few departmental engines). These locomotives dated from 1870 and although rapid inroads were made into them as the LMS standard Class 3F 0—6—0Ts came into service, a few did manage to survive in departmental use until as late as 1959.

    * N.B. There were also some Webb 0—4—2 crane tanks but these were never allocated LMS capital stock numbers.

Plate 133 This delightful picture is an example of a Ramsbottom 0—4—0ST No. 7216 in post-1928 livery, Code C16. Note that the lid of water tank is open, the Ramsbottom smokebox door, and the bracing rod to the cab front.

Real Photographs

Plate 134 Later to become No. 7468 this picture illustrates No. 6418 in its first LMS livery. As noted, this class was originally numbered within the passenger tank series but they were soon altered to a more logical series within the freight tank numbers. Note the smokebox numberplate, later removed. Livery Code C5 — note that the position of the number and 'LMS' panel has been reversed.

Real Photographs

Plate 135 The numerous Ramsbottom 'Special' tanks lasted many years and this picture of No. 7438 in pre-1928 livery Code C4 is interesting in that the position of the number and 'LMS' panel (usually found on the cabside) has been reversed. Livery Code C4.   *Authors' Collection*

Most of them had, however, gone by 1934 and only some 20 long-term survivors received LMS duplicate numbers.

The other saddle tank design (LMS 7458–502) was a saddle tank version of the Webb 0–6–0 'Coal' engines. As tank engines, these locomotives dated from 1905 but basically they had started life as tender engines to a design dating from 1873. Rather a higher proportion of these engines reached the LMS duplicate list than did the Ramsbottom design although, of course, the total number was fewer. One only (LMS 27462) reached BR but never received its allotted number (58870). They exhibited a similar "square" saddle to the 0–4–2STs.

The most numerous design of LNWR freight tank was the Webb 0–6–2T design of 1881 (LMS 7550–841). The 'Coal' tanks were a familiar sight over the whole system and to call them freight tanks was something of a misnomer. Many were used for passenger work and a few were fitted for push-pull passenger working. A goodly number reached the duplicate list in 1934 and 58 were allocated BR numbers although not all received them. Like most LNWR classes, many were slow to be renumbered by the LMS in the early post-group period.

The LNWR freight tank list was completed by 60 eight-coupled engines of two types — both derived from the contemporary 0–8–0 tender classes. The older design was the Bowen-Cooke 0–8–2T of 1911 (LMS 7870–99) which lasted until 1953. This type was developed by Beames into the 0–8–4T design of 1923 which only lasted until 1951. The latter engines (LMS 7930–59) were not actually delivered until after the grouping and only fifteen had been allocated genuine LNWR numbers before the LMS took over. Some of these, in fact, entered service with LNWR numbers but with LMS markings on the tank side. Perhaps the most surprising feature in the early days was the delivery of six of these engines (7943–9) in the fully lined LMS crimson lake livery! None of the 8-coupled tanks ever received cut-back cabs and were, therefore, entirely excluded from the Midland Division.

Total ex-LNWR freight tank engines at grouping:*

0–4–0 type	17
0–4–2 type	20
0–6–0 type	283
0–6–2 type	292
0–8–2 type	30
0–8–4 type	30 †
Total	672

* Not counting departmental engines but including post-1922 building to LNWR design.

† LMS built.

Plate 136 (Above) This picture of No. 27496, Livery Code C16, is an example of an 0—6—0 tender engine rebuilt to a pannier tank and carrying its post-1934 number when placed upon the duplicate list. *BR LMR*

Plate 137 The LNWR 'Coal Tanks' were to be found all over the Western Division and they displayed a variety of liveries during the LMS period. This picture of No. 7763 taken at Crewe South on 1st May, 1938, displays the most common post-1928 livery, Code C18, for this class of locomotive. No. 7763 is fitted for working motor trains; note the two vacuum pipes on the front buffer beam. Note also 2—4—2T No. 6676 in Livery Code B10. *L. Hanson*

Plate 138 The large 0—8—2Ts of Bowen-Cooke design were intended for shunting and trip freight working. No. 7880, photographed in Crewe Works Yard on 14th April, 1935, and carrying Livery Code C17, still has its smokebox door numberplate. *L. Hanson*

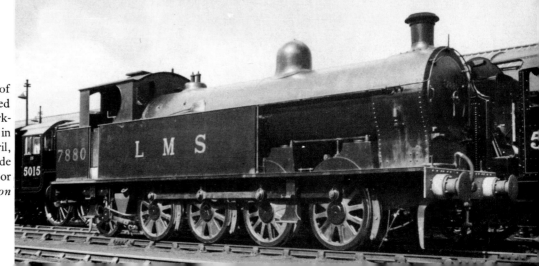

Freight Tender Engines

Unlike the MR, the LNWR was not totally wedded to one wheel arrangement for its main line freight services and although six-coupled engines were numerically in the ascendant at the grouping, the company also possessed well over 600 eight-coupled locomotives.

The LMS inherited 624 engines of 0—6—0 wheel arrangement from the LNWR and a further 170 of the 4—6—0 type. Oldest of the six-coupled group were the last of the celebrated Ramsbottom 'DX' Class (LMS 8000—87), the eldest of which went right back to 1858. These veterans had been built in their hundreds and withdrawals had been extensive for over 20 years prior to the grouping. In consequence, not many of the residual 88 members of the class survived long enough to receive LMS numbers and all were gone before 1931.

The Webb 0—6—0s on the other hand, although still fairly venerable, lasted well into BR days in spite of continuous withdrawals throughout the whole LMS period. Two classes of engine were involved; the 17″ 'Coal' engines of 1873 (LMS 8088—314) and the famous 'Cauliflowers' (LMS 8315—624 excluding 8328/9—blank) dating from 1880. Withdrawals of the 'Coal' engines started well before 1923 but the 'Cauliflowers' were all but intact at that year. Examples of both types lasted long enough to go onto the LMS duplicate list in the 1940s (during the large scale building of Stanier Class 8F 2—8—0s) and well over 100 of the Webb 0—6—0s were allocated BR 58xxx numbers — most carried them. The 'Coal' engines finally became extinct in 1953 and the 'Cauliflowers' in 1955.

The final LNWR six-coupled goods engines were not so long lived as their predecessors. These were the 170 George Whale 4—6—0s, generally referred to as '19 in Goods' engines (LMS 8700—869). One suspects that, like so many other Whale engines, they had been well and truly exploited during their first 20 years of life and by the 1930s stood no chance of competing with the new range of standard engines. Intact in 1931, the class had gone by 1950 — swept aside, like so many others, by the ubiquitous Stanier breed.

The ex-LNWR eight-coupled freight tender engines handed over to the LMS presented a strange contrast in types. On the one hand there was a motley collection of asserted 2—8—0 designs and compound 0—8—0s and on the other there was the highly successful final LNWR 0—8—0 design (the 'G2' Class) which was destined not only to outlive its LMS standard derivative (the Fowler Class 7F 0—8—0) but also to become the last of the LNWR standard gauge types to survive in main line service.

The 2—8—0 engines were of two main types, either Webb four-cylinder compounds (Classes 'E' and 'F') or Robinson Great Central Railway type ex-ROD 2—8—0s, acquired by the LNWR after the First World War. The Webb 2—8—0s (LMS 9600—15) started life just after the turn of the century as 0—8—0 compounds but were converted to 2—8—0 during the George Whale period. After the grouping, half were scrapped quite quickly as 2—8—0s but the other eight were rebuilt to the final LNWR 0—8—0 simple arrangement and renumbered 8892—9. In this form, they matched the remaining LNWR 0—8—0s (see below) and lasted into the 1960s.

The ex-ROD engines (LMS 9616—65) were acquired by the LNWR and LMS before and after the grouping. Of the LNWR acquisitions (9616—45), many did not enter service until too late to receive their allotted LNWR series numbers. The LMS did not seem very enthusiastic about these engines, in spite of their relative newness, and scrapping commenced in 1928. In 1931, 28 of the residual 31 survivors were renumbered 9455—82 to avoid clashing with the numbers of the new Fowler 0—8—0s. All had gone by 1932 and it is interesting to contrast the fate of these engines on the LMS with their considerable success on the LNER and GWR systems. To be fair to them, however, they were faced with extensive LMS route restrictions, being prohibited from virtually the whole of the ex-LYR and ex-MR lines.

There were three basic classes of LNWR 0—6—0s in existence at the grouping and we have illustrated the earliest and final designs in this section. **Plate 139 (left)** shows a Ramsbottom DX Class as rebuilt by Webb carrying both its final LNWR number 3085 and its LMS number 8072. The majority of this class were withdrawn without carrying their allocated LMS numbers.

A.G. Ellis

Plate 140 (Above) The LNWR crested goods, generally known as 'Cauliflowers', were a long lived class and ran with both round top and Belpaire boilers. No. 8350 is seen here in early LMS livery – Code C5 is in the 'correct' livery for the pre-1928 period. *Real Photographs*

Plate 141 The LNWR owned a few 2–8–0s at the time of the grouping and this picture of No. 9601, carries only a smokebox door numberplate. Some doubt must exist about this picture, the locomotive may have been coupled to a tender from another locomotive and therefore attracted the attention of the photographer. On the other hand many unusual 'livery' combinations were to be found on ex LNWR locomotives during the early years of the LMS.

Authors' Collection

Plate 142 The War Department owned a considerable number of 2–8–0s based upon Robinson's GCR design and a number were operating on the LNWR at the time of the grouping. No. 9462 was originally LNWR No. 2093, becoming LMS No. 9629, and, with the arrival of the Fowler 0–8–0s numbered in the 9600 series, it became 9462 before final withdrawal. Livery Code C16.

Real Photographs

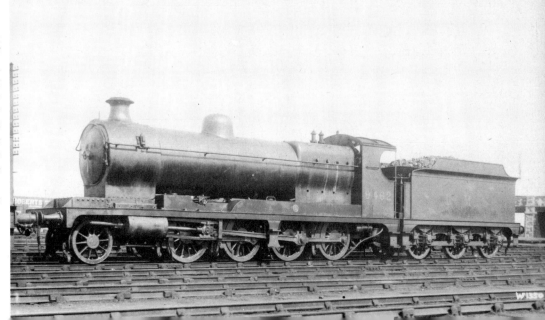

The LNWR 0—8—0 classes (LMS 8900—9454 plus 8892—9 above) had a complex history well outside the scope of this survey. The distribution of the various types (by LMS running numbers) at the time of the grouping is given in *Table 5* — page 42. Essentially, the series had started with a Webb two-cylinder simple design of 1892. This was followed by several series of Webb three and four-cylinder compound variants and finally by the Whale and Bowen-Cooke developments (Classes 'G' and 'G1') which reverted to two-cylinder simple propulsion and culminated in Bowen-Cooke's 'G2' Class of 1921.

Parallel with building new two-cylinder engines, Whale and Bowen-Cooke also pursued a policy of rebuilding the Webb compounds to the two-cylinder simple layout and this process went on right up to and after the grouping. Some of the Webb compounds were also converted to 2—8—0 type (see above). These compounds which were not rebuilt to simple form were scrapped during the 1920s, including the 2—8—0 variants but the rebuilds had a much longer life. The following summary should clarify the situation:

LMS 8892—9	Ex-2—8—0 compounds rebuilt to 0—8—0 Class 'G1' by the LMS. Class 'B' compounds mostly rebuilt
8900—52	to Class 'G1' by the LMS.
8953—67	Whale Class 'C' simples (rebuilt ex-Webb compounds) a few of which were again rebuilt to Class 'G1' by the LMS.
8968—9001	Whale Class 'C1' simples (rebuilt ex-Webb compounds), never subsequently rebuilt and scrapped quite early by the LMS.
9002—64	Whale Class 'D' simples (ex-Webb compounds), all rebuilt again to Class 'G1' by the LMS.
9065—153	Whale Class 'G' simples built as such, all rebuilt to Class 'G1' by the LMS.
9154—394	Bowen-Cooke Class 'G1'
9395—454	Bowen-Cooke Class 'G2'

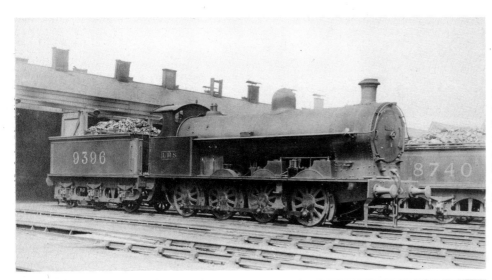

Plate 143 LNWR 0—8—0 No. 9396 was built as a Class G2 No. 742 and this picture shows it running in pre-1928 livery carrying a smokebox door numberplate. Unlike No. 9162 in Plate 144 which has been fitted with LMS buffers, No. 9396 retains its original LNWR buffers.

Authors' Collection

Plate 144 This shows LNWR 0—8—0 No. 9162 with a cut down cab coupled to a tender with coal rails in post-1928 livery, Code C18. No. 9162 was originally a Class G1, LNWR No. 2001.

L. Hanson

By the time of nationalisation, further LMS rebuilding had reduced the varieties to either 'G1' type (with 160 lb boilers) or 'G2'/'G2A' type (with 175 lb boilers). The 'G2As' were rebuilds of the 'G1' Class with 'G2' type boilers. In all, therefore, some of the LNWR 0—8—0s had undergone several stages of rebuilding during the 1920s and 1930s and many of them were, in most essentials, relatively new engines — hence their longevity over nominally younger engines. It is finally, perhaps, also worth recording that to generations of locomen, *all* ex-LNWR 0—8—0s of 'G1', 'G2' or 'G2A' type were known as 'Super Ds' in reference to their original derivation from Whale's Class 'D' engines.

Like the larger LNWR passenger engines, the LNWR 0—8—0s received cut down cab fittings to clear the LMS composite loading gauge and many of them were also fitted with Belpaire boilers, tender cabs and other modifications before finally being scrapped. Some 400 or so of the engines survived to receive BR numbers and many of them soldiered on for almost the whole of the BR steam period, the type finally becoming extinct (except for the preserved 9395) in 1964.

The rebuilding of the LNWR 0—8—0s was a massive and on-going activity and lasted well into the Stanier era. It presented a marked contrast to the normal 'scrap and build' philosophy of the LMS and was a much more significant activity than many of the more celebrated rebuilding programmes of other British railways at the same time. The LNER (very much wedded to rebuilding) never attempted anything on the scale of the LNWR 0—8—0 programme.

Total ex-LNWR freight tender engines at grouping:

0—6—0 type	624
4—6—0 type	170
0—8—0 type	553
2—8—0 type	
LNWR	48
LMS acquired	20
Total	1415

THE WIRRAL RAILWAY

The seventeen tank engines which were added to the LMS stock list by the Wirral Railway are tabulated as part of *Table 5* (page 42). Other than the 2—4—2Ts, four of which were originally of LNWR and one of LYR origin, the Wirral engines were built specifically for that company. They did not long survive grouping and only one genuine Wirral engine (0—4—4T No. LMS 6776) is thought to have been given its allotted LMS number.

The most long lasting ex-Wirral locomotive was 2—4—2T No. 6762 (ex-LYR type) which lasted until 1952. It was correctly numbered in the Western Division list but a vacant number (10638) was, additionally, left in the Central Division 2—4—2T series amongst its LYR contemporaries. This number was never taken up.

Plate 145 The Wirral Railway owned two 0—6—4Ts built by Beyer Peacock and this picture illustrates No. 13 in Wirral Railway livery. Allocated LMS No. 6949, the number was never carried, the locomotive being withdrawn in 1923.

Real Photographs

THE NORTH LONDON RAILWAY

The North London Railway, actually absorbed by the LNWR prior to the grouping, contributed 109 tank engines to LMS stock of which by far the largest proportion was represented by a group of 78 distinctive 4—4—0Ts (LMS 6435—512). The first four of these, survivors of a design by Adams, dated back to 1865 and had inside cylinders, whereas 6439—512 had outside cylinders. This latter group, designed by Park, were also fairly venerable machines. Although officially dating back to 1886, most of them were rebuilds of older engines going back to 1871. In consequence, neither variety of 4—4—0T had a long post-group life. The Adams engines never received LMS numbers and had gone by 1925. Many of the Park engines also failed to receive their LMS numbers and of those that did, the majority still kept their pre-group livery. All were withdrawn by mid-1929.

All but one of the remaining NLR engines were 0—6—0Ts designed by Park in 1887 (LMS 7503—32). These fared much better than the 4—4—0Ts, 23 receiving LMS 275xx numbers and 15 surviving to BR (14 renumbered). The final survivor, preserved on the Bluebell Line as LNWR 2650, was withdrawn in 1960 (LMS 27505, BR 58850), having served out its final years on the Cromford and High Peak Railway in very demanding conditions.

Even more resilient than the 0—6—0Ts was the final NLR engine, the celebrated 0—4—2 crane tank (LMS 7217). As a crane tank, this engine dated from 1872 but its origins actually went back to 1858 when it was built as an 0—4—0ST. In 1951, when it was withdrawn as BR 58865, it is thought to have been the oldest standard gauge steam engine in service on British Railways.

Total ex-NLR engines at grouping:

4—4—0T	78
0—6—0T	30
0—4—2CT	1
Total	109

Plate 146 The North London passenger tanks were all of 4—4—0T wheel arrangement and we have selected this picture of No. 6462 to represent this type. Originally NLR No. 68, it became LNWR No. 2854 before carrying its LMS number, but many of the early members of the classes never carried their allotted numbers. This picture displays Livery Code A4. *W. Beckerlegge*

Plate 147 The North London Railway owned a number of 0—6—0Ts which lasted many years and this picture of No. 7528 in pre-1928 livery shows a locomotive with its original North London chimney and a small 'LMS' on the bunker, Livery Code C6. No. 7528 was originally NLR No. 93, later LNWR No. 2893, before becoming LMS 7528. *Authors' Collection*

Chapter 6   Pre-Group Locomotives – Central Division

The LMS Central Division locomotive number series (10000–12999), originally Western 'B', was allocated to five pre-group railways located in an area extending from the industrial areas of Lancashire and the West Riding to the mountains and fells of the Lake District and the North-West. Of the more than 1,800 engines involved, over 90% came from the LYR (or LYR design) with the Furness Railway providing three quarters of the remainder. The Maryport and Carlisle added a further 33 while the Cleator and Workington Junction and the Knott End Railways each contributed a handful.

Because the 1923 LMS renumbering was based on power class and age, the smaller companies' engines occasionally interrupted the predominantly LYR series of engine numbers but this brief survey will treat each company separately.

THE LANCASHIRE AND YORKSHIRE RAILWAY

Locomotive Superintendents:

W. Hurst	1868–1876
W. Barton-Wright	1876–1886
John A. F. Aspinall	1886–1899
H. A. Hoy	1899–1904
George Hughes	1904–1921

(amalgamated with LNWR in 1922)

The LYR can lay fair claim to have been the most compact and concentrated of all the major constituent companies at the grouping. Although officially merged with the LNWR some twelve months prior to the formation of the LMS, it had hardly lost any of its identity during this short period. In fact, its followers could claim that with George Hughes appointed firstly as CME of the enlarged LNWR and then as first CME of the new LMS, the LYR had, in fact, taken over the other concerns. Fate was, of course, to decree that such was not quite the case but it is, nevertheless, true to say that Horwich did have more influence on LMS matters than did Crewe. This was first instanced in the contribution of such classes as the highly successful Class 5F 2–6–0s to the LMS standard list but no less by the provision of such experts as Coleman, Cox and others to Stanier's highly successful team of the 1930s. Students of these matters could also, perhaps, see something of Horwich in the valve events of such classes as the 'Royal Scots' and Fowler 2–6–4Ts, not to mention the well liked Stanier cab which patently drew much of its inspiration from that first fitted to the 'Horwich Moguls'.

Be that as it may, the LYR engines themselves contributed materially to the LMS stock and, in their own areas at least, some of the classes proved to be considerably more resilient than those from more 'illustrious' concerns. Indeed, it was not entirely unheard of for the products of a certain locomotive establishment on the South East corner of the Pennines to find themselves mysteriously boxed into the corner of the ex-LYR sheds thus necessitating the use of the LYR types which were more conveniently accessible – such are the ways of locomotive men! A not dissimilar fate was to await those BR standard 4–6–2s which found their way onto the Western Region of BR after nationalisation!

An interesting feature of the LYR was the extent to which it had managed to concentrate the bulk of its traffic into the care of a relatively small number of engine classes. This was particularly marked in the field of passenger tank engines where the ubiquitous 2–4–2T reigned unchallenged.

Plate 148 No. 10000 was originally built by the LNWR for the LYR and this broadside picture displays ex-LYR No. 731 in LMS livery, Code A4.
BR LMR

Passenger Tender Engines

Not even its friends could call the 'Lanky' an express passenger line. Its passenger services were numerous and often heavily loaded and although it had some very tightly timed intermediate distance workings, nowhere did it have the opportunity to provide that long distance haulage at high speed which was exhibited on the majority of the large LMS constituents. That being so, it is perhaps a little surprising that the last of the LYR passenger tender classes (the Hughes 4—6—0) should have been adopted, for a few years at least, as a quasi-LMS standard type. Perhaps it was George Hughes having a final fling in the face of pressures from Derby — we shall never know!

At the grouping, the new 4—6—0s represented but a small proportion of the LYR passenger tender engine collection, most of which was of 4—4—0 or 4—4—2 type. These four-coupled designs were mostly of Aspinall origin, there being 71 4—4—0s of two basic types and a class of 40 4—4—2s.

The oldest engines were a series of 4—4—0s with 6 ft 0 in driving wheels (LMS 10100—30). The earliest of these (10100—1) were the last survivors of a design dating back to the Barton-Wright era in 1885 but the bulk of them were built during the Aspinall régime from 1888 onwards. Apart from a premature accident withdrawal, this group came intact to the LMS. All 31 engines were renumbered by the LMS and the later series, in spite of being over 30 years old at grouping, managed to survive intact until 1930. However, all had gone by 1945.

The remaining 4—4—0s (LMS 10150—83; 10190—5) were far less fortunate. These were Aspinall engines of 1891 design with 7 ft 3 in driving wheels of which 10190—5 had been rebuilt by Hughes with larger cylinders and superheaters. All were withdrawn between 1925 and 1930, many before being renumbered.

The Aspinall Atlantics (LMS 10300—39) dated from 1899 when they achieved acclaim as the first inside cylinder English 4—4—2s. They had 7 ft 3 in driving wheels like the later series of 4—4—0s and were universally known as 'Highflyers'. This nickname seemed not to impress the LMS management and all were scrapped between 1926 and 1934, some without ever receiving LMS numbers.

The 4—6—0 type was introduced to the LYR by George Hughes in 1908. His first essay took the form of twenty non-superheated engines with Joy valve gear and four cylinders. Five only of these engines (LMS 10400—4) remained as built at the time of grouping and these were quickly scrapped before getting their LMS numbers. The other fifteen were rebuilt (see below). These twenty engines were the only LYR 4—6—0s until 1921 when Hughes introduced the first of what was to become a large class of superheated four-cylinder engines with Walschaerts valve gear (LMS 10405—74). Fifteen of the earlier Joy valve gear engines (LMS 10405—19) had been rebuilt to this type along with the fourteen new engines (LMS 10420—33) at the time of grouping and the LMS itself added 41 more to the total between 1923 and 1925.

The Lanky 'Dreadnoughts' as they were known, survived intact as a class for less than ten years. Until the advent of the 'Royal Scots' and LMS standard Class 5XPs, they shared the heavier West Coast services with the LNWR 'Claughtons' — especially north of Crewe but, like the 'Claughtons', they proved no match for the LMS replacements. Withdrawal commenced in 1934, only seven survived to BR of which only one (10455) received its BR number and the class was extinct by 1951.

The only other LYR passenger 'tender' engine was the pioneer LMS No. 10000. This engine, was in fact, an ex-LNWR 2—4—0 dating from Ramsbottom days and bought from the LNWR in 1873. It had been rebuilt and fitted with an integral tender-cum-saloon to form the CME's personal coupé. After Hughes had reached the end of his working career, the engine was scrapped in 1926.

Total ex-LYR passenger tender engines at grouping:

2—4—0 type	1
4—4—0 type	71
4—4—2 type	40
4—6—0 type	75 *
Total	187 *

* Including LMS built examples

Plate 149 The LYR owned a number of 4—4—0s and examples in LMS livery are rather rare. We have chosen this picture of LYR No. 1228, later LMS 10173, to represent the Aspinall 4—4—0s. *Real Photographs*

Plate 150 (Above) The LYR 4—4—2s were known as 'Highflyers' and this works grey picture of No. 10327 illustrates livery details as used on this class when painted red, Livery Code A3. There are some additional embellishments added for photographic purposes. *NRM*

Plate 151 (Below) Ex-LYR No. 1662 in battleship grey with 'LM&SR' in yellow is not typical of the livery of the Hughes 4—6—0s, but this picture has been included for its historical interest. *NRM*

Passenger Tank Engines

To many people, the LYR was typified by a train of suburban coaches, with the inevitable horsehair cushions, hauled by a 2—4—2 radial tank. Indeed, it is quite remarkable how the LYR had achieved such a degree of standardisation in this area. Virtually the whole of its stopping passenger traffic — and not a few express workings — was in the charge of this not unduly powerful class of engine.

The type had its origins in 1889 when Aspinall first pioneered the design and by 1923, 330 engines had been built of which one had been sold to the Wirral Railway (see page 93). At the grouping, the engines were allocated numbers 10621 — 10950 and almost immediately, four of the non-superheated engines (10826/32/6/46) were rebuilt into the superheated type and given new LMS numbers 10951—4 (not the same order). There was a fifth blank number in the lower part of the series (10638) which was reserved for the Wirral engine but which was never, in the event, taken up.

Basically, the LYR 2—4—2Ts exhibited various permutations of long/short bunkers, Belpaire and round top boilers and saturated or superheated steam. The detailed ramifications are outside the scope of this survey but a basic summary of the 1923 position is as follows:

10621—821	Original short bunkered saturated type, some with Belpaire boilers but mostly round-topped.
10822—99	Long bunkered version of 10621—821.
10900—50 (plus 10951—4)	Hughes development with superheater, Belpaire boiler and extended smokebox (some with long bunkers).

This tidy pattern was somewhat complicated by further conversions to superheated type in LMS days. Unlike 10951—4 (above), these later conversions retained their original LMS running numbers. Well over 100 ex-LYR 2—4—2Ts survived to BR days and the type only became extinct in 1961.

Plate 152 (Above) The 2—4—2Ts of the LYR worked the bulk of the local passenger trains on the system and this picture of No. 10919 in works grey has been included to show details which would be less visible on a correctly liveried locomotive and to indicate the lining employed when in crimson lake livery, Code A3. *NRM*

Plate 153 (Left) By way of contrast to Plate 152, No. 10621 is an example of an earlier member of the class of 2—4—2Ts and the shorter bunker should be compared with that of No. 10919, Plate 152. No. 10621 is carrying Livery Code B3. *Photomatic*

Plate 154 The large 4—6—4Ts of LYR design did not enter traffic until after the grouping and this picture shows No. 11116 carrying Livery Code B1. *A.G. Ellis*

Plate 155 The LYR numbered these railmotors in a special series of coaches and locomotives but the LMS numbered them at the beginning of the Central Division passenger tank stock. No. 10600 is in Livery Code C15 (no 'LMS'). *BR LMR*

Apart from the 2—4—2Ts, ex-LYR passenger tanks proper were non-existent at grouping. However, a design did exist for a 4—6—4T development of the Hughes 4—6—0 tender type and this new design emerged during early LMS days (LMS 11110—19). These ten very massive machines were destined to have a somewhat short life. Built in 1924, withdrawal commenced only fourteen years later and all were extinct by 1942. Like so many other small classes of engine, they fell victim to the widespread standardisation policy of the 1930s. It was originally the intention to build twenty further 4—6—4Ts but the parts were actually used in the construction of the final batch of Hughes 4—6—0s (LMS 10455—74).

The last LYR passenger engines to be considered were not true tank engines but were, of course, the well known Hughes railmotors of 1906 (LMS 10600—17). The engine portion was a reasonably conventional 0—4—0 side tank which was, in traffic, permanently coupled to a coach unit fitted with trailing bogie only, the front end being supported by the engine portion. The combined units were numbered into the LMS engine series (unlike all other LMS self-propelled railcar type vehicles which carried coaching stock numbers) and the passenger portions of the LYR railcars were therefore somewhat unusual in being the only LMS passenger carrying vehicles to carry engine numbers on the side panels as well as their carriage stock numbers.

The railmotors enjoyed rather a longer life than many other similar designs elsewhere in the country. Although the first withdrawal was as early as 1927, one long term survivor (LMS 10617) just lasted until BR days but was withdrawn in 1948 without being renumbered.

Total ex-LYR passenger tank engines at grouping:

2—4—2 type	329
4—6—4 type	10 *
0—4—0 railmotor	18
Total	357

* LMS built engines

Freight Tank Engines

As with all other generic types of LYR engine, the bulk of the total of freight tanks was contained in but few classes — in this case 0—4—0STs and 0—6—0STs. However, unlike the passenger tanks where standardisation on one type was all but universal, there were still a few subsidiary classes of freight tank in service when the LMS was formed.

The smallest engines were 58 0—4—0STs (LMS 11200—57), all but one of which were to the Aspinall 1891 design. The odd man out (LMS 11200) was a somewhat older engine of slightly smaller proportions and an early withdrawal. The main class, however, formed a resilient group of engines. Some 23 survived to reach BR and the last one was not withdrawn until 1963.

Continuing up the scale in terms of size, the next group of engines was the familiar 0—6—0STs, again to an Aspinall design of 1891 (LMS 11303—532). These engines had, in fact, started life as Barton-Wright 0—6—0 tender engines as far back as 1876 but the continual building of further tender types provided an economical way of producing shunting tanks without the need for completely new machines. All 230 engines were in existence in 1923 and withdrawals were only gradual from 1926 onwards. As a result, over 100 reached BR and it was not until 1964 that the final withdrawal was made (Horwich works shunter, LMS 11305, never renumbered by BR).

What might be termed the 'non-standard' LYR freight tanks were all of side tank configuration and mostly six-coupled. The smallest (physically) were the short wheelbase Aspinall 0—6—0 dock tanks of 1897. Fourteen of the original twenty reached the LMS (LMS 11533—46) and withdrawal was relatively slow. Five reached BR, one of which (11537) was reputedly the last ex-LMS engine to receive its allotted BR number. The class became extinct in 1961.

The oldest LYR freight tanks at grouping were the survivors of a quite extensive series of Barton-Wright 0—6—2Ts (LMS 11600—21). These engines, which dated back to 1881, had been heavily depleted during the years between 1906 and 1923. All had 5 ft 1 in driving wheels except the first two which had 4 ft 6 in wheels. Most members of this class lasted but a short time in LMS days and all had gone by 1932, some before receiving LMS numbers.

The final two ex-LYR freight tank designs were something in the nature of oddities. Firstly there were the 2—6—2Ts built to a design by Hoy in 1903/4. It is generally thought that these engines were an attempt to enlarge the highly successful 2—4—2T design but in the event they were not a success — nor did they share the neat visual lines of the 2—4—2Ts. Seventeen out of twenty reached the LMS (LMS 11700—16) but only two were renumbered (11704/11) and all had been withdrawn by late 1926.

A somewhat similar fate lay in store for the five gargantuan 0—8—2Ts dating from 1908 (LMS 11800—4). These engines, built as a tank engine version of the large boilered Hughes 0—8—0, were somewhat lacking in versatility and the LMS had scrapped them all by late 1929, only 11803 having received its LMS number.

Total ex-LYR freight tank engines at grouping:

0—4—0 type	58
0—6—0 type	244
0—6—2 type	22
2—6—2 type	17
0—8—2 type	5
Total	346

Plate 156 (Opposite) The LYR 0—4—0 were used for shunting in docks, etc., many lasted until after nationalisation. This picture of No. 11247 displays the correct pre-1928 livery, Code C4.
Real Photographs

Plate 157 The LYR owned a considerable number of 0—6—0STs rebuilt from tender locomotives and used them for shunting work. This picture of No. 11353 in post-1928 livery, Code C13, can be considered as typical for the class during the post-1928 period. Examples of the class moved off the Central Division and this picture of No. 11353 was taken at Bletchley on 25th June, 1938. *L. Hanson*

Plate 158 A number of 0—6—2Ts of Barton Wright design were in existence in 1923 and this picture shows No. 11610 in pre-1928 livery, Code C3. *Real Photographs*

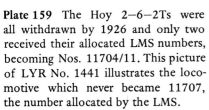

Plate 159 The Hoy 2—6—2Ts were all withdrawn by 1926 and only two received their allocated LMS numbers, becoming Nos. 11704/11. This picture of LYR No. 1441 illustrates the locomotive which never became 11707, the number allocated by the LMS.
Real Photographs

Freight Tender Engines

Almost exactly half of the LYR engine stock at grouping consisted of freight tender engines and of the 830 engines taken over by the LMS, only two basic types were represented; 0—6—0s and 0—8—0s. The 0—6—0 group was divided by age and power class at the grouping and this did not form a consecutive LMS number series.

The oldest engines (LMS 12015—64) were the fifty residual Barton-Wright 0—6—0s which had not been rebuilt to 0—6—0ST by Aspinall (above). Already 36 years old at grouping, the class still had many years to go, withdrawal of the survivors being very slow. Half of them reached BR in 1948 but thereafter, withdrawal speeded up a little and the class was extinct in 1959.

The biggest single group of LYR 0—6—0 engines was represented by the Aspinall design of 1891 vintage (LMS 12083—12467). These engines were an enlarged development of the Barton-Wright engines and many of them carried Belpaire boilers by the time of the formation of the LMS. Withdrawal commenced in 1931 but well over 200 reached BR and the class was not finally extinct until 1961.

The superheated engines dating from 1909 formed the last group of ex-LYR 0—6—0s (LMS 12515—619). Some of these engines (12517—56) were new engines designed by Hughes but the remainder were superheated Hughes rebuilds of the earlier Aspinall design. All but one of the first 22 engines had round topped boilers, the exception being 12528, but engines numbered 12537 upwards had Belpaire boilers. Like the saturated engines, the superheated machines had a long life. Withdrawal commenced in 1933 but was not complete until 1962.

Along with the LNWR, the LYR was the only major user of the 0—8—0 tender type amongst the LMS constituents. Almost 300 engines were in existence at the grouping (LMS 12700—994); but although many survived for quite a long time, they were not as resilient as the LYR 0—6—0s and forty of them never received LMS numbers.

The oldest engines were the 60 surviving small boilered Aspinall engines introduced in 1900 (LMS 12700—59). Many more had been built but the bulk of the remainder had been rebuilt to the larger size (below) before 1923. Scrapping of the small boilered engines commenced in 1926 but one example (12727) did reach BR, being withdrawn in 1950. One of these 0—8—0s formed the prototype for the second group of LYR eight-coupled goods engines when it was rebuilt to compound form by Hughes in 1907. Together with ten new engines of the same type, this class of four-cylinder compounds (LMS 12760—70) formed the smallest group of LYR freight tender engines and, possibly for this reason, did not seem to find much favour. All were withdrawn between 1926 and 1927.

The largest single group of LYR 0—8—0s were the large boilered Hughes engines (LMS 12771—994). Most of these were superheated (12840 upwards) but the first 69 employed saturated steam. Many of the early examples of both variants were rebuilds of the original small boilered Aspinall engines. Although relatively new engines by comparison with most of the 0—6—0s, the large boilered 0—8—0s did not long remain intact after 1923. Scrapping commenced in 1926 and both varieties were rendered extinct in 1951. To a large extent, these engines were superseded by the Fowler LMS standard 0—8—0 type — an interesting contrast with the ex-LNWR lines where the 'native' 0—8—0 design managed to outlive the LMS standard engines.

Total ex-LYR freight tender engines at grouping:

0—6—0 type	535
0—8—0 type	295
Total	830

Plate 161 The LYR 0—6—0s were long lived and the oldest locomotives of this wheel arrangement to come into LMS ownership were the Barton-Wrights. No. 12046 is shown here in post-1928 livery, Code C15. Note that it is still carrying a smokebox door numberplate.

Authors' Collection

Plate 162 The bulk of the 0—6—0s were of Aspinall design and this picture of No. 12321 in post-1928 livery, Code C15, was taken at Bletchley on 25th June, 1938. Examples of this class were to be found on both the Western and Midland Division as well as the parent Central Division. *L. Hanson*

Plate 163 The final design of LYR 0—6—0 were the Hughes locomotives and this picture of No. 12517 shows the pre-1928 livery, Code C4.

A.G. Ellis

Plate 167 Furness Railway 2—4—0 No. 44A was allocated the number 10002 but the locomotive was withdrawn before the number could be carried. This picture, taken at Barrow on 25th July, 1925, shows the locomotive prior to withdrawal. *Authors' Collection*

THE FURNESS RAILWAY

The Furness Railway contributed 120 engines to LMS capital stock and, as with many of the smaller LMS constituents, it was very much a regional system. Its territory was well defined and its locomotives rarely ventured far afield. Like so many small companies, standardisation was not particularly in evidence at grouping, no fewer than nine wheel arrangements and twice that number of classes being represented. To the extent that standardisation had been achieved, it is probably worth mentioning that almost 50 of its engines were of 0—6—0 tender type and it also had a reasonably homogeneous collection of 0—6—0 and 0—6—2 tank engines.

LMS policy being what it was, it is not really surprising to relate that most Furness engines had vanished during the 1920s and 1930s and only a handful (all 0—6—0s) managed to reach BR — even these had been rebuilt almost beyond recognition. As with the smaller companies considered in Chapter 4, it has been thought most appropriate to give a semi-tabular presentation in the summary of ex-FR engines which follows.

Running Numbers	Description
10002	This engine was the last survivor of a class of 2—4—0s dating from 1872. It never received its LMS number.
10131—4	These four engines were small wheeled 4—4—0s of rather ancient appearance although dating back only to 1890. Although renumbered by the LMS, all were scrapped by 1927.
10135—42	There were sixteen Pettigrew 4—4—0s on the Furness Railway and these eight represented the largest single type. They had 6 ft 0 in driving wheels and dated from 1896. All were scrapped between 1929 and 1931.
10143—6	These four engines were to a later Pettigrew design of 1900 and were 6 ft 6 in 4—4—0s of somewhat North Eastern Railway lineaments. They survived only until 1931.
10185—8	The final Pettigrew 4—4—0s reverted to 6 ft 0 in driving wheels and were much newer and somewhat larger than the other FR 4—4—0s. Although built as late as 1913—14, they lasted little longer than the older engines, all being scrapped between 1932 and 1933.

Total passenger tender engines   21

◀ **Plate 164 (Opposite top)** The LYR 0—8—0s were employed to haul the heaviest coal trains and while there was a number of variations, basically they were either small- or large-boilered locomotives. This picture of No. 12739 in pre-1928 livery, Code C1, is interesting inasmuch as it shows a feed water heater. *NRM*

◀ **Plate 165 (Opposite centre)** An example of a large-boilered locomotive is shown in this picture which illustrates No. 1427 in ex-works LYR livery, but with block style 'LM&SR' on the tender similar to that carried by 4—6—0 No. 1662, Plate 151. No. 1427 later became LMS No. 12990. *NRM*

◀ **Plate 166 (Opposite bottom)** Ex-LYR 0—8—0 No. 12941 is in pre-1928 livery, Code C1, and illustrates a locomotive without side windows in the cab, and it should be compared with No. 1427, Plate 165. Basically, all these locomotives were members of the same class of 0—8—0. *NRM*

10619—20	These were the last two of a class of seven 2—4—2Ts rebuilt in 1891 from 2—4—0s dating back to 1875. They were scrapped by 1924 without being renumbered.
11080—5	These six engines were particularly neat 4—4—2Ts designed by Pettigrew in 1915. Again relatively new engines, they did not survive the impact of standard designs and were withdrawn between 1930 and 1933.
11100—4	The Furness 4—6—4Ts were by far the most recent of the FR passenger designs, having been built as late as 1920. They thus enjoyed a slightly longer post-grouping life but even so were all gone by 1940.

Total passenger tank   13

11258	This engine was the sole ex-FR 0—4—0ST to reach the LMS. One of a pair built in 1874, it never carried its LMS number.
11547—8	These two engines had started life with the Whitehaven, Cleator and Egremont Railway in the 1870s. They were 0—6—0STs and did not receive LMS numbers, being withdrawn by 1925.
11549—52	Of contemporary age to the WCER engines (above) were these four 0—6—0Ts of 1871—3. Withdrawn by 1926, none are thought to have received LMS numbers.
11553—62	These ten 0—6—0Ts represented quite a large class by FR standards. Built by Pettigrew from 1910—16, they remained intact until 1930 and withdrawal was not complete until 1943.
11622—40	These engines were Pettigrew 0—6—2Ts dating from 1898. All were essentially of one type but the first three had smaller driving wheels and were early post-group casualties. The remainder fared a little better and the last survivor lasted until 1945.
11641—4	These later and larger Pettigrew 0—6—2Ts of 1912 were not as fortunate as the older engines and all were scrapped between 1929 and 1934.

Total freight tank engines   40

12000—14	The first fifteen of the FR 0—6—0s were to a Sharp Stewart design dating back to 1866. Over 50 had been built and several had been rebuilt by Pettigrew (below). Withdrawal of the original engines was rapid and all had gone by 1927, many probably before receiving LMS numbers.
12065—76	These twelve engines were the Pettigrew rebuilds of the above mentioned Sharp Stewart engines. Even as rebuilds they were somewhat elderly (1871—83) and by 1930, all were scrapped.
12468—79 12480—3	These sixteen Pettigrew 0—6—0s were of two basically similar classes. The last four had larger wheels (5 ft 1 in against 4 ft 8 in) and higher boiler pressure. Dating from 1899—1907, the engines were withdrawn between 1928 and 1936.
12494—512	The only FR engines to enjoy any degree of longevity were the final Pettigrew 0—6—0s built between 1913 and 1920. Although the first withdrawal was made in 1930, six survived to BR and were all renumbered. These late survivors had all been rebuilt with the final type of LYR Belpaire 0—6—0 boilers by the time of withdrawal. The last survivor went for scrap in 1957.

Total freight tender engines   62
Total ex-FR engines absorbed by the LMS   136

Plate 168 These Furness Sharp Stewarts looked very elegant in crimson lake, Livery Code A1. This class was similar to locomotives supplied to the Cambrian Railway by the same builders.

Real Photographs

Plate 169 The large Furness 4—4—0s only lasted until the early 1930s and this works grey picture of No. 10187 has been selected to illustrate details not normally visible in correctly liveried pictures, and also shows lining details on these locomotives when in crimson lake condition. *NRM*

Plate 170 The Furness owned six 4—4—2Ts and this picture of No. 11085 shows a locomotive in crimson lake livery, Code A1. Note the shovel on the roof, not the normal carrying position! *Real Photographs*

Plate 171 The Furness Railway provided the LMS with two 2—4—2Ts which, although allocated numbers 10619/20, never carried their new numbers. This picture of No. 71, later 71A, shows the locomotive which would have become 10619 if it had remained in service for a longer period. *Real Photographs*

Plate 172 This ex-works picture of No. 11101 shows the lining employed when in crimson lake livery and also illustrates some of the finer details not normally so visible in more usual pictures. *NRM*

Plate 173 No. 12476 in pre-1928 livery, Code C1 or C2 (but no cab panel), was an example of a Pettigrew design and should be compared with **Plate 174** which shows No. 12510, of the same class but now rebuilt with a LYR Belpaire boiler and carrying post-1928 livery, Code C14. Note con rods, sandboxes, cab front, and tender coal rails, all giving a different visual appearance.

Plate 173 Author's Collection
Plate 174 British Rail

Plate 175 No. 10013 in crimson lake, Livery Code A1, was one of four 0—4—2s accorded passenger livery by the LMS. These ex-Maryport and Carlisle locomotives were interesting in so far as they were at one time fitted with extra buffers for propelling chaldron wagons and the holes where these buffers had been mounted can be clearly seen in this picture.

Stephen Collection — NRM

THE MARYPORT AND CARLISLE
AND THE CLEATOR AND WORKINGTON JUNCTION RAILWAYS

These two companies added 39 engines to the LMS total, all but six being of M & CR design or origin. Only 34 were allotted LMS numbers and in LMS numerical sequence the types were as follows:

Running Numbers	*Description*
10005—7	M & CR 2—4—0s built to a design by Smellie in 1874—8 and withdrawn 1924—5 without being renumbered.
10010—13	M & CR 0—4—2s, again to a design by Smellie and dating from 1879. Although classed as passenger engines and painted red by the LMS, these engines had quite small driving wheels (5 ft 7½ in) and had, at one stage, extra low-mounted buffers for propelling chaldron type wagons in collieries and the like. All were withdrawn in 1928.

Total passenger tender   7

10618	This engine was the only surviving M & CR passenger tank. Of 0—4—4 type, it was built in 1897 and scrapped in 1924 without receiving its LMS number.

Total passenger tank   1

11259—60	M & CR 0—4—0Ts built in 1880 and withdrawn in 1924 without receiving LMS numbers.
11563	This engine was an ex-M & CR 0—6—0T built in 1907 from an 0—4—2T of 1865 vintage. It was withdrawn in 1927.
11564—8	These engines were five C & WR 0—6—0STs of varying ages. All were named and, considering their highly non-standard nature, lasted longer than many of their contemporaries. Withdrawals took place between 1926 and 1932 but the last to go (11568) was sold out of LMS service and remained in colliery service until 1956.

Total freight tank   8

Plate 176 More than half of the M&CR stock absorbed by the LMS were 0—6—0 tender goods engines and this picture of No.12486 carrying Livery Code C6 has been chosen to represent this group of locomotives. Note the open splashers, a most distinctive feature. *Stephen Collection — NRM*

Plate 177 No. 11566 was an ex-Cleator and Workington 0—6—0ST built by Peckett in 1907, shown here in LMS freight livery, Code C4. These 0—6—0Ts varied, and illustrations of other members of the class will appear in *Volume II*.

Real Photographs

12077—82	These engines were six somewhat elderly M & CR 0—6—0s (built 1866—73) which had a short post-grouping life, all being withdrawn by 1929.
12484—93	These ten engines, the largest M & CR class, were 0—6—0s of 1875 design, although some were built much later. All withdrawals took place between 1925 and 1930.
12513—14	The last two M & CR engines were 0—6—0s of 1921 vintage. Although new engines, they only lasted ten years or so and were scrapped in 1933/4.

Total freight tender	18	
Total ex-M & CR engines absorbed by the LMS	29 + 4	not numbered
Total ex-C & WR engines absorbed by the LMS	5 + 1	See *Table 1*

THE KNOTT END RAILWAY

This tiny independent concern in NW Lancashire added but four engines to LMS stock. Three of them (LMS 11300—2) were 0—6—0Ts, the first two being Hudswell-Clarke saddle tanks and the last a Manning Wardle side tank. The KER never numbered its engines and all were known by name only. All were withdrawn between 1924 and 1926 and only No. 11300 *Jubilee Queen* was numbered into the LMS list.

The final KER engine was not only a unique machine, it was also of a unique 2—6—0T wheel arrangement. Built by Manning Wardle, named *Blackpool* and numbered 11680 by the LMS, it lasted until 1927.

Chapter 7   Pre-Group Locomotives – Northern Division

The Northern Division of the LMS consisted of its Scottish routes with the addition of the Anglo-Scottish link from Carlisle to Gretna. Three constituent companies were concerned and the 1923 LMS number series allocated to their engines ran from 14000–17997. Unfortunately, from the standpoint of locomotive identification, the policy of renumbering by power class tended to split up the various companies' engines even within a single wheel arrangement (e.g. the various Caledonian 4–4–0 types were 'punctuated' by batches of GSWR and HR 4–4–0 engines). However, members of a single class of locomotive did, for the most part, receive a consecutive number allocation. In this survey, each company will be considered separately but a few general comments will first be made in order to put the Scottish pre-group companies into some sort of perspective.

The Caledonian Railway was the largest of the Scottish constituents of the LMS and of the three Scottish companies it seems fair to say that its influence on LMS matters was greater than that of the other two. In fact, in one respect the Caledonian outshone all the English constituents too and this was in the realm of locomotive longevity. Viewing the LMS stock as a whole, a smaller proportion of ex-CR engines was scrapped during the 1920s and 1930s than of any other LMS constituent and several classes of Caledonian origin (particularly freight classes) remained essentially intact throughout the LMS period.

The reasons for this longevity are a little hard to identify with precision. Certainly the Caledonian engines were in the main robust and well built, but in terms of age they were broadly comparable with those of other LMS constituents and in terms of mechanical efficiency, no more remarkable than many other classes of non-Caledonian origin. There is some evidence that the generally softer Scottish water may have had a beneficial effect on boiler maintenance costs during an increasingly cost-conscious period but offsetting this there is also evidence that an engine had to be somewhat more run-down in Scotland before it was proposed for major repairs at the works. This would tend to give a superficial appearance of larger mileages between general works repairs but possibly with shed repairs proving more expensive in consequence.

Two other aspects should also be borne in mind. Firstly, the LMS often seemed, at least outwardly, to be pursuing a policy which implied that the English lines should receive a higher priority for re-equipment than the Scottish ones. It is certainly true that new engine types were often first seen south of the border, as, indeed, were new coach types but this apparent neglect of the Scottish lines was only superficially true. The LMS tended increasingly to view its system as a whole as the years went by and this had important ramifications in the locomotive operating departments. New and more complex locomotive and stock rostering made it increasingly beneficial to regard the Anglo-Scottish routes as single units and, in consequence, through workings of locomotives from well south of the border became more commonplace. Thus one had such features as Crewe engines working through to Glasgow and Perth and from the Midland Division, Leeds engines working through onto the GSWR lines north of Carlisle. Indeed, the latter city tended to become less important as a locomotive changing point as the years went by.

It can therefore be seen that, at least in terms of long distance working, new LMS standard equipment was represented in Scotland from quite early days, but much of it was based south of the border and the bulk of the remainder at places like Glasgow and Perth. It is not, therefore, without significance that included in the early post-group locomotive scrapping lists in Scotland was a fair proportion of larger passenger engines. For example, the ex-CR 4–6–0s fared little or no better than those of the GSWR in terms of post-group life span. In general, therefore, it was not until much later in the 1930s and 1940s that many of the lesser workings in Scotland received a sizeable quota of LMS standard types.

The second relevant aspect may possibly be attributable to the widespread influence of the Drummond family north of the border. All three Scottish constituents contributed Drummond designed (and Drummond inspired) engines to the LMS stock list. Their family resemblance was remarkable, not only within one company but between companies and this may have suggested to the economy minded LMS a kind of 'second-level' standardisation in Scotland for the smaller types of engine based upon Drummond and derived designs. The Caledonian had by far the largest total of engines in this category and it would obviously be economical to 'standardise' these types. Furthermore, rationalisation of maintenance eventually led to St Rollox assuming a more and more dominant role in the repair of *all* Scottish based LMS engines. It thus became quite common practice after the grouping to find, for example, CR type boilers fitted to ex-Highland Railway Drummond classes like the 'Ben' class 4–4–0s. It is also worth recording that E.S. Cox in his 1946 paper 'A Modern Locomotive History' records that a strong case was made north of the border for the retention of Caledonian types which were claimed to be especially suited to Scottish condition.

Whatever the reasons may be, the fact remains that the characteristic 'Caley' lineaments remained strongly represented well after the close of the LMS phase and almost to the end of the steam period itself. This should not, of course, be taken to imply that no LMS standard classes made an appearance but merely that their general penetration north of the border seems to have been at a slightly lower rate than in England. After all, several areas of Scotland received LMS standard types at a relatively early period – particularly in terms of 4–4–0s for the GSWR and CR lines and somewhat more powerful engines for the HR main line between Perth and Inverness. Even by the 1930s, there were few areas in Scotland which did not have at least some LMS standard engines, even if it was only the (statutory?) quota of Class 2P 4–4–0s and Class 4F 0–6–0s!

THE CALEDONIAN RAILWAY

Locomotive Superintendents:

Robert Sinclair	1847—1856
Benjamin Connor	1856—1876
George Brittain	1876—1882
Dugald Drummond	1882—1890
Hugh Smellie	1890
J. Lambie	1890—1895
J. F. McIntosh	1895—1914
William Pickersgill	1914—1923

The Caledonian Railway contributed 1,069 engines to the LMS in 1923 and this represented almost 65% of the total from Scotland. By the time of the grouping, the gradual evolution of designs from the Drummond/Lambie era through to McIntosh and Pickersgill had given to the company a wide measure of standardisation and this was reflected in the numerically large size, by pre-group standards, of some of the classes. It should be noted that several CR locos on the departmental list (including the famous 4—2—2) were later reinstated to capital stock — see *Table 2*.

Passenger Tender Engines

The Caledonian was predominantly a 4—4—0 line and had but few 4—6—0s, these being mainly confined to main line expresses and freight and the Oban line.

The 4—4—0 wheel arrangement contained representatives spanning some 40 years of design. Oldest were the eight survivors of the ten 'Oban Bogie' 4—4—0s designed by Brittain and introduced in 1882 (LMS 14100—7). These lasted only a few years after grouping and had gone by 1930, as indeed had the next two series of 4—4—0s (LMS 14108—15; 14290—310). These engines were the last eight of the small-wheeled Drummond 4—4—0s of 1888 together with the 21 survivors of the Drummond/Lambie design of 1884—94.

The remaining Caledonian 4—4—0s were the various series of engines derived from the famous McIntosh 'Dunalastair' type of 1896 which culminated in the final Pickersgill design of 1916. These series of engines were intact (with but one exception) at grouping and the types are summarised below as they existed in 1923:

LMS Numbers	Type		Introduced	Withdrawn First	Last
14311—25	Dunalastair I		1896	1930	1935
14326—36	Dunalastair II		1897	1936	1947
14337—48	Dunalastair III	Saturated	1899	1932	1947
14349—65	Dunalastair IV		1904	1937	1948
14430—3	Dunalastair II		1914 *	1935	1937
14434—7	Dunalastair III	Rebuilt with superheaters	1914 *	1928	1948
14438—9	Dunalastair IV		1915 *	1955	1958
14440—60	Dunalastair IV	Built new with superheaters	1910	1946 †	1957
14461—508	Pickersgill type		1916	1953	1963

* Date rebuilt from saturated state

† Except for one accident victim (Quintinshill 1915)

Caledonian 4—6—0 passenger engines were somewhat less standardised and considerably less numerous than the 4—4—0 engines. No fewer than eight classes were represented at the grouping from three separate designers, yet they totalled less than 50 engines. Even with the addition of twenty more Pickersgill '60' Class engines by the LMS, they represented scarcely more than one third the total of 4—4—0 engines. The Caledonian 4—6—0s will be considered by designer and not in LMS number order.

Dealing first with the McIntosh engines, LMS 14600—8 were the nine '55' Class 4—6—0s with very small driving wheels (5 ft 0 in) dating from 1902 and generally reserved for working the stiff gradients of the Oban line. They remained intact until 1928 but were all withdrawn by 1937, during the early part of the Stanier period. A largely similar fate was in store for the somewhat larger McIntosh '908' Class with 5 ft 9 in wheels (LMS 14609—18). Ten of these were built in 1906 and survived intact until 1930 but five years later all had gone. CR No. 909 *Sir James King* (LMS 14610) was a member of this class.

The other McIntosh engines were approximately contemporary with the smaller wheeled engines but had 6 ft 6 in driving wheels. LMS 14750—1 were the two '49' Class engines dating from 1903 of which CR No. 50 *Sir James Thompson* (LMS 14751) was probably the better known. They were scrapped in 1930. The final McIntosh design was the celebrated '903' or 'Cardean' Class (LMS 14752—5), dating from 1906. Five of these engines had been built but CR No. 907 (the last of the series) was scrapped after the Quintinshill disaster. The four survivors to the LMS did not fare very well and had all gone by 1930.

The numerically largest group of CR 4—6—0s, was the Pickersgill engines. Three designs were involved, of which the most numerous and successful were the 26 members of the '60' Class, dating from 1916. Often nicknamed 'Greybacks', only six of these engines existed at the grouping (LMS 14650—5) but twenty more were built some two or three years later (LMS 14630—49). They remained intact until 1944, all but three passed to BR and the class was not extinct until 1953.

Unlike the '60' Class, other Pickersgill designs were not so fortunate. The '191' Class (LMS 14619—26) was introduced in 1922 and was a small wheeled engine type with 5 ft 6 in driving wheels for the steeper graded lines. The engines were not particularly successful and were scrapped between 1939 and 1945. The largest (physically) of the Pickersgill designs was the '956' Class of 1921. These were three-cylinder engines of which only four were built (LMS 14800—3). Although very impressive in looks, they turned out to be one of the most feeble designs of 4—6—0 in the country and were scrapped between 1931 and 1935.

The final CR 4—6—0s were the six 'River' Class engines (LMS 14756—61). Built in 1915 to a design by Smith for the Highland Railway, they were found to be too heavy for the HR system and only two were delivered as HR engines. They never worked on the Highland Railway and all were sold to the Caledonian. They were amongst the best of the Scottish 4—6—0 types and withdrawal did not commence until 1936. All had gone by 1945. Oddly enough, during LMS days they did eventually work the ex-HR lines for which they had been designed.

The only other Caledonian passenger tender engine was the famous 4—2—2 built by Nielson & Co in 1886 (CR 123 — later 1123; LMS 14010). This engine achieved fame during the railway 'races' to the north in the later 19th century and was, of course, restored to working order for enthusiast specials in the 1950s. It is now preserved in the Glasgow Transport Museum. Although its lines are very much in the classic Drummond style, it is, in a sense, an untypical representative of CR passenger engine design.

Total ex-CR passenger tender engines at grouping:

4—2—2 type	1
4—4—0 type	171
4—6—0 type	69 *
Total	241

* including 20 LMS built examples

Plate 178 The 'Oban Bogies' did not survive long after the grouping but CR No. 1182 is shown here after renumbering to 14103, Livery Code A1. Note the wooden buffer beam, unusual arrangement of footstep and handrail on the tender and the wooden side doors between engine and tender. *Authors' Collection*

Plate 179 No. 14309 was a Lambie 4—4—0 and is shown here when carrying LMS crimson lake, Livery Code A1.

Stephen Collection — NRM

Plate 180 No. 14447 was a 'Dunalastair IV', the final development of this series, and this locomotive was built new with a superheater. Illustrated in pre-1928 passenger livery, Code A1, its condition is typical for CR passenger locomotives for this period.

Stephen Collection — NRM

Plate 181 No. 14604 was an example of the '55' Class and is shown here in post-1928 livery. Pictures of Caledonian locomotives often show tenders well coaled and this picture is no exception. It was good practice to coal tenders high where some form of mechanical coaling was available, particularly if the coaling facilities were more primitive at the destination. Livery Code A1.

Authors' Collection

Plate 182 The Caledonian '191' Class was introduced in 1922 but they lasted only until 1945. This picture of No. 14620 displays Livery Code A1.

Stephen Collection — NRM

Plate 183 The final Caledonian class of 4—6—0 to be illustrated is No. 14800, a member of the '956' Class and is shown in crimson lake livery, Code A1. Note the lining on the buffer beam and how it is cut back slightly following the line of the edge of the beam.

Stephen Collection — NRM

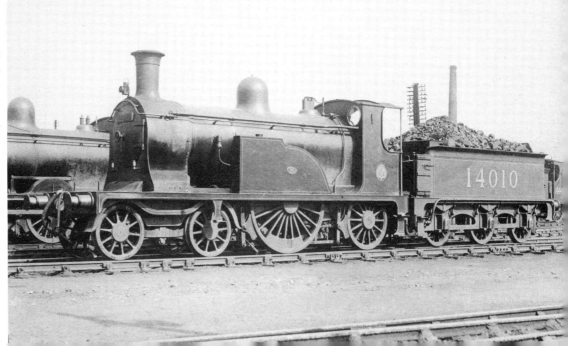

Plate 184 No. 14010. The last example of a single driver to run in service in the British Isles. Photographed in crimson lake, Livery Code A1, the picture clearly shows livery on the bogie 'mudguards', a rather unusual feature.

Authors' Collection

Passenger Tank Engines

Caledonian passenger tank designs totalled 177 engines of which the vast majority were of the 0—4—4 wheel arrangement. There were, however, three other smaller groups and these will be dealt with first.

The smallest engines were two 0—4—2STs (LMS 15000—1), designed by Drummond in 1885 and used on the Killin branch. Although numbered in the passenger series, they were essentially similar to the 0—4—0STs in the freight lists. Although one was scrapped in 1928, No. 15001 survived until 1947. Some eight years after the Killin 'Pugs' had been introduced, Lambie designed a particularly neat series of 4—4—0Ts which survived intact as a class to become LMS 15020—31. They survived for a further four years before scrapping started in 1927 and all had gone by 1938.

What might be termed the third 'non-standard' group of CR passenger tanks were the twelve rather handsome Pickersgill 4—6—2Ts of 1917 (LMS 15350—61). Generally used for the Wemyss Bay services and contemporary with the same designer's '60' Class 4—6—0s, these 4—6—2Ts had a similar life span to the tender engines, being withdrawn between 1946 and 1953, most of them receiving their BR numbers. Latterly, they were best known as banking engines on Beattock.

Plate 185 No. 15028 in crimson lake livery, Code A1 or B1, with crest. These CR 4—4—0Ts remained in service until 1938 and were latterly used for shunting coaches at main stations. *A.G. Ellis*

Plate 186 Sometimes referred to as 'Wemyss Bay' tanks, the handsome appearance of these locomotives was enhanced by St. Rollox style livery, Code B1, as carried by No. 15351. Note the twin vacuum and Westinghouse pipes on the buffer beam and the steam heating pipe hanging down. *W.L. Good*

Turning now to the much more numerous 0—4—4T series, the oldest engines were those designed by Drummond in 1884. All told, 24 were built of which fifteen reached the LMS (15100—14). Withdrawal was comparatively slow, the last survivor not going until 1944. The Drummond engines were quite small machines with 5 ft 0 in driving wheels but the bulk of succeeding CR 0—4—4Ts were much larger 5 ft 9 in engines dating from 1895.

These engines continued building with but detail modifications right through both the McIntosh and Pickersgill periods and into LMS days, the last examples appearing in 1925. All were very similar in outward appearance, the later engines being mainly distinguished by higher boiler pressure and/or larger cylinders. The series is summarised below:

LMS Numbers	Type	Introduced	Withdrawn First	Last
15115—24	McIntosh '19' Class	1895	1946	1961
15125—46	McIntosh '92' Class	1897	1946	1961
15159—226	McIntosh '439' Class	1900	1946	1962
15227—40	Pickersgill development of '439' Class	1915	1961	1962
15260—9	LMS built engines	1925	1961	1962

These engines were highly characteristic of the CR lines, particularly during the last 20 years of the pre-group period and an example of the '439' Class (CR 419; LMS 15189) has been preserved. All survived to the LMS and during the LMS period they roamed far from their parent system. They were tried, with limited success, on the ex-MR London suburban lines in early post-group days but some 20 years later they met with a much better reception when some were drafted to the West Riding. On their home metals, they resisted the onslaught of LMS standardisation to a remarkable degree and were only made finally redundant by the electrification of the Glasgow suburban services.

The final CR 0—4—4T designs were the twelve McIntosh 4 ft 6 in engines of 1899, built for the Balerno branch services (LMS 15147—58). Although typically 'Caley' in style they were somewhat 'non-standard' by comparison with the 5 ft 9 in engines and were scrapped between 1929 and 1938.

Total ex-CR passenger tank engines at grouping:

0—4—2ST	2
4—4—0T	12
0—4—4T	151 *
4—6—2T	12
Total	177

* including ten LMS built examples

Plate 187 The principal Caledonian class of passenger tank was the 0—4—4T wheel arrangement and this picture of No. 15132 can be considered typical of the class in the pre-1928 livery period. Later they were to receive stove pipe chimneys and this development will be illustrated in *Volume II*. Livery Code A1.   *Stephen Collection — NRM*

Plate 188 This ex-CR 0—4—4T is No. 15154, a member of the class sometimes referred to as 'Balerno tanks'. The number is just visible on the original print: therefore the locomotive displays Livery Code A3. *BR LMR*

Freight Tank Engines

Just as the passenger tanks were dominated by the McIntosh 0—4—4 types, the Caledonian total of 250 freight tanks was largely composed of a homogeneous series of the same designer's 0—6—0 side tanks whose longevity was of an even higher order than that of the 0—4—4Ts. Once again, therefore, it seems simpler to deal first with the smaller 'non-standard' groups.

The smallest (physically) of the CR freight tanks were the 0—4—0STs (LMS 16000—39). The first of these was an odd man out in the form of an Andrew Barclay engine of 1896 vintage. This very small engine was scrapped in 1924. The remaining 0—4—0STs of Drummond/McIntosh design were much more resilient. Although dating back to 1878, the design was repeated over the next 30 years and withdrawal was equally long drawn out. All 39 reached the LMS, withdrawal commenced in 1923 but 14 reached BR and the last survivor did not disappear until 1962.

Another non-standard group were the three small-wheeled Drummond 0—6—0 dock saddle tanks of 1888 (LMS 16100—2) and the odd Brittain 0—6—0ST of 1881 (LMS 16150). These four engines lasted until 1938/9. The larger group of Drummond 0—6—0STs of 1887 (LMS 16200—24) and their Lambie derivatives (16225—9) were also short lived engines. Some of the Drummond engines had gone before the grouping and both types were extinct by 1929/30.

The last of the smaller groups of ex-CR freight tanks were the six McIntosh 0—8—0Ts of 1903 (LMS 16500—5). Renumbered 16950—5 in 1926 to make way for LMS standard 0—6—0Ts, these engines lasted until the 1930s, being withdrawn between 1932 and 1939.

Perhaps the most surprising feature of the 170 McIntosh 0—6—0 side tank engines is the fact that all of them not only survived grouping but nationalisation as well and withdrawals did not commence until 1952, some 57 years after the first examples had appeared. All received both LMS and BR series numbers and two classes were involved. LMS 16151—73 were the 23 smaller short wheelbase dock tank engines with 4 ft 0 in wheels dating from 1911 while LMS 16230—376 were the 4 ft 6 in engines dating from 1895. The larger engines were withdrawn between 1952 and 1962, the smaller ones being scrapped during the 1958—62 period.

Total ex-CR freight tank engines at grouping:

0—4—0ST	40
0—6—0ST	34
0—6—0T	170
0—8—0T	6
Total	250

Plate 189 No. 16211, in post-1928 livery, was an example of a Drummond 0—6—0ST in its final years. Good pictures of these locomotives are not plentiful so this view has been included to show details of construction; in particular note the wooden sides to the bunker and the notice, 'Speed 12 mph'. An LMS works plate is on the side of the front sandbox.   *BR LMR*

Plate 190 These 0—4—0STs of Drummond/McIntosh design often ran with 'tenders' to increase coal capacity and further illustrations will be found in *Volume II*. This picture displays No. 16004 in post-1928 freight livery, Code C4. Note the dumb buffers, location for the fire irons, tool box under the framing below the cab side sheets and position of the water capacity plate.

Authors' Collection

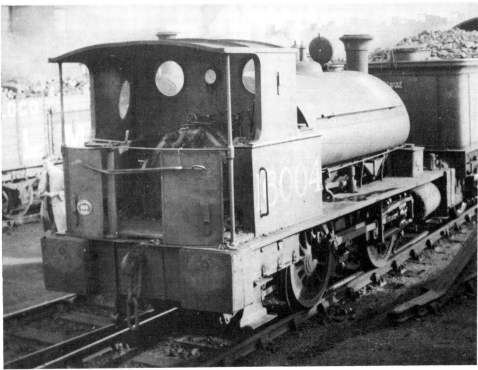

Plate 191 (Below) The principal Caledonian shunting tank locomotives were the McIntosh 0—6—0Ts and this picture of No. 16347 is in pre-1928 livery, Code C1. Note the LMS works plate which reads: Built 1912, St. Rollox.   *BR LMR*

Freight Tender Engines

Of the major LMS constituents, the Caledonian was second only to the Midland Railway in the emphasis it placed on the 0—6—0 type for freight working and out of a total of 439 freight tender engines, no less than 89% were of 0—6—0 type.

The 50 other engines were to five different designs, four of them by McIntosh and the fifth by Brittain. This latter group was the oldest and numerically largest of the five types and dated from 1878 (LMS 17000—20). They were very distinctive outside cylindered 0—4—2 engines whose visual lines were no longer typical of the CR by the time of the grouping. Nevertheless, some of the survivors managed to last for almost ten years until 1932 saw their final demise.

The next oldest of the non-standard engines were the eight McIntosh 0—8—0s of 1901—3 (LMS 17990—7). These were somewhat similar to the contemporary 0—8—0Ts but did not last as long, being withdrawn between 1927 and 1929. Until the adoption of the 2xxxx duplicate series numbers, the running numbers given by the LMS to the CR 0—8—0s were the highest in the LMS stock list.

Two other McIntosh designs were the 4—6—0 freight engines of 1906 (the '918' Class) and 1913 (the '179' Class). The '918' Class (LMS 17900—4) had 5 ft 0 in wheels while the '179' Class (LMS 17905—15) had 5 ft 9 in wheels. Broadly contemporary with and similar in general concept to the same designer's 4—6—0 passenger designs, these engines, like the passenger 4—6—0s, offered but token resistance to the LMS standard classes. The small engines were withdrawn in 1929/30 before the Stanier period had even started while the '179' Class succumbed to the Stanier Class 5s during 1935—46.

In 1912, McIntosh also developed a small series of 2—6—0s (LMS 17800—4). In all essentials these were basically 0—6—0s with a pair of leading wheels to carry the extra weight of the superheater but whose external appearance suggested they had been added as an afterthought. They were scrapped during 1935—7.

Turning now to the Caledonian 0—6—0 designs, these engines were yet another group whose longevity was to prove remarkable. Apart from two ex-Solway Junction Railway engines (LMS 17101—2) dating from 1868 and scrapped in 1927/8, all the CR 0—6—0s could trace their ancestry back to the basic Drummond design of 1883. Some 244 of these were built during the Drummond/Lambie/McIntosh period and all reached the LMS (LMS 17230—473). These Drummond 'Jumbos' remained intact until 1946, only a handful failed to reach BR and they did not become extinct until 1962.

McIntosh enlarged the basic 'Jumbo' in his '812' Class of 1899 and this variation contributed another 96 engines to the total (LMS 17550—645). All survived to BR and withdrawal took place between 1948 and 1963.

Oddly enough, the newest and most powerful Caledonian 0—6—0s were less resilient than the older engines and this may well have been symptomatic of the general trend of LMS replacement policy alluded to on page 111. Some 47 engines were involved, four by McIntosh (the '30' Class; LMS 17646—9) and the remainder by Pickersgill (LMS 17650—92). The McIntosh engines were scrapped between 1935 and 1946, the Pickersgills between 1934 and 1963. There were 29 survivors of the Pickersgill series in 1948 and all received BR numbers.

Plate 192 Ex-CR 0—4—2 No. 17013, pictured in pre-1928 freight livery (Code C5), has been selected to represent this group of Brittain locomotives. Examples of this class remained in service until 1932 when the final member was withdrawn. Note the footstep on the tender and wooden side doors between tender and locomotive.

Authors' Collection

Total ex-CR freight tender engines at grouping:

0—4—2 type	21
0—6—0 type	389
2—6—0 type	5
4—6—0 type	16
0—8—0 type	8
Total	439

Plates 193-195 These photographs represent three numerically small classes of McIntosh goods engines.

Plate 193 (Opposite top) shows an 0—8—0 ▶ No. 600, later to beocme LMS 17990 in its condition prior to repainting in LMS livery. These eight 0—8—0s had all been withdrawn by 1929 one of which, No. 605, remaining in CR livery to the end and was the last member of the class to be withdrawn. *Authors' Collection*

Plate 194 (Opposite centre) The Caledonian ▶ '918' Class lasted only a few years after the grouping and this picture of No. 17902 displays Livery Code C1.

Stephen Collection — NRM

Plate 195 (Opposite bottom) The Caledonian built five 2—6—0s and this picture illustrates No. 17803 in post-1928 freight livery, Code C14. Note the pipe connecting the front and rear vacuum brake pipes and the slacking pipe hooked through the handrail on the cabside. *Authors' Collection*

Plate 196 The Caledonian Railway Drummond 'Jumbo' 0-6-0s were a long lived type and as such exhibited many detail variations; many are illustrated in *Volume II*. This picture of No. 17423 being prepared at Stirling on 6th July, 1933 can be considered as typical for this class during this period of their history. Livery Code C14.   *A.G. Ellis*

Plate 197 This picture of No. 17595 is an example of the McIntosh 'Jumbo' which was an enlarged version of the earlier Drummond design. Photographed at Kingmoor on 31st August, 1939. Livery Code C21.   *A.G. Ellis*

Plate 198 The Pickersgill 0—6—0s are represented by this picture of No. 57652 in British Railways livery. Photographed at Dawsholm c1961. Note the prominent rivet detail at the front end.   *Authors' Collection*

THE GLASGOW AND SOUTH WESTERN RAILWAY

Locomotive Superintendents:

Patrick Stirling	1853—1866
James Stirling	1866—1878
Hugh Smellie	1878—1890
James Manson	1890—1912
Peter Drummond	1912—1918
Robert Harben Whitelegg	1918—1923

The GSWR was something of an odd man out amongst the LMS constituents. Its total of 528 engines was too large to be discounted yet it was too small and consisted of too many old and separate classes for there to be any real prospect of a quasi-standardisation along the lines adopted for the CR engines. In the event, although numerically quite considerable, the GSWR engine stock tended, in the main, to suffer a similar fate to that undergone by most of the smaller LMS constituents such as the Furness and North Staffordshire Railways. In consequence, post-group standardisation was probably in evidence at an earlier date and to a greater extent in the ex-GSWR territory than almost anywhere else in Scotland. This resulted in quantities of the early LMS standard engines taking over responsibility from a whole variety of older engines. In particular, the LMS standard 4—4—0s (both simple and compound) plus the Fowler Class 4Fs and to some extent the Hughes/Fowler 'Crabs' were early arrivals. Since the GSWR had, before the grouping, adopted the carriage colours of its English ally, the Midland, there was more than a superficial air of 'Lesser Derby' about the railway scene of South West Scotland!

The GSWR was very much a tender engine line with only a small proportion of tank engines in its lists (less than 16%). Although only two wheel arrangements (4—4—0 and 0—6—0 tender) accounted for over two thirds of the engines involved, the overall number of different classes contained within the GSWR stock was considerable. Moreover, the LMS renumbering seemed to be a little illogical at times. For this reason, a semi-tabular presentation along similar lines to that adopted for the smaller English railways has been selected for this review of the GSWR engines.

Running Numbers	*Description*
	Passenger Tender Engines
14000	This number was allocated to the last survivor of ten Stirling 2—4—0s dating from 1870. The number was never carried and the engine was withdrawn in 1923, along with another survivor which never even received an LMS number allocation.
14001—2	Out of twelve 2—4—0s designed by Smellie in 1879, two survived to the grouping. Neither engine survived to carry the numbers, both being scrapped in 1923.
14116—37	These numbers were allotted to a series of elderly 4—4—0s designed by Hugh Smellie in 1882 — the 'Wee Bogies'. Originally fitted with small domeless boilers and Stirling type cabs (LMS Class 1P), the majority had, by the time of the grouping, been rebuilt with larger domed boilers and new cabs (LMS Class 2P). Of the few which retained the small boilered configuration, one or two had acquired a dome by 1923. The whole group of engines was extinct by 1934.

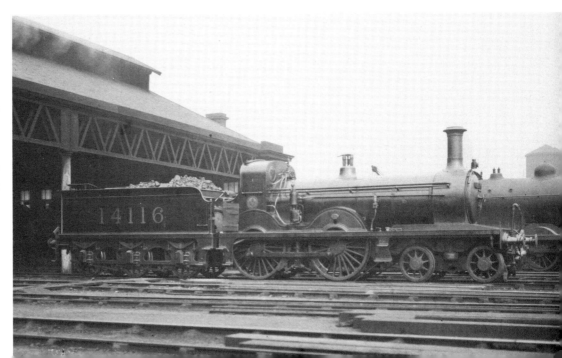

Plate 199 This picture of No. 14116 shows a Smellie 4—4—0 in original condition carrying crimson lake livery, Code A1. Many members of the class were later rebuilt with domed boilers and certain locomotives acquired larger, all-over, cabs.

Photomatic

14138—56	This later design of 4—4—0 by Hugh Smellie dated from 1886 and was basically a larger wheeled version of the older design. Once again, these engines started life in domeless condition with Stirling type 'round cabs' but most had received larger domed boilers and new cabs by the time of grouping. As with 14116—37, the odd example carried the original cab with a small domed boiler. There was one accident withdrawal before 1923 and the main class was withdrawn during 1925—35.
14157—227 14244—70	These numbers were allocated to a series of older Manson 4—4—0s from the 1829—1906 period. Some had been rebuilt with larger boilers; and two wheel sizes, together with several cylinder size/boiler pressure variations were exhibited. In simplified summary they were as follows:

14157—202	Engines with 6 ft 9½ in driving wheels, built between 1892 and 1904
14203—27	6 ft 1¼ in engines built 1895—9
14244—5 14249—53 14266—70	As per 14157—202
14246—8 14254—65	Later 6 ft 9½ in engines built 1904—6 with larger boilers from new

The rebuilding of the earlier engines with larger boilers was by no means complete at grouping but a greater proportion of the large wheeled engines had received the larger boilers than had the small wheeled engines. The LMS classified the larger boilered engines as 2P, the remainder as 1P.

These Manson 4—4—0s were intact at grouping, there being 72 large and 25 small wheeled engines. All were scrapped between 1925 and 1933.

14228—43	These engines were the sixteen survivors of 22 Stirling-designed 4—4—0s dating from 1873. Most were domeless engines but one or two had domed boilers. Why they were numbered so high up the LMS sequence is not known. The class was extinct in 1930.
14366—78	These engines were a further series of Manson 4—4—0s dating from the 1907—12 period. They were dimensionally all but identical to the large boilered, large wheeled examples from the earlier series above (14157—14227; 14244—70) and were scrapped during a similar period (1925—32).
14509	This engine held the distinction of being the first four-cylinder simple expansion locomotive in Britain. It was a 4—4—0 design dating from 1897 and extensively rebuilt in 1922 by Whitelegg. Named *Lord Glenarthur*, it was the only named GSWR engine and was scrapped in 1934.
14510—21	The newest and possibly the best of the GSWR 4—4—0s were the twelve Drummond engines of 1914—15. They were withdrawn between 1934 and 1937.
14656—74	These 19 engines were the 4—6—0s introduced by James Manson in 1903 and built in small numbers until 1911. Designed for the heavier main line services, they did not long outlive the GSWR, being scrapped during 1928—34 and replaced, mainly by standard Compound 4—4—0s, before even the Stanier engines were introduced.

Total ex-GSWR passenger tender engines at grouping:

2—4—0 type	3
4—4—0 type	181
4—6—0 type	19
Total	203

Passenger Tank Engines

15241—4	These were a class of four 0—4—4Ts of Stirling design dating from 1879. Withdrawn in 1925/6, none are thought to have carried their LMS numbers.
15245—54	These 0—4—4Ts were to a Manson design of 1893. They did not long survive grouping, all being scrapped between 1930 and 1932.
15400—5	These six massive 4—6—4Ts were amongst the newest of the GSWR designs. Built by Whitelegg in 1922, their imposing appearance somewhat belied their ability and, being non standard, they did not last long, being withdrawn during 1934—5.

Total ex-GSWR passenger tank engines at grouping:

0—4—4T	14
4—6—4T	6
Total	20

Plate 200 (Above) The Manson 4—4—0s are represented by No. 14172 in post-1928 livery, Code B2, illustrating a 6′ 9½″ driving wheel locomotive.
BR LMR

Plate 201 (Right) The 1886 Smellie design was basically a larger wheeled version of the 1882 class illustrated in Plate 200. This picture of No. 14140 shows a locomotive in post-1928 livery, Code B3, after rebuilding with a domed boiler and new larger cab. *Photomatic*

Plate 202 No. 14377 is an example of the Manson 4—4—0s of 1907 and in this picture, displays pre-1928 freight livery (Code C2) on a passenger locomotive. *A.G. Ellis*

Plate 203 The Drummond 4—4—0s of 1913 were the final design of this wheel arrangement to be built by the GSWR and this picture of No. 14518 was taken on 10th October, 1931 at Newton-on-Ayr and shows post-1928 livery, Code B4.

A.G. Ellis

Plate 204 No. 15246 in crimson lake, Livery Code A1, illustrates an 0-4-4T of 1893 Manson design. These handsome 0—4—4T locomotives, along with the majority of GSWR designs, did not survive long in LMS ownership. Photographed on 13th June, 1931. *A.G. Ellis*

Plate 205 The massive 4—6—4Ts were introduced just before the grouping but were all withdrawn by 1935. This picture shows No. 15401 in St Rollox livery, style Code B1.

Photomatic

Freight Tank Engines *

16040—3   These were an assorted group of 0—4—0STs of three types and were scrapped during 1924—32. They were contractors' locomotives built by outside firms.

16044—9   These six engines were Manson 0—4—0 side tanks built during 1907—9 and withdrawn during 1930/31.

16080—5   These six dock tanks by Manson, introduced in 1906, were somewhat unusual in being the only tank engines of 0—4—4 wheel arrangement in the LMS freight tank list. They were scrapped between 1925 and 1932.

16103—17   These Manson 0—6—0Ts were built during 1896—1914. All 15 reached the LMS but were scrapped between 1928 and 1932.

16377—9   There were but three Drummond 0—6—0Ts in the GSWR lists but they had an interesting post-group history. No. 16377 was scrapped in 1932 but the other two were sold out of service in 1934. Thirty years later it was realised that 16379 (now doing colliery duty in Wales) was the only surviving ex-GSWR engine in existence and it was rescued and restored for preservation in Glasgow Museum as GSWR 324. Although it is good that the GSWR is represented by at least one engine, it cannot really be said that the Drummond 0—6—0T was a typical GSWR machine.

16400—27   This group of 28 0—6—2Ts built by Drummond and Whitelegg formed the largest class of GSWR tank engines and, in the event, turned out to be the longest surviving GSWR type (tank or tender). Built during 1915—1919, these typically Drummond looking engines were intact at the grouping and until 1936. They were renumbered 16900—27 in 1926 to make way for standard Class 3F 0—6—0Ts. One of them (16905), was the sole GWR engine to achieve BR ownership but was scrapped in 1948 before being renumbered.

Total ex-GSWR freight tank engines at grouping:

0—4—0T/ST	10
0—4—4T	6
0—6—0T	18
0—6—2T	28
Total	62

* *Note:*   Two ex-Glasgow and Paisley Joint Railway engines were numbered next to the GSWR freight tanks. These were two 0—4—0STs and allocated LMS 16050—1. They were scrapped in 1924.

Plate 206   0—4—0ST No. 16043 in pre-1928 freight livery, Code C4, has been selected to represent the four 0—4—0STs inherited by the LMS from the GSWR.   *BR LMR*

Plate 207 0—4—4Ts for freight work were unusual and this Manson design was the only type to be inherited by the LMS. Note the unusual bogie design. Livery Code C4.

BR LMR

Plate 208 This class of 0—6—2T was the longest lived of all GSWR locomotives in LMS ownership. No. 16924 is in the St Rollox style Code B1 but there is no lining on this particular locomotive. Note the handrail along the tank top and the cranked vacuum pipe. *A.G. Ellis*

Freight Tender Engines

17021—75   These engines were the survivors of a considerable number of 0—4—2 tender engines designed both by Patrick and by James Stirling. Dating back to the 1860s and 1870s, several of them had undergone rebuilding at the hands of James Manson and the following summary is in outline only:

17021—2   The two remaining Patrick Stirling engines of 1866, withdrawn by 1924.

17023—7   James Stirling engines of 1873, withdrawn in 1923.

17028—34   The seven survivors of 20 James Stirling engines of 1870/1 rebuilt by Manson in 1900. They lasted until 1930.

17035—45   These were later Stirling engines of 1874—8 but in unrebuilt form. All were early casualties after grouping and none are thought to have been given LMS numbers.

17046—75   These thirty engines were Manson rebuilds of another group of Stirling engines of the same type as 17035—45. The rebuilding took place in 1901—3 and the class was intact at grouping. Withdrawal took place between 1925 and 1931.

17100   This was the last surviving Patrick Stirling 0—6—0 of 1866—9 vintage. Eight reached the LMS but 17100 was the only one allotted an LMS number. It never received it, being scrapped in 1923.

17103—11   These nine 0—6—0s were also elderly engines, being designed by James Stirling in 1877. Originally twelve strong, nine only reached the LMS and the class was extinct by 1928.

17112—84
17203—12   These 0—6—0 designs by Hugh Smellie, built during 1881—92, were, like the contemporary 4—4—0s, a little confusing. They had started life as small boilered domeless engines of essentially Stirling lineaments; some were rebuilt with small domed boilers and original Stirling type cabs while others had received larger domed boilers with all-over cabs. All three varieties were well represented and all but one reached the LMS. Withdrawals were complete by 1935.

17185—202   These were Manson 0—6—0s of 1897—9 vintage. All survived to the LMS but were scrapped between 1925 and 1933.

17474—524   These were much larger Manson 0—6—0s, built mostly during the 1900—10 period but 17523—4 in 1921. Some were rebuilt with large boilers and most of the 17508—24 series had large boilers from new. Despite their relative modernity by GSWR standards, and their fairly considerable numbers, scrapping started in 1928 and was complete by 1937.

Plate 209   A variety of 0—4—2 designs were taken over by the LMS in 1923 and this picture of No. 17047 is an example of a Stirling design as rebuilt by Manson. Note the deep buffer beam, lack of running plate on the tender, and cabside doors. Livery Code C1.

Stephen Collection — NRM

Plate 210 (Above) This picture of 0−6−0 No. 17117 is an example of a Smellie locomotive with a small domed boiler and original cab. Pre-1928 freight livery, Code C2.

BR LMR

Plate 211 (Below) No. 17514 was a Manson 0−6−0 from the 1900−10 period with a large domed boiler. Photographed in pre-1928 freight livery, Code C1. This locomotive is coupled to a flat sided tender.

Stephen Collection − NRM

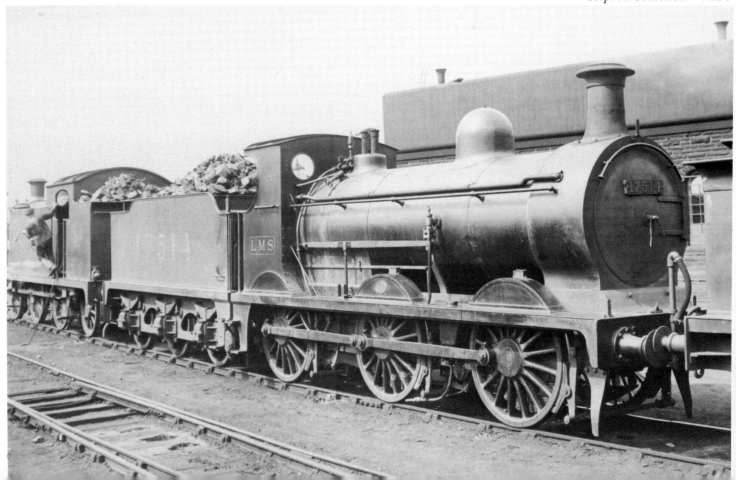

Plate 212 The most powerful Scottish 0—6—0s were the Drummond locomotives of 1913. This picture shows No. 17764 in post-1928 livery, Code C14. *A.G. Ellis*

17750—64   The only Drummond 0—6—0s on the GSWR were 15 engines built in 1913. Intact at grouping, they were scrapped during 1930—3. These engines were by far the most powerful of any of the Scottish 0—6—0s acquired by the LMS. They were probably too big to be 'standardised' by using Caledonian type replacement components as happened to some of the Highland Railway types.

17820—30   These engines dated from 1915 and were to all intents and purposes a 2—6—0 derivative of the Drummond 0—6—0 design. They were much better than the 0—6—0s and were amongst the more long lasting of the GSWR types; for although scrapping started in 1935, the last did not disappear until 1947.

Total ex-GSWR freight tender engines at grouping:

0—4—2 type	55
0—6—0 type	177
2—6—0 type	11
Total	243

Plate 213 The 2—6—0s outlived the 0—6—0s of GSWR design and the final member of the class of eleven was not withdrawn until 1947. This plate shows No. 17827 which is carrying post-1928 freight livery, Code C1. *A.G. Ellis*

THE HIGHLAND RAILWAY

Locomotive Superintendents:

William Stroudley	1866–1869
David Jones	1869–1896
Peter Drummond	1896–1911
F. G. Smith	1912–1915
C. Cumming	1915–1923

If the ex-GSWR engines inherited by the LMS were chiefly remarkable for the rate at which they were scrapped, bearing in mind their relatively large numerical strength, then the Highland Railway engines were equally remarkable for their post-group resilience. The Highland Railway contributed only 150 engines to the LMS number list which put it on a par with such systems as the North Staffordshire or the Furness Railway; but its engines fared much better than those of the comparably sized English systems.

One of the reasons for the tolerably good survival rate of many ex-HR engines (quite apart from their compatibility with many ex-CR designs — see page 111) was that they were well built and of good design. In its time, the HR had attracted the services of several of Britain's most celebrated locomotive engineers and they often made significant advances in locomotive design when faced with the peculiar and difficult operating conditions north of Perth. The outside framed 'Crewe Type' locomotive, whose ancestry goes back to Buddicom and Francis Trevithick in the 1840s, was probably developed by the Highland Railway to a finer degree than anywhere else in Britain by David Jones; while he was also the pioneer of the British 4–6–0 in the shape of his HR 'Big Goods' engines.

In general, the HR was predominantly a tender engine railway and, proportionally, placed heavier emphasis on the 4–6–0 type than did most LMS constituents. In fact, by LMS standards, the Highland could almost be said to have had a 'big engine' policy. However, it must be stated that the most common single HR wheel arrangement was the 4–4–0 and in 1923, some of these were very small and elderly.

Highland Railway passenger engines were numerically much stronger than freight types. In fact, the HR did not hand over a large number of purely freight engines to the LMS. This was not because of a lack of goods traffic but largely stemmed from the fact that the passenger types themselves were usually given quite small wheels to cope with the gradients and were thus well able to cope with freight traffic in addition to passenger trains. Mixed trains were also common on the Highland and it is probably not too fanciful to postulate that the HR experience may well have been relevant to the overall LMS policy of building large numbers of mixed traffic types for the whole system.

As with the other smaller LMS constituents, the following review is presented in semi-tabulated form.

| Running Numbers | Description |

Passenger Tender Engines

14271—6
These six 'Strath' Class locomotives represented one of several variants of a very characteristic Highland type — the so-called 'Crewe Type' 4—4—0. The 'Straths' dated from the 1890s and had 6 ft 3 in driving wheels. Originally twelve in number, six reached the LMS and all had gone before 1931.

14278
This was the sole survivor of the earlier 6 ft 3 in wheeled 'Bruce' Class 4—4—0 dating from 1886. It was withdrawn in 1930.

14277
14279—85
The third 'Crewe Type' 4—4—0 tender design was the famous 'Skye Bogie' Class with smaller (5 ft 3 in) driving wheels. Nine were built to operate on the Kyle of Lochalsh route and all but one reached the LMS. No. 14277 was numbered out of sequence because it was mistakenly assumed to have been another 'Bruce' Class 4—4—0. All the 'Skye Bogies' were withdrawn between 1922 and 1930.

14379—96
These 18 locomotives were the Jones 'Loch' Class 4—4—0s, 15 having been introduced in 1896 and the remainder in 1917. All reached the LMS. Many were rebuilt after 1923 with larger Caledonian type boilers and their survival rate was good. Withdrawal began in 1930 but two of the larger boilered rebuilds (14379/ 85) survived to BR days until 1950. Neither carried BR numbers.

Plate 215 No. 14271 *Sir George* pictured here in crimson lake livery (Code A1), was a member of the 'Strath' Class of 1892. This class was extinct by 1931.

Authors' Collection

Plate 214 (Opposite) The Highland 'Skye Bogies' are represented by this picture of No. 14284 resplendent in crimson lake livery, Code A1. Note the front coupling hook in the upright position and the vacuum pipe laid back, common Highland practice.

Stephen Collection — NRM

Plate 216 No. 14391 *Loch Shin* in post-1928 livery, Code B7 or B4, illustrates a member of the 'Loch' Class rebuilt with a larger Caledonian Railway boiler.

Photomatic

Plate 217 The Drummond 4—6—0 'Castles' were the principal express passenger locomotives of Highland design and this picture shows No. 14681 *Skibo Castle* in post-1928 livery, Code B6.

Photomatic

14397—416 14417—22	The Drummond 4—4—0 was represented on the HR by the two 'Ben' Classes. The first 20, dating from the turn of the century were the 'Small Bens' and the last six (built 1908—9) were the 'Large Bens' with bigger boilers. Like the 'Lochs', the 'Bens' also benefited from the already mentioned semi-standardisation policy evident in Scotland and many received CR type boilers. The 'Large Bens' lasted until 1937 but ten of the smaller type reached BR, three being renumbered (54398-9/404). One of them (54398 *Ben Alder*) was retained for many years, scheduled for preservation, but was eventually broken up under rather mysterious circumstances during the 1960s — a somewhat unfortunate and foolish move in the light of subsequent preservation activity.

14522—3   These two 4—4—0s were designed by Cumming in 1916 but were destined to last only until 1936. Named *Snaigow* and *Durn*, they were amongst Britain's most modern 4—4—0s at the time, having outside cylinders and Walschaerts valve gear; but the fact that there were only two of them undoubtedly contributed to their early demise.

14675—93   The Drummond 'Castle' Class 4—6—0s, built from 1900—1917, were the mainstay of the heavier Highland trains, particularly between Perth and Inverness. All but three had 5 ft 9 in driving wheels but the last of the series had 6 ft wheels. The engines had obvious affinities with the earlier 'Jones Goods' 4—6—0 type and a variant of the design was adopted to a limited extent in France. All the HR 'Castles' reached the LMS and withdrawal was slow and steady between 1930—46. As with many other pre-group designs, they fell victim to the ubiquitous Stanier Class 5.

14762—9   The eight Cumming 'Clan' Class 4—6—0s, dating from 1919, were the Highland's most powerful passenger locomotives and a very successful design. They had much in common with the earlier Cumming 4—4—0s (above) but they did manage to survive the initial onslaught of the Stanier era. Withdrawal took place between 1944 and 1950, one of them (54767) receiving its BR number.

Total ex-HR passenger tender engines at grouping:

4—4—0 type	61
4—6—0 type	27
Total	88

Passenger Tank Engines

15010—12   These three engines were 4—4—0T versions of the 'Crewe Type' design and used for branch line work. Rather similar to the 'Skye Bogies' but with smaller cylinders, they dated from the 1880s when they were introduced as rebuilds of earlier 2—4—0Ts. They were withdrawn between 1928 and 1932.

15013—17   These five 4—4—0Ts were built by Dübs & Company in the early 1890s for the Uruguay Eastern Railway but never delivered. Bought by the HR, they had neat visual lines but had little family affinity with the rest of the HR fleet. Used mainly for branch line work, they were withdrawn between 1924 and 1934.

134

Plate 218 (Above) The Cumming 'Clan' Class of 1919 was the most powerful Highland 4—6—0 design, and this picture of No. 14762 *Clan Campbell*, in crimson lake livery, Code A1, clearly shows the pre-1928 lining style employed for this class of locomotive.

Stephen Collection — NRM

Plate 219 (Below) 4—4—0T No. 15011 in crimson lake livery, Code A3, is one of three locomotives which could be described as 'tank versions' of the 'Skye Bogies' (see Plate 214).

Stephen Collection — NRM

Plate 220 Drummond 0—4—4T No. 15054 was a member of the final design of Highland locomotive to remain in service. Note the absence of links on the front coupling hook. Livery Code B3.

Authors' Collection

15050—4 The five HR 0—4—4Ts were of two types. No. 15050 was a solitary Jones engine, built in 1890 as a saddle tank and rebuilt to side tank in 1901. The remaining four were Drummond engines with slightly bigger driving wheels (4 ft 6 in as opposed to 4 ft 3 in) but sharing several similarities with the unique Jones engine. No. 15050 was withdrawn in 1929, but two of the Drummond engines (55051/3) lasted as late as 1956, working the Dornoch branch, and in so doing were the last ex-HR engines to remain on book stock.

15300—7 These eight machines were big 0—6—4Ts built by Drummond between 1909—11 and shared many visual similarities with his 0—6—2Ts built at a later date for the GSWR. Their most noteworthy use was in banking heavy trains over Drumuichdar Summit between Blair Atholl and Aviemore. Although very much in the Drummond tradition, these engines did not fare so well and the last example was withdrawn in 1936. Ironically, the withdrawal of the rather similar GSWR tanks did not commence until that year.

Total ex-HR passenger tank engines at grouping:

4—4—0T	8
0—4—4T	5
0—6—4T	8
Total	21

Plate 221 The Highland Railway owned eight 0—6—4Ts of Drummond design and many were used for banking duties. This picture of No. 43, later to become 15304, illustrates a member of this class just prior to grouping.

Stephen Collection — NRM

Freight Tank Engines

16118—19
16383
These three 0—6—0Ts were the Stroudley HR forerunners of his famous Brighton 'Terrier' tanks. No. 16383 was wrongly numbered in 1923 and the mistake was never rectified. It could have taken 16120, which remained vacant, but this was never done. All three engines were scrapped between 1927 and 1932.

16380—2
These three 0—6—0Ts emerged during the Drummond period in 1903—4. They were rather massive outside cylindered engines and designed to utilise available spare parts held in stock. For this reason, they were always known as 'Scrap' tanks. They were withdrawn between 1930 and 1932.

Total ex-HR freight tank engines at grouping:

0—6—0T   6

Freight Tender Engines

17693—704
These were a class of twelve 0—6—0s, built by Drummond between 1900 and 1907 and generally known as 'Barneys'. Visually almost identical with many of the ex-CR 0—6—0s, they were mostly fitted in due course with CR type fittings and, like the ex-HR 4—4—0s of similar vintage, enjoyed a long post-group life. Withdrawal took place between 1936 and 1952, seven reaching BR and three being renumbered (57695/7—8).

17916—30
The 15 'Jones Goods' were Britain's pioneer 4—6—0 type, dating from 1894. Possibly the most significant locomotives to emerge from the Highland Railway, the engines remained intact as a class for 35 years before withdrawal started in 1929. The final withdrawal was in 1940, but the pioneer engine (HR 103 — LMS 17916) was preserved when withdrawn in 1934 and is now, happily, in the Glasgow Transport Museum.

17950—7
These eight 4—6—0 engines, built between 1917—19, were designed by Cumming and were the freight equivalent of his contemporary passenger 4—6—0s. For this reason they were usually known as 'Clan Goods'. Like the 'Clans' themselves, the goods engines lasted well, scrapping taking place between 1946 and 1952. All but two reached BR.

Total ex-HR freight tender engines at grouping:

0—6—0 type	12
4—6—0 type	23
Total	35

Plate 222 No. 16118, an 0—6—0T of Stroudley design preceded his 'Terrier' Class for the LB&SCR. Seen here at Strathpeffer in Livery Code C4.

Stephen Collection — NRM

Plate 223 (Above) 0—6—0T No. 16382 was one of three locomotives sometimes referred to as 'Scrap Tanks', being partly built from spare components available at the time of their construction in 1903/4. They were extinct by 1932. Livery Code C4.

BR LMR

Plate 224 The Highland owned 12 0—6—0s known as 'Barneys' and No. 17693, photographed at Corkerhill on 25th June, 1949, displays post-1928 livery, Code C14.

A.G. Ellis

Plate 225 The 'Clan Goods' of Cumming's design lasted until 1952 and, in this view at Kyle, No. 17951 displays post-1928 livery, Code C15.

Authors' Collection

Chapter 8   New Locomotives — 1923 Onwards

In addition to the 10,000 odd locomotives acquired by the LMS in 1923 and the non-standard designs built after 1923, already considered, there were added more than 5,000 additional units before LMS designs were superseded by BR equivalents in 1951. These locomotives, which ultimately replaced about 7,000 of the pre-group total, were to LMS standard design or to Midland design modified as an LMS standard. They are reviewed below in ascending order of wheel arrangement and are summarised in chronological order of introduction in *Table 9* at the end of the chapter. For the sake of completeness, this table also includes the non-standard designs built during the LMS period.

0—4—0 Tank

Very few locomotives were built to this wheel arrangement by the LMS and the only justification for calling them 'standard' engines is the fact that they were new designs. They had little influence on LMS policy.

The only conventional type involved was a Class 0F 0—4—0ST — a Kitson design built to LMS requirements and introduced in 1932. Five were built (1540—4) and since they post-dated Stanier's arrival on the scene, they were, officially, 'Stanier' designs. It is questionable whether he had anything to do with them at all. These five were renumbered 7000—4 in 1934 and, after nationalisation, five more examples with increased tank capacity and other detail changes were built during 1953—4 (47005—9).

The other 0—4—0T designs were geared Sentinel locomotives. Four two-speed locomotives were introduced in 1930 and one single speed machine in 1932. Originally numbered 7160—4, the locomotives became 7180—4 in 1939. One oil fired Sentinel-Doble engine (7192) was added in 1934.

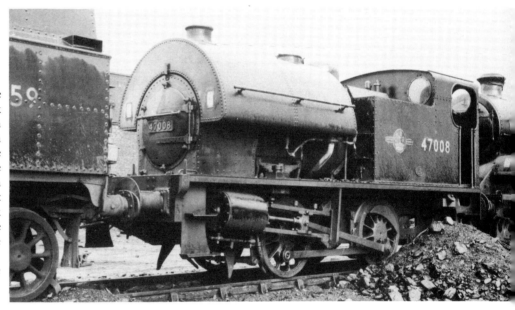

Plate 226 The LMS added five 0—4—0STs of Kitson design to stock in 1932 and a further five with enlarged tank capacity were built in 1953/4, the final LMS designs to be produced by British Railways. We have chosen to illustrate this type with No. 47008, a British Railways built locomotive photographed at Lostock Hall on 7th October, 1964. The original design is featured in Plate 22.

Authors' Collection

Plate 227 No. 7160 was the first of a series of five Sentinel locomotives and this picture shows a locomotive in original condition. Livery Code C14, with countershaded 'LMS'.

Authors' Collection

Plate 228 The final design of 0—4—4T to be built in Great Britain was a class of ten which was basically a modification of the Johnson 0—4—4Ts of the Midland Railway. Originally built with stovepipe chimneys and numbered 6400-9 they received new chimneys during the early 1940s and were then renumbered in 1946, and the picture of No. 41901 illustrates a locomotive in British Railways ownership.

Authors' Collection

0—4—4 Tank

As with the 0—4—0T arrangement, the 0—4—4T can hardly be considered a significant LMS standard design. Only ten engines were built and, emerging as they did in 1932, were again officially 'Stanier' engines. They were essentially a modernised version of the Midland 0—4—4T using second hand ex-MR boilers and their external appearance was in line with the Fowler lineaments of the first and second generation LMS standard parallel boiler classes. The stovepipe chimney fitted at first was the only obvious innovation. Originally 6400—9, the engines were renumbered 1900—9 in mid-1946 to make way for Ivatt standard 2—6—0s.

4—4—0 Tender

Two varieties of 4—4—0 locomotive were built by the LMS. Most numerous were the 195 LMS built examples of the Midland Class 4 Compound type. The LMS examples were numbered 1045—1199 and 900—939. In most external details they were all but identical to the Midland version but had 6 ft 9 in driving wheels instead of 7 ft 0 in. The first 20 LMS examples had the taller chimneys and domes of the MR locomotives but the remainder had reduced height fittings. Finally, all but the first 40 of the LMS built engines employed left hand rather than right hand drive.

The other 4—4—0 design was an LMS version of the Midland Class 2 type. The engines were numbered 563—700 and, as with the Compounds, the LMS engines had 6 ft 9 in driving wheels and other detail differences from the MR locomotives. They were also paired with Fowler LMS standard tenders rather than the pre-group Johnson pattern tenders fitted to the ex-MR Class 2s.

Plate 229 This picture of standard Compound No. 938, the penultimate Compound to be built by the LMS, was taken at Perth in August 1939 prior to the locomotive working the Royal Train. Note the block style replacement smokebox numberplate and the retention of the water deflector plates under the front buffer beam. Many Compounds were fitted with exhaust injectors, the pipe coming out of the smokebox confirms that 938 was so equipped. Livery Code A15.

G.L. Wilson

Plate 230 The standard LMS steam shunting tank locomotives were developed from the 1900—59 series of Midland Railway 0—6—0Ts after this design had been equipped with a Belpaire boiler. There were numerous variations to the class and they are fully illustrated in *Volume III*. To represent this class in *Volume I*, we have selected a view of No. 47667 in traffic when allocated to Carlisle Upperby. Note the three rain strips on the cab roof — originally there was only one. Some were built as 'steam brake only' but No. 47667 has a vacuum brake and has been equipped for steam heating of coaches.

BR LMR

0—6—0 Tank

Two designs of 0—6—0T were evolved by the LMS. By far the most numerous was the Class 3 shunting tank which was developed from its MR predecessor. The LMS examples had a slightly altered coal bunker compared with the MR engines. The LMS examples were built as 7100—56 and 16400—764, being completely renumbered into the 7260—7681 series in the same order from 1934 onwards.

The other 0—6—0Ts were ten Fowler Class 2F dock tank locomotives with a very short wheelbase. These were built in 1928 to replace older pre-group engines but the design was never repeated. It is, however, worth noting that the class was always listed as a design to be perpetuated in the various lists of standard types issued from time to time by the LMS. The dock tanks were built as 11270—9 and were renumbered 7100—9 during 1935—7 (usually when the corresponding Class 3F 0—6—0T in the 71xx series had been renumbered). Finally, in 1939, they were again renumbered to 7160—9 which numbers they retained — plus 40000 after 1947.

Plate 231 The LMS built ten 0—6—0Ts for dock shunting. Originally Nos. 11270-9, they became 7100-9 and finally 7160-9, before British Railways added a further 40000 to their original numbers. This official picture shows their original condition when built and carrying Livery Code C13.

BR LMR

Plate 232 (Left) This picture of No. 4224 displays a basic standard Class 4F 0–6–0 in mid-1930s condition, carrying freight livery, Code C13. Note the tender with a solid bulkhead, no coal doors, tail rod housing on the front buffer beam, later removed by Stanier, and original chimney. This locomotive is equipped with an exhaust injector (note the pipe coming out of the smokebox) and the injector just below the running plate near the rear driving wheels.

Real Photographs

Plate 233 (Opposite) No. 13000 was the pioneer 2–6–0 to be built by the LMS and this locomotive later became No. 2700. This picture illustrates No. 13000 before being painted in crimson lake livery, adopted for the first 100 locomotives to be built.

NRM

0–6–0 Tender

One of the most numerous classes to be built by the LMS was the Midland Class 4 0–6–0 'heavy goods' engine. The LMS built 575 units to add to the existing 197 MR and S & DJR locomotives and the differences between the two types were mostly matters of small details (splasher beading, tender type, left or right hand drive, etc). The LMS examples were mostly built before 1930 but, somewhat surprisingly, examples of the type were constructed as late as 1940/1. The full number range of the LMS built engines was 4027–4606, excluding 4557–61 which were the ex-S & DJR engines of pre-1923 date.

Counting pre- and post-group examples, there were eventually 772 Class 4Fs which class total was only exceeded by the Stanier Class 5 4–6–0 and Class 8F 2–8–0 types (but see page 53 regarding the number of '8Fs' which actually ran with LMS numbers).

2–6–0 Tender

The 2–6–0 tender engine was not a popular choice among the LMS pre-group constituents but after 1923, no less than four designs of 2–6–0 were standardised by the LMS.

The first was the Hughes/Fowler Class 5P/4F design of 1926, 245 of these engines being built between 1926 and 1930 – the most numerous of the LMS 2–6–0 types. In 1932, these engines were followed by 40 more of a taper boiler version – the first 'proper' Stanier design of locomotive. The combined total of 285 locomotives was numbered 13000–284 until 1934 when they became 2700–2984 in the same order.

From this point until 1946, no further 2–6–0 locomotives emerged but in the latter year, the Ivatt Class 2 2–6–0 was introduced (originally Class 2F). This design was to meet a requirement for economical motive power in a low power class and represented the change in locomotive philosophy mentioned at page 25. The Ivatt Class 2 eventually totalled 128 locomotives (46400–527) although only 20 had entered service before nationalisation. The design was adopted, almost unaltered, as a BR standard class and 65 more were built to this latter designation.

The final LMS 2–6–0 design was the Ivatt Class 4 of 1947 (originally Class 4F). This was the post-war design replacement for the ubiquitous Class 4F 0–6–0 in the list of LMS basic types and 162 were eventually built, 43000–161. Only the first three (3000–2) were in service as *LMS* engines.

2–6–2 Tank

Three hundred and thirty-nine 2–6–2Ts were built to three LMS designs. The earliest were 70 Class 3P engines of Fowler design, introduced in 1930 and for which two LMS diagrams were issued – one of which covered a condensing version for use on the Moorgate lines in London. The engines were originally numbered 15500–69, later becoming 1–70 in the same order.

In 1935, Stanier designed a taper boiler version of the Class 3P 2–6–2T and 139 of these were eventually built (Nos. 71–209). A few were given larger boilers in 1941.

The final LMS Class of 2–6–2T was a Class 2 tank engine (originally Class 2P), equivalent to the Ivatt Class 2 2–6–0 (above). The philosophy behind the design was the same and, like the tender engines, the type was again adopted, almost unchanged, as a BR standard type. One hundred and thirty examples were built of the LMS version (41200–329), the first 20 being in service before nationalisation.

2—6—4 Tank

This wheel arrangement became an almost universal LMS replacement for the considerable variety of medium and large sized passenger tank engines of pre-group origin. Essentially there was but one original LMS concept, from which stemmed the remaining designs.

The type originated with the two-cylinder Fowler Class 4P parallel boiler version of 1927, of which 125 were built, Nos. 2300—424. These were followed by the Stanier taper boiler derivatives which were of two principal variants. The first 37 were three-cylinder engines (2500—36) which were used mainly on the LT & S section; while 206 were two-cylinder locomotives (2425—94; 2537—672). The final version was a Fairburn designed shorter wheelbase variant of the Stanier two-cylinder design, 277 of which were built from 1945 onwards (2673—99; 2050—299). Many of them were placed in service after the LMS ceased to exist.

All told, 645 Class 4P 2—6—4Ts of LMS design were constructed and to this total could well be added the 155 more engines built from 1951 onwards to the BR standard design which stemmed from the Fairburn version of the LMS type.

Plate 234 The Fowler 2—6—2Ts, originally numbered in the 155xx series (see Plate 14) were later re-numbered 1-20 and this picture illustrates No. 28 carrying Livery Code B4. This locomotive was one of the class fitted with a condenser and used in the London area.

Authors' Collection

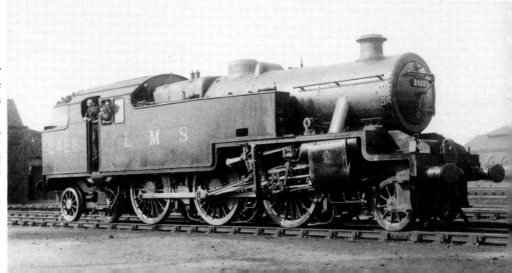

Plate 235 The Stanier 2 cylinder 2—6—4Ts were developed from the earlier Fowler locomotives and this picture of No. 2428 at Bedford on 8th June, 1936, carrying Livery Code B4, displays their first livery style: many members of this class entered traffic carrying the 1936 block style. Note the access hole in the tank side.

A.G. Ellis

4—6—0 Tender

LMS standard design 4—6—0 tender engines eventually totalled 1,156 units and fell into two distinct series — 314 three-cylinder locomotives and 842 two-cylinder machines.

The series started with the parallel boiler Class 6 'Royal Scot' design of 1927. Seventy of these engines were built in two separate batches (6100—49; 6150—69) and they established a basic three-cylinder express passenger 4—6—0 chassis layout which remained recognisably intact until the cessation of LMS designs.

In 1930, the basic 'Royal Scot' chassis layout was 'married' to the new large boiler of the rebuilt LNWR 'Claughton' Class to produce the prototype of the parallel boiler 'Patriot' Class 5XP design of which, eventually, 52 examples were built (5500—51). These were nominally 'rebuilds' of some of the small boilered 'Claughtons' although, in fact they were virtually new locomotives. Before 1934, the 'Patriots' carried the running numbers of the 'Claughtons' they had replaced.

The advent of Stanier brought taper boilers to the three-cylinder 4—6—0 layout and the first visible evidence of this was seen on the '191' Class 5XP locomotives (numbered 5552—5742) built between 1934 and 1936. When these were named (1935 onwards), they became known as the 'Jubilee' Class and were, in general terms, the taper boiler equivalents of the 'Patriots'.

Taper boilers did not generally start to appear on Class 6P 4—6—0s until 1942 when two 'Jubilees' were rebuilt with larger boilers and double chimneys (5735/6). These two engines were reclassified 6P and utilised a modified version of the boiler fitted by Stanier to 4—6—0 No. 6170 *British Legion* in 1935. This unique locomotive — in effect the 71st member of the 'Royal Scot' Class — stemmed from the rebuilding of the experimental high pressure 4—6—0 No. 6399 *Fury* which had 'blown up' in 1929 with fatal results — for full details see the appropriate chapter in *Volume III*.

Experience with 6170 and the two rebuilt 'Jubilees' convinced the LMS management that to rebuild all standard three-cylinder 4—6—0s to Class 6P taper boiler style was a desirable policy. Accordingly, a start was made with the oldest loco-motives — namely the parallel boiler 'Royal Scots'. The general rebuilding of this class started in 1943 but it was 1955 before the last was converted, the advent of nationalisation having considerably slowed down the process.

In 1946, a start was made on fitting the next oldest class (the 'Patriots') with taper boilers. Eight had been converted to Class 6P before nationalisation but the onset of BR standard designs caused a revision of the rebuilding policy. In conse-quence, only ten more 'Patriots' were rebuilt. The remaining parallel boiler engines and all the 'Jubilees' (except 5735/6) thus ended their days at Class 5XP rather than Class 6P (LMS power class ratings, *not* the later BR version — see page 151).

The 842 two-cylinder 4—6—0s were all of the Stanier Class 5P/5F type — albeit with many minor variations. The original design appeared in 1934 and by 1947, several variations of domed/domeless and high/medium/low superheat engines had emerged. From 1947 to 1950, a quite formidable experimental programme involving the Class 5s was under-taken. The experiments involved valve gears and wheel bearings and sundry combinations of the two — all being aimed at increasing mileage between repairs and reducing the cost of maintenance. Some of the final versions of the class built during this experimental phase bore little resemblance to the neat design which had sired them.

All these variations are covered in the class chapter on these engines but it is also interesting to note that the BR standard Class 5 4—6—0 of 1951 was essentially a Stanier Class 5 with some post-nationalisation variations.

Plate 236 The Class 5 4—6—0s were subject to a variety of modifications and these are fully covered in *Volume III*. To represent the class in this section we have selected a member of the Armstrong Whitworth batch of 227 locomotives numbered between 5225 and 5451 which was the largest single lot constructed. No. 45305 is shown in British Railways livery when allocated to 10D — Plodder Lane.

R.D. Clarke

Plate 237 Two 4—6—0 'Jubilee' Class locomotives were rebuilt with larger boilers in 1942 and reclassified 6P. No. 45736 *Phoenix* at Chester is shown here in BR condition in September 1955 with the addition of smoke deflector plates which produced, apart from the cabside sheets, a rebuilt 'Scot' appearance. *A.G. Ellis*

4—6—2 Tender

Unlike the LNER, the LMS did not, at first, pin its faith on the 4—6—2 type of tender engine for the most onerous of passenger duties. Fowler had toyed with the idea of a compound 4—6—2 in the 1920s — indeed, the design was all but ready to commence production — but the operating staff of the time preferred a 4—6—0, which emerged as the 'Royal Scot' Class. It was not until 1933, a year after Stanier assumed office, that the first LMS 4—6—2 emerged. Two principal classes of 4—6—2 engine were designed by Stanier, together with one very noteworthy experimental locomotive. Although in terms of tractive effort, the first LMS Pacifics were the most powerful in the country and the final design of Stanier 4—6—2 was an outstanding success, the LMS never whole-heartedly adopted the 4—6—2 type and only 51 locomotives were built to LMS design. The company could certainly have used more.

The first design was the 'Princess Royal' Class of 1933. Two only were built (Nos. 6200/1) of an original order for three machines for evaluation purposes. The design was impressive but not an instant success and a new boiler had to be built and the two original boilers converted to match before the first pair of Pacifics satisfied their designer.

Meanwhile, the frames of the third prototype (6202) had been set aside for building an experimental turbine driven 4—6—2. 'Turbomotive' as this engine was always called (although never named as such), proved a very 'near miss' in the field of locomotive design and it is arguable that, but for the war, the design might have been multiplied. In 1951, 'Turbo' was rebuilt to a reciprocating type, *Princess Anne,* coming to a sad end in the frightful Harrow double collision of October 1952.

Work on Nos. 6200/1 had pointed the way to further desirable changes for the main 'Princess Royal' Class (6203—12) and these engines emerged in 1935. The main visible change was a longer firebox and shorter boiler but there were other detail changes too — see class chapter in *Volume III*.

Plate 238 'Princess Royal' Class 4—6—2 No. 6207 *Princess Arthur of Connaught* is carrying Livery Code A6 and is coupled to a nine ton coal capacity tender, later to be exchanged for one with a ten ton capacity. *Photomatic*

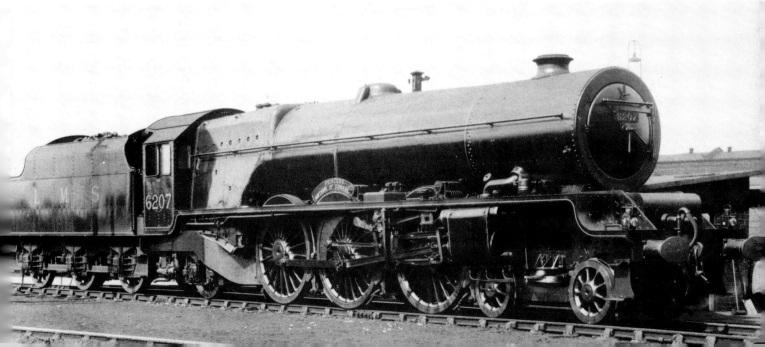

Plate 239 Blue streamlined 'Coronation' Class 4−6−2 No. 6223 *Princess Alice* on the down 'Coronation Scot' at Bolton-le-Sands in 1939.

G.L. Wilson Collection

Plate 240 (Opposite) The 0−8−0 Class ▶ 7F freight locomotives were all steam brake locomotives, and this picture shows No. 9563 carrying Livery Code C16, possibly C13 and is coupled to a Fowler tender with coal doors.

Authors' Collection

In 1937, the final LMS 4−6−2 design emerged − the famous 'Princess Coronation' Class − variously referred to as the 'Coronation' or 'Duchess' Class. The first examples were streamlined but in 1938, a non-streamlined version was also built. Double chimneys were fitted from 1939 to both streamlined and non-streamlined versions and, retrospectively, to existing single chimney members of the class.

All told, 24 streamliners were built (6220−9; 6235−48) and 12 non-streamlined engines (6230−4; 6249−55) before the final Ivatt version of 1947 introduced further mechanical and visual changes (6256 and 46257).

After the war, streamlining was removed and all the class were fitted with smoke deflectors. The 38 'Coronations' underwent many visual changes during their short lifetime and all these aspects are considered in the class chapter in *Volume III*.

2−6−6−2 Tank

In an attempt to reduce the traditional double-heading of coal trains on the Midland Division Toton-Brent route, Fowler arranged with Beyer-Peacock in 1927 to produce a 2−6−6−2 Garratt design of articulated engine. Three machines were delivered in 1927 and a main batch of 30 engines in 1930. The resulting 33 locomotives (4967−99) were the only *class* of Garratts to run in regular service in Britain − the LNER design never, of course, being multiplied beyond the one proto-type locomotive.

The LMS Garratts basically employed two sets of 'Crab' cylinders and motion, but with inferior valve settings and fed by a large boiler of somewhat 'Midland' character. They were the most powerful LMS standard locomotives but were never allocated a numerical power class. Shortly before the Class 5 4−6−0s were likely to 'overflow' into the 49xx number series, the Garratts were renumbered 7967−99 in the same order as originally numbered.

0−8−0 Tender

Although the Midland Railway never felt the need for a larger goods engine than the Class 4 0−6−0, the other two large English constituents of the LMS (the LNWR and LYR) had both employed a considerable number of 0−8−0 freight engines. In 1929, the need was felt for further examples of this wheel arrangement and the Fowler Class 7F 0−8−0 was the result. Eventually 175 were built and, in simplified terms, the design employed a boiler derived from the final 'G2' version of the LNWR 0−8−0 series but fitted to a chassis which had more in common with the standard Class 4F 0−6−0. This factor, together with the 'Midland' cab and Fowler standard tender, made the final product look far more like a Midland engine than a North Western machine.

Some sources refer to the Class 7F 0−8−0s as the 'G3' Class but, as far as has been ascertained, this designation was unofficial and was not in common usage by the LMS.

2—8—0 Tender

In 1935, as part of his standardisation programme, Stanier introduced a taper boiler 2—8—0 freight locomotive with many parts of the engine common to those used on the Class 5 4—6—0. The first few 2—8—0s were designated Class 7F but this was soon altered to 8F, which classification was maintained until scrapping.

Early construction was somewhat limited and the number of engines had only risen to fill the 8000—8125 series by the outbreak of war. However, the design was adopted as a War Department standard and hundreds more 8Fs were built during the war years. The grand total included WD engines, a considerable number of engines built by all four British railway companies on behalf of the LMS, plus some further examples built for the LNER.

The full history of the 8Fs is rather complicated and is covered in more detail in the class chapter in *Volume III.* Suffice it to say at this stage that, all told, 719 locomotives ran with LMS numbers before 1948 while another 133 were never included in the LMS lists. Many engines were lost at sea or remained overseas but the grand total of 852 units makes the Class 8F the numerically largest LMS standard class by a slight margin over the 842 Class 5s.

Plate 241 This picture of a Class 8F illustrates the use of the small snowplough which was a feature carried upon a number of LMS locomotives. In addition, attention is drawn to the block style numberplate and position of the power classification below the running number. Livery Code C22 (yellow shaded red but cabside figures seem unshaded, possibly even gilt).
BR LMR

TABLE 9. NEW STEAM LOCOMOTIVES ADDED TO STOCK — 1923 ONWARDS

Notes:
i) This table is arranged by classes in order of appearance of the first locomotive in each class. It includes post-nationalisation locomotives of LMS design built 1948-54.
ii) Individual classes are described in outline only, without reference to major or important variations within the class.
iii) Classes introduced prior to 1928 are shown with the classification adopted in 1928.
iv) Classes introduced from 1928 onwards are shown with their original classification.
v) Where BR numbers are shown, it should be understood that not all engines received their allotted numbers and that a number of engines did not survive to be taken over by BR.
vi) All engines built by BR are shown with their BR numbers, although several engines built early in 1948 were turned out at first with a four figure LMS series number, usually with a prefix letter 'M'. They later received the correct five figure 4xxxx series numbers as did all new locomotives to LMS design built from mid-1948 onwards.
vii) Of the non-standard locomotives built during 1923, many received numbers in the appropriate pre-group series, the correct LMS series numbers being applied later. This group also received a variety of non-standard hybrid liveries which are covered in detail elsewhere.

Date Introduced	Wheel Type	Number Built	Description	Final LMS Numbers	BR Number Allocation
Jan. 1923	4—6—0	41	Class 5P 4-cylinder Hughes parallel boiler LYR design, introduced 1920. The last 20 engines were larger and intended to be 4—6—4T — see March 1924 entry. Locomotives built 1923-5.	10434-10474	50455 only
Feb. 1923	0—8—4T	30	Class 7F 2-cylinder Beames parallel boiler LNWR design, introduced 1923. Tank engine version of LNWR Class 'G2' and built 1923-4.	7930-7959	47930-47959
May 1923	4—4—2T	35	Class 3P 2-cylinder parallel boiler engines to LTSR design as modified by the Midland Railway. Built 1923-30. These were never regarded as a standard type, not being of pure Midland design.	2110-2134 2151-2160	41928-41952 41969-41978
1923	0—6—2T	4	Class 3F 2-cylinder parallel boiler engines to a modified NSR 1913 design. All built 1923.	2270-2273	None
Feb. 1924	4—4—0	195	Class 4P Compound, almost identical to the Midland 3-cylinder design of 1905, as superheated 1913. LMS standard type built 1924-32.	900-939 1045-1199	40900-40939 41045-41199
Mar. 1924	4—6—4T	10	Class 5P 4-cylinder Hughes parallel boiler design based on LYR 4—6—0 of 1920. All built 1924 and originally intended to be 30 in number — see Jan. 1923 entry.	11110-11119	None
1924	4—6—0	1	Class 4P 2-cylinder parallel boiler LNWR 'Prince of Wales' type with Joy valve gear replaced by outside Walschaerts gear but retaining inside cylinders. First LMS number 5845.	25845	None
Jul. 1924	0—6—0T	422	Class 3F 2-cylinder parallel boiler shunting engines. LMS standard design by Fowler but essentially based on the largest of the ex-MR 0—6—0Ts. Engines built 1924-31 and total includes seven built for S&DJR in 1928-9 which came into LMS stock in 1930. First LMS numbers: 7100-56 (7150-6 were ex-S&DJR) and 16400-764.	7260-7681	47260-47681
Nov. 1924	0—6—0	575	Class 4F 2-cylinder parallel boiler to MR 1911 design with minor modifications. LMS standard type built 1924-41.	4027-4556 4562-4606	44027-44556 44562-44606
1925	4—6—0	20	Class 4P parallel boiler outside 2-cylinder engines to Caledonian '60' Class of 1916 with minor modifications. Built 1925-6.	14630-14649	54630-54649
1925	0—4—4T	10	Class 2P 2-cylinder parallel boiler engines to Caledonian '439' Class of 1900 with slight modifications. All built 1925.	15260-15269	55260-55269
May 1926	2—6—0	245	Class 5P4F parallel boiler outside 2-cylinder design by Hughes/Fowler. LMS standard type built 1926-32; first LMS numbers: 13000-244.	2700-2744	42700-42944
Apr. 1927	2—6—6—2T	33	Garratt (unclassified). New design by Fowler/Beyer Peacock & Co with four outside cylinders. Regarded as LMS standard type and built 1927-30. First LMS numbers: 4967-99.	7967-7999	47967-47999
Jul. 1927	4—6—0	70	Class 6P 3-cylinder parallel boiler 'Royal Scot' type. New LMS standard design by Fowler/N.B. Loco. Co. Built 1927-30 and rebuilt with taper boilers 1934-55.	6100-6169	46100-46169
Dec. 1927	2—7—4T	125	Class 4P parallel boiler outside 2-cylinder design by Fowler using MR Class 3P 4—4—0 boiler design. New LMS standard type, built 1927-34.	2300-2424	42300-42424
Mar. 1928	4—4—0	138	Class 2P 2-cylinder parallel boiler engines, basically to the 1912 MR design with minor modifications. LMS standard type built 1928-32. Total includes three	563-700	40563-40700

Date Introduced	Wheel Type	Number Built	Description	Final LMS Numbers	BR Number Allocation
			transferred to S&DJR in 1928 and returned to LMS stock in 1930 — see page 74.		
Dec. 1928	0–6–0T	10	Class 2F parallel boiler outside 2-cylinder design by Fowler. New LMS standard design but never multiplied beyond the first ten, built 1928-9. First LMS numbers: 11270-9, later 7100-9.	7160-7169	47160-47169
Mar. 1929	0–8–0	175	Class 7F 2-cylinder parallel boiler design by Fowler based on LNWR 0–8–0 but with many MR type detail fittings. New LMS standard type built 1929-32.	9500-9674	49500-49674
Mar. 1930	2–6–2T	70	Class 3P parallel boiler outside 2-cylinder design by Fowler. New LMS design but utilising superheated version of existing MR boiler type. Built 1930-2, first LMS numbers: 15500-69.	1-70	40001-10070
Jun. 1930	0–4–0T	4	Sentinel two-speed type (unclassified). Sentinel 2-cylinder 100 hp chain driven design. First LMS numbers: 7160-3.	7180-7183	47180-47183
Nov. 1930	4–6–0	52	Class 5XP 3-cylinder parallel boiler 'Patriot' type. New LMS standard design by Fowler. First two engines rebuilt 1930 from ex-LNWR 'Claughton' 4–6–0, 40 nominal 'Claughton' rebuilds during 1932-3 and ten new engines built 1934. First 42 engines originally carried number of 'Claughton' from which 'rebuilt'. During 1946-9, 18 were rebuilt with taper boiler as per 'Royal Scot' class.	5500-5551	45500-45551
Jan. 1932	0–4–0T	1	Sentinel single speed type (unclassified). Sentinel 2-cylinder chain driven design. First LMS number: 7164.	7184	47184
Nov. 1932	0–4–0ST	10	Class 0F parallel boiler outside 2-cylinder design by Kitson & Co. Five engines built 1932 and five modified examples by BR in 1953-4. First LMS numbers (1932 batch): 1540-4.	7000-7009	47000-47009
Dec. 1932	0–4–4T	10	Class 2P 2-cylinder parallel boiler design nominally attributed to Stanier. Built 1932-3, first LMS numbers: 6400-9.	1900-1909	41900-41909
Jul. 1933	4–6–2	12	Class 7P 4-cylinder taper boiler 'Princess Royal' type. New LMS standard design by Stanier, built 1933-5.	6200-6201 6203-6212	46200-46201 46203-46202
Oct. 1933	2–6–0	40	Class 4F taper boiler outside 2-cylinder design by Stanier. These were the first true Stanier engines although the first two 'Princess Royals' preceded them into service. Built 1933-4, first LMS numbers 13245-84.	2945-2984	42945-42984
Apr. 1934	2–6–4T	37	Class 4P 3-cylinder taper boiler engines. New LMS standard design by Stanier, all built 1934.	2500-2536	42500-42536
May 1934	4–6–0	191	Class 5XP 3-cylinder taper boiler 'Silver Jubilee' type. New LMS standard design by Stanier, built 1934-6. Two rebuilt in 1942 with larger boilers.	5552-5742	45552-45742
Sep. 1934	4–6–0	842	Class 5P5F taper boiler outside 2-cylinder design by Stanier. New LMS standard type, built 1934-51.	4758-5499	44758-45499
Nov. 1934	0–4–0T	1	Sentinel-Doble (unclassified). Oil fired 4-cylinder 200 hp Sentinel design — withdrawn 1943.	7192	None
Feb. 1935	2–6–2T	139	Class 3P taper boiler outside 2-cylinder design by Stanier. New LMS standard type, built 1935-8. Six rebuilt with larger boilers 1940-56.	71-209	40071-40209
Jun. 1935	2–8–0	852	Class 8F taper boiler outside 2-cylinder design by Stanier. New LMS standard type built 1935-46. Many of these engines were built for the WD and did not receive LMS series numbers. For fuller details of these engines, see page 53.	8000-8479 8490-8495 8500-8559 8600-8772	48000-48775 (non-continuous)
Jul. 1935	4–6–2	1	Class 7P taper boiler experimental turbine driven design by Stanier. Rebuilt in 1952 as orthodox 4-cylinder reciprocating locomotive.	6202	46202
Oct. 1935	4–6–0	1	Class 6P 3-cylinder taper boiler design by Stanier, incorporating material from experimental locomotive No. 6399 Fury. In effect, this Stanier rebuild formed the prototype for the rebuilt 'Royal Scots', 'Patriots' and 'Jubilees'.	6170	46170
Dec. 1935	2–6–4T	206	Class 4P taper boiler outside 2-cylinder design by Stanier, based on the 3-cylinder 1934 design. New LMS standard type built 1935-43.	2425-2494 2537-2672	42425-42494 42537-42672
Jun. 1937	4–6–2	38	Class 7P 4-cylinder taper boiler 'Princess Coronation' type. New LMS standard design by Stanier built 1937-48. Of these engines, 24 were originally streamlined, the casings being removed between 1946 and 1949.	6220-6256	46220-46256 46257

Date Introduced	Wheel Type	Number Built	Description	Final LMS Numbers	BR Number Allocation
Mar. 1945	2—6—4T	277	Class 4P taper boiler outside 2-cylinder design by Fairburn, being a modification of the 1935 Stanier design with shorter wheel-base and reduced weight. LMS standard type built 1945-8.	2187-2189 2200-2299 2673-2699	42187-42189 42200-42299 42673-42699 42050-42186 42190-42199
Dec. 1946	2—6—0	128	Class 2F taper boiler outside 2-cylinder design by Ivatt. New LMS standard type built 1946-53.	6400-6419	46400-46419 46420-46527
Dec. 1946	2—6—2T	130	Class 2P taper boiler outside 2-cylinder design by Ivatt. Tank version of 2F 2—6—0 (above). New LMS standard type built 1946-52.	1200-1209	41200-41209 41210-41329
Dec. 1947	2—6—0	162	Class 4F taper boiler outside 2-cylinder design by Ivatt, being the planned replacement of the Class 4F 0—6—0 (see Nov. 1924 entry). New LMS standard type built 1947-52.	3000-3002	43000-43002 43003-43161

Numerical Summary of engines built

Wheel Arrangement	Non-standard 'Pre-Group' designs built by or for the LMS	LMS standard designs built by or for the LMS	LMS designs built by or for BR	Totals
0—4—0T	—	11	5	16
0—4—4T	10	10	—	20
4—4—2T	35	—	—	35
0—6—0T	—	432	—	432
0—6—2T	4	—	—	4
2—6—2T	—	219	120	339
2—6—4T	—	498	147	645
4—6—4T	10	—	—	10
0—8—4T	30	—	—	30
2—6—6—2T	—	33	—	33
4—4—0	—	333	—	333
0—6—0	—	575	—	575
2—6—0	—	308	267	575
4—6—0	62	1056	100	1218
4—6—2	—	50	1	51
0—8—0	—	175	—	175
2—8—0	—	719	133*	852*
Totals	151	4419	773*	5343*

* Includes 133 Class 8F 2—8—0s built during World War II which never ran with LMS series numbers.

Chapter 9   Locomotive Classification and Naming

POWER CLASSIFICATION

The LMS management was primarily concerned with what a locomotive could perform in the way of work rather than what its specific type happened to be. As a result, from 1923 onwards, LMS locomotives were classified into standard power classes on a numerical scale.

This system had its origins on the Midland Railway, being directly related to the new traffic and locomotive numbering policies introduced in 1907. These policies had given rise to such a marked improvement on the Midland system that it is not surprising that the predominantly Midland management of the early LMS decided on the general adoption of the Midland power class system. It is worth noting that for some years prior to 1907, the MR had been using various power classification systems before the 1907 scheme was settled.

The principles were fairly simple. A numerical scale from 1 to 4 was linked to the tractive effort of the locomotive — the most powerful carrying the highest power class numbers. In theory, any locomotive could perform a duty appropriate to its own or a lower power class. Initially, the MR applied the system to its main line engines — i.e. the tender types — and mounted a brass figure on the cabside to indicate the power class. Tank engines were not classified for power and so did not carry brass figures. There was no distinction made between passenger and freight types, save, of course, for their actual utilisation in traffic.

At grouping, this system was applied across the board to virtually all the pre-grouping stock including tank engines. Only a few minor classes due for early withdrawal, together with the 0—4—0 saddle tank classes were excluded. The absorption of engines more powerful than the Midland types caused an extension of the number scale upwards to Class 6; while the eventual inclusion of *all* tank engines led to the insertion of a Class 0 designation to cover the very smallest machines. New standard classes were given the appropriate power classification from their date of building.

The original power classes into which the pre-group locomotives were placed are given as part of *Table 5* (page 42). It should be mentioned that there was some confusion in this operation and the power class quoted was not always strictly correct.

It should, at this stage, be pointed out that although classified for power, it was somewhat rare to see pre-group locomotives (other than ex-MR examples) actually carrying a visible indication of their power class until 1928 and afterwards. In that year, the system was refined by adding a suffix letter (P or F) to the power class number in order to define the primary utilisation of the locomotive — passenger or freight. Some classes — e.g. the Horwich 2—6—0s — eventually carried both types of marking, viz. 5P4F.

It is, nowadays, well appreciated that the pure tractive effort figure is no more than a theoretical calculation based on cylinder and wheel size, together with boiler pressure. It bears no relation to the actual power which a locomotive can develop in service which depends, *inter alia*, upon such considerations as the efficiency of use of the steam, the ability of the boiler to make steam and, not least, the skill of the fireman in realising the available potential of the locomotive. Not surprisingly, therefore, the pure tractive effort classification produced some power class anomalies — perhaps the classic and best known being to rate the LNWR 'George the Fifth' 4—4—0 as no better than the Johnson 'Belpaire' of the Midland. Admirable though the latter were, the LNWR 'Georges' were a quite outstanding British 4—4—0 for their period and regularly put up performances which matched, if not exceeded, those of nominally much more powerful types.

The building of larger locomotives caused further upward extension of the numbering and by the close of the LMS period, the power classifications ranged from 1P to 7P (with Class 5XP inserted between Classes 5P and 6P) and from 0F to 8F. Of the LMS standard classes, only the Garratts were not assigned a power class — why is not known. Curious also was the case of the famous Stanier 2-cylinder 4—6—0 design. These ran for many years as Class 5P5F but shortly before Nationalisation were reclassified as Class 5 without letter suffix — full circle indeed.

After Nationalisation, BR adopted a modified form of the LMS power class system. The anomalous Class 5XP was rationalised in 1951 by slightly modifying the system to run from 1P to 8P classifications and in the freight series, a 9F designation was added but did not affect LMS designed locomotives. In addition to these alterations, the BR system also introduced an 'MT' suffix (Mixed Traffic) which was applied to many ex-LMS types which had, hitherto, been officially 'P' or 'F'. On numerous occasions, the 'MT' suffix did not actually appear on the cabside which simply carried a plain figure.

CLASS DESIGNATION

Unlike the LNER and to a lesser extent the SR, where locomotives were classified by letters and suffix numbers to denote the exact type, the LMS had no such system. Neither did it entirely follow the common GWR policy of referring to classes by name (e.g. 'Castle', 'Grange' etc) or by the running number block allocated to a new type (e.g. 45xx).

The pre-group constituents had not been much better than the LMS in this respect. In general, employees continued to refer to pre-group designs by their pre-group classifications — not always officially endorsed either! Thus one had at least two types referred to, colloquially, as 'Jumbos' (the ex-LNWR 2—4—0s and the ex-CR 0—6—0s), while such endearing terms as 'Pug', 'Jocko', 'Jinty' and the like either carried different meanings in different areas or were purely divisional or even district phenomena. These terms were indiscriminately mixed with rather more official classifications like the ex-LNWR 'DX' Class 0—6—0s or the ex-CR '60' Class 4—6—0s. Then there were the nickname classes like the ex-LYR 'Little Egberts', the ex-LNWR 'Cauliflowers' or the ex-HR 'Barneys'. One assumes that the locomen knew to what they were referring even if no-one else did.

The Midland, as a result of its power classification principle, was tending to refer to its engines by power class towards the end of the pre-grouping period, albeit with many exceptions and refinements. For example, the term 'Class 4' seems to have been reserved fairly exclusively for the 0—6—0 goods engine. The two other Class 4 types were usually referred to as '990s' (the Deeley simple expansion 4—4—0) or 'Compounds'. The Johnson single driver engines were rarely 'Class 1s' but usually 'Spinners' while 'Class 3' could be either a Johnson 'Belpaire' 4—4—0 or a Deeley 0—6—0 goods. To precisely define the type one had to specify the wheel arrangement — and so it went on.

The LMS officially adopted the power class method of referring to standard locomotives but it must have made things simpler when the P and F suffixes were introduced. With the advent of named classes, it became more common and officially correct, to refer to 'Royal Scots' and 'Princess Royals' rather than Class 6P 4—6—0s and Class 7P 4—6—2s. Even so, the new classes were by no means spared from the long established individuality of the enginemen. A Stanier 'Jubilee' was far more commonly referred to as a '5X' than anything else — even after BR had altered the classification to 6P. Class 4F 0—6—0s continued to be referred to as 'Class 4s' by the crews, ignoring the 'F'; while the standard Class 3F 0—6—0T became almost universally known as a 'Jinty' or 'Jocko'. Since the former was basically an enthusiast nickname and the latter a regional term used to denote *any* shunting engine, it cannot have clarified matters very much for the uninitiated.

The Hughes/Fowler, or Horwich 2—6—0 tender engines became known to enthusiasts as 'Crabs' (because of their distinctive exposed outside motion), so much so that the Stanier derivative was often called a 'Stanier Crab' or even, to our certain knowledge, a 'Taper Crab' — visions of some quite unique crustacean! The original rebuilt ex-LNWR 'Claughton' Class 4—6—0s were officially called 'Patriots' once No. 5500 had been thus named but the enginemen had already dubbed them 'Baby Scots' because of their considerable resemblance to the 'Royal Scot' type and this nickname tended to stick. The new standard Class 7F 0—8—0s, which used an LNWR derived boiler on a Midland inspired chassis, were sometimes referred to unofficially as the 'G3 Class' (continuing the LNWR 0—8—0 classification — see page 92), but far more commonly as 'Austin Sevens' — a somewhat unflattering pun on their power classification one feels.

Regional nicknames were also quite common. North of the border, the Highland enginemen christened the Stanier Class 5s 'Hikers' — conceivably a flattering tribute to their ability to go anywhere and do almost anything — while in the North West at least, the two Stanier 4—6—2 designs were known as 'Lizzies' (the original 'Princess Royal' type) or 'Big Lizzies' (the later 'Coronation' type). Indeed, as late as 1965, one of the authors encountered a driver who did not recognise 'Coronation Class 4—6—2' as any machine *he* had ever encountered — and he was driving them during their year of withdrawal in 1964! It was, of course, also in the North West that the new Ivatt 2—6—0s were christened 'Penrith Lizzies' (see page 25) which indicated that even in the final years, the inventiveness of locomen was still to the fore. These same lightweight 2—6—0s (and their 2—6—2T derivatives) were also referred to as 'Mickey Mice' while the somewhat ungainly looking Class 4 2—6—0s were often called 'Doodlebugs'.

It is really rather surprising that such a standardised company as the LMS should not have introduced a more logical nomenclature for its locomotives — but it never did. Officialdom frowned upon the nicknames as a general rule but, except possibly in the case of the term 'Patriot' which gradually usurped 'Baby Scot', little success was achieved. For all its size, the LMS was not without its human side.

No apology is offered for the foregoing excursion into the more light-hearted side of LMS locomotive matters. The presence or absence of a pet name frequently reflected an attitude to the locomotive on the part of the men who had to operate the machine and this may, on occasion, have been important. For example, it does not seem entirely without significance that the Fowler and Stanier Class 3P 2—6—2Ts seem never to have been given any accolade by the enginemen. If they were, it was probably unprintable since the engines themselves could hardly be considered the most memorable of the LMS designs.

In this book, it will be our normal policy to refer to the LMS standard classes by the quasi-official titles given in *Table 7* — page 53. However, we trust that our motives will be understood if, on occasion, we lapse into the more individual designations which, in some cases, were more familiar than the officially correct terms.

LOCOMOTIVE NAMING

The LMS did not seem at first to be greatly enamoured of the idea of naming its more imposing engines and in May 1923, a decision was made that although named pre-group engines would continue to carry their names, there would be no naming of new locomotives. This was, of course, in line with existing Midland policy — the MR had only ever had two named locomotives. Even so, some pre-group engines did lose their names especially if they were only painted on.

It was probably the increasing publicity rivalry with the other railway companies which caused the change of heart in the later 1920s when names re-appeared with the 'Royal Scots' in 1927. There was then a break until the middle 1930s when some 'Scots' were renamed and a few 'Patriots', together with the whole of the Stanier 5XP Class (the 'Jubilees') were given names. All but one of the LMS 4—6—2s were given names and four Stanier Class 5s were named in Scotland. One 2—6—4T (2313) was named *The Prince* for a short period — see *Volume III*.

242

243

244

245

246

247

Plates 242-249 These pictures illustrate nameplates carried by Fowler locomotives at varying stages of their existence.

Plate 242 Original name carried by 'Royal Scot' No. 6142 later renamed *The York & Lancaster Regiment*.   *Authors' Collection*

Plate 243 Two-row 'Royal Scot' name without crest, No. 6160.

Plate 244 Single-row 'Royal Scot' name without crest but with a spacing plate, No. 6159.

Plate 245 Single-row 'Royal Scot' name with crest below the nameplate of No. 6122.

Plate 246 Double-row 'Royal Scot' name with crest above the nameplate of No. 6148, originally *Velocipede*.

Plate 247 Single-row 'Royal Scot' name with crest above the nameplate of No. 6133, originally *Vulcan*.

Plate 248 'Patriot' No. 5501 – photographed on 4th June, 1938.
                                        L. Hanson

Plate 249 'Patriot' No. 5526.

All BR LMR except where noted

248

249

250

251

252

253

254

255

256

257

Plates 250-257 This selection illustrates nameplate styles carried by Stanier locomotives.

Plate 250 'Silver Jubilee' 4—6—0 No. 5595.

Plate 251 'Silver Jubilee' 4—6—0 No. 5706, with crest.

Plate 252 'Silver Jubilee' 4—6—0 No. 5616 *Malta G.C.*, originally *Malta*.

Plate 253 'Silver Jubilee' 4—6—0 No. 5739 *Ulster*, after the addition of the crest.

Plate 254 One of the four Class 5 4—6—0s to be named, No. 5157.

Plate 255 'Princess Royal' 4—6—2 No. 6203.

Plate 256 'Princess Coronation' Class 4—6—2 No. 6252.

Plate 257 'Princess Coronation' Class 4—6—2 No. 6254, with coat of arms.

All Photographs BR LMR

Most LMS nameplates were cast in brass but there were exceptions. When de-streamlined, some of the 'Coronations' were, apparently, given rather fragile alloy plates but no record is available to indicate how many. The LMS nameplates themselves were neatly cast but, perhaps, a little uninspiring, lacking something of the character of the old LNWR nameplates. The favoured finish was to polish the plate and give it a black backing. The plates themselves were generally concentric with the splasher and, for the greater part, set on a plate which raised them a little above the top of the splasher — not always however. They were usually fitted above the leading splasher of the three cylinder 4-6-0s but the positions varied on other classes. The few named Class 5s had the nameplate mounted on the footplate above the leading driving wheel, while the 'Princess Royal' 4-6-2s had nameplates surmounting the centre splasher. The 'Coronation' 4-6-2s had the most imposing LMS nameplates and these were straight and set on the side of the boiler centred over the middle driving wheel. This arrangement somehow seemed to look much more imposing than that of the somewhat insignificant nameplates carried by members of other standard classes with rather short names.

The majority of the nameplates were cast at Crewe but Derby cast its own for the few 'Royal Scots', 'Patriots' and 'Jubilees' built there. St Rollox made the plates for the four named Class 5s and also those for a few of the 'Jubilees' which were working in Scotland when this class was given names. The St Rollox plates were instantly recognisable, the letters being of slightly different and less substantial shape. Among them are believed to have been included the following: 5576 *Bombay*, 5577 *Bengal*, 5580 *Burma*, 5581 *Bihar and Orissa*, 5584 *North West Frontier*, 5644 *Howe* and 5645 *Collingwood*.

A few individual peculiarities are worth noting. Firstly, 25 of the original 'Royal Scots' (6125-49) were given plates bearing names of old engines from the early pre-group companies with a facsimile reproduction of the original engine which had first carried the name on an oval plate just below the main nameplate. This distinctive feature disappeared when these engines were given new regimental type names in the mid-1930s. The 'military' plates themselves were interesting as some of them carried a double row of lettering (because of the long name) and at a later stage, many had regimental crests added to the nameplate. The combination of a double row nameplate and a regimental crest could produce quite an imposing effect. Within the 'Royal Scot' Class, *The Old Contemptibles* (6127) and the unique *British Legion* (6170) had nameplates which were handsome cast reproductions of the respective badges. In the case of 6127, these were cast in solid copper.

The 'Coronation' 4-6-2s originally had brass nameplates (see above) but the first 25 (6220-44) had them chrome plated with either dark blue (6220-4) or black backgrounds, while 6220's were also surmounted by a crown. The later engines, named on the 'City' theme, occasionally carried the city coat of arms above the nameplate and *City of Sheffield* is reputed to have carried Sheffield steel nameplates at some time.

During the war, the background colour of LMS nameplates was often changed to vermilion while, from 1946 onwards, engines carrying the post-war express livery had their plates painted maroon with the raised letters rendered in straw coloured paint. Examples of most of these variations can be seen displayed at the National Railway Museum, York.

Turning now to the choice of names, it cannot be said that the LMS entirely distinguished itself. It did not, thankfully, follow the GWR example of theme repetition, nor did it commit some of the absurdities which the LNER followed with its 'racehorse' names and which led to magnificent engines like the Gresley 'A3' being called *Pretty Polly*, *Spearmint* and the like! However, bearing in mind the legacy of the often splendid LNWR locomotive names, one feels that the LMS missed a great opportunity. The above mentioned renaming of 25 'Royal Scots' removed some fine historic names while the obsession with the 'colonial' theme on the Stanier Class 5XPs produced some pretty feeble names. Equally, it must be admitted that the adoption of 'naval' inspired names for the later series of these engines gave rise to some very appropriate choices. There was hardly a bad name in the whole of the series between 5688 *Polyphemus* and 5738 *Samson*. Some of them were positively inspiring.

The named 'Patriots' were, generally speaking, an uninspired collection with neither thematic consistency nor verbal resonance to commend them. They were almost redeemed by *Illustrious* (5532) but the choice of *Lady Godiva* for the unfortunate 5519 was on a par with the worst of the LNER racehorses.

Fortunately, the LMS 4-6-2s carried reasonable names. Arguably, the 'City' theme on the final 'Coronations' was a little overdone but at least it gave no offence. The 'Duchess' series of names, on the other hand, was a happy choice. The theme more than adequately symbolised these most majestic and regal of locomotives, so much so that most references to the class as a whole tend to use the unofficial class designation 'Duchess' when describing the engines even though only ten of them carried 'Duchess' names. The 'Princess' theme for the earlier 4-6-2s was also reasonable (even though it contained one Queen, one Duchess and one Lady!), but the nameplates themselves were a little insignificant by comparison with the size of the locomotives.

Finally, it should be noted that a few LNWR style nameplates (with sunken wax-filled letters) were made after the grouping for any ex-LNWR engines which received replacement plates and these had 'LMS' engraved instead of 'LNWR'.

Considering that the sole function of a tender was to carry coal and water, the ramifications of tender types fitted to each class of locomotive, not to mention the switching of tenders between locomotives, can cause considerable confusion to any student who is anxious to know exactly what the situation was at any point in time. Since this can be of particular significance to the modelmaker it seemed sensible to try and give some sort of basic outline of LMS tender 'policy', if, by such word it may thus be dignified. Where possible, the class by class situation will be summarised in the detailed reviews of types in *Volumes II* and *III* but the general situation merits explanation at this stage to avoid overmuch repetition.

In general, two aspects warrant amplification; firstly the matter of tender numbering and secondly the question of precise tender types. We are, of course, mainly concerned with LMS built tenders but some preliminary background comments are necessary to explain the inherited 1923 situation.

Of the constituent companies, only two (the LNWR and LYR) numbered their tenders and this was by means of a cast numberplate – *Fig. 4*. It is not known whether on the LYR, when tenders were exchanged, their numbers were also altered but the LNWR pursued a deliberate policy of tender changing and numbered its tenders separately from the engines. This was because at general repair, a tender took less time in shops than a locomotive and therefore, provided the engine was given a suitable tender, it did not have to be the same one as fitted at the start of the repair.

Plate 258 This works grey picture of the tender coupled to 4—6—0 'Prince of Wales' No. 5751 has been included to illustrate the rear view of a Bowen-Cooke tender. Note the position of the lining which gives a good impression of the red livery applied to these tenders.
NRM

Plate 259 This picture is noteworthy for illustrating a black engine with a blue tender. The locomotive, No. 17588, is coupled to the tender off CR 0—6—0 No. 859, later to become LMS No. 17597. Note the small centre link to the coupling and the handrail 'on the corner' but no steps at the end of the vehicle. *Authors' Collection*

Figure 4

TENDER NUMBERS AND PLATES

A LMS Standard pattern
B LNWR pattern
C LYR pattern
(*all drawn by Arthur Whitehead*)

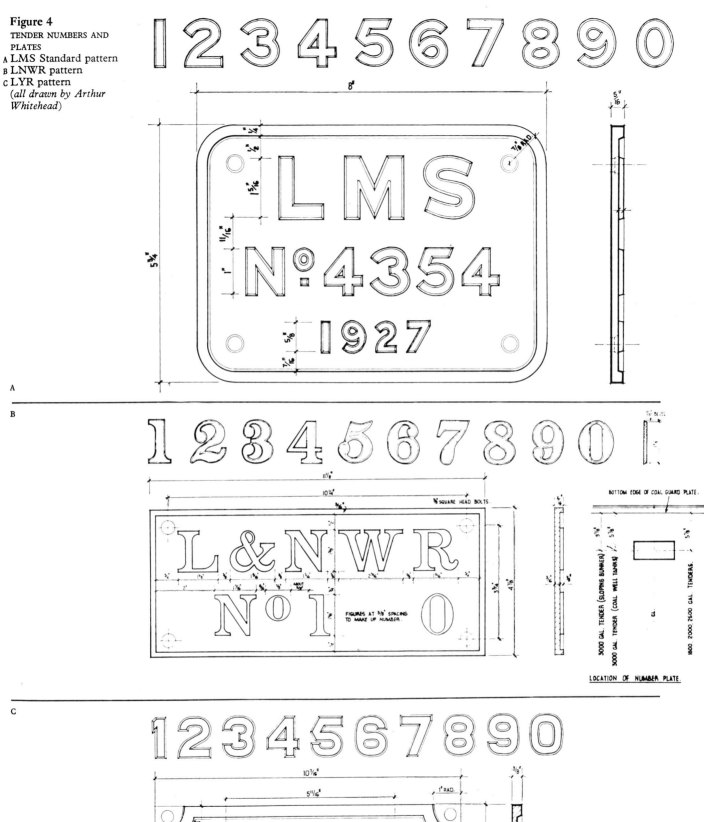

A

B

C

LOCATION OF NUMBER PLATE

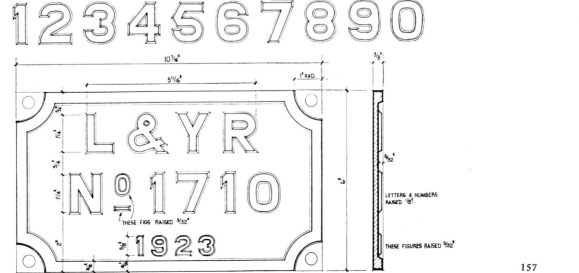

NOTE · YEAR TO BE OMITTED IF BUILDING DATE UNKNOWN.

157

Plate 260 Midland Compound 4—4—0 No. 1028 coupled to a Midland Deeley 3,500 gallon tender which differed from the later Fowler 3,500 gallon tenders, see Plate 263. Note the cut back of the footplating along the tank bottom, the arrangement at the rear upon which the fireman stands. Worthy of note are the lamps carrying the locomotive's number, three-link not screw coupling and finally, although not obvious, the fact that the wheelbox was unequal, being 7′ 0″ x 6′ 9″.

BR LMR

As explained more fully in Chapter 11, the Midland Railway policy, when later adopted by the LMS, of placing the locomotive number on the tender began to cause problems and arising from the confusion, a 'distinctive tender number' policy was adopted in 1928 whereby the total stock of tenders was numbered and new construction was numbered in sequence from the outset. This policy was, *inter alia*, one of the principal causes of the radical livery change also explained in detail in Chapter 11.

The full details of the tender numbering scheme are too complex to be included in this survey but a brief note on the principles adopted will not be out of place.

Plate 261 This shows an ex-Midland Railway tender, probably of 2,350 gallon capacity, coupled to Class 2F No. 3230. Note the tender springs above the framing. The picture was taken to illustrate the method of securing the storm sheet to the tender. Note the low bulkhead and twin tool boxes.

BR LMR

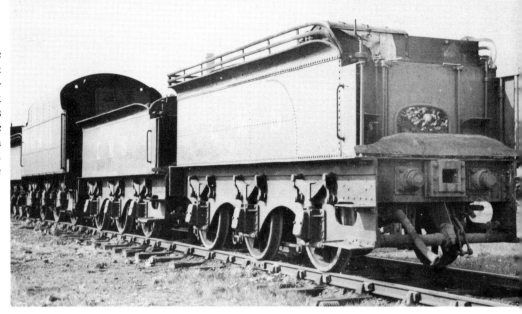

Plate 262 A row of tenders, the first two being of Lancashire & Yorkshire origin. Note the intermediate buffers, pipe from tank to injectors, handbrake, two levers to control the water mix for the injectors and twin tool boxes. On this picture the lap plate has been folded back. *Authors' Collection*

The LNWR and LYR tenders kept their own numbers and plates but all other pre-group tenders plus the LMS standards were allotted new LMS numbers. The series started with 1,500 gallon tenders (1-5) and continued through to 3,500 gallon tenders (2661-3945) with but a few small gaps. A large gap was then left (for new 3,500 gallon tenders) and the series resumed at 6000 for 3,560 gallon tenders and larger sizes. The ex-ROD tenders came after this latter series.

Initially, of course, new LMS tenders had followed the Midland practice of the tender carrying the locomotive number. Photographic evidence proves that the MR and the Midland Division of the LMS were not totally averse to exchanging tenders but it is not known with certainty whether tenders were then repainted or exchanged back again as soon as possible. The latter is thought more probable since it would be an easier solution than supplying all sheds with a supply of transfer numerals and/or signwriters! Furthermore, if such exchanges were permanent, the intervals between tender overhauls would vary considerably — an undesirable feature in terms of LMS thinking.

Within each water capacity group, the new distinctive tender numbers were allotted usually in the order MR, NSR, CR, GSWR, HR, Barrow (FR and M & CR). The SMJR tenders were probably numbered in the MR series. The only exception to this principle seems to have been in the 3,500 gallon series where the Scottish tenders came first, followed by MR and LMS tenders. The tenders were supposed to be numbered in engine number sequence which, in the case of certain LMS standard locomotives coupled to either MR or LMS standard tenders, caused the MR tenders to be mixed up with LMS standards in the 3,500 gallon series. Unfortunately, St Rollox made a further mess of things by numbering the tenders behind 0—6—0 engines in engine number order regardless of tender type so the issue was more than a little confused.

The S & DJR 3,500 gallon tenders were numbered in the LMS series in 1930 and its smaller tenders were fitted into gaps in the MR series. Fortunately, most of the LMS standard tenders escaped these ramifications and a full and comprehensive number list can be found in Appendix 4 to *Engines of the LMS* by J.P. Rowledge. We shall, therefore, confine our comments to amplifying the matter of tender types, covering the pre-group designs in the appropriate sections of *Volumes II and III* and concerning ourselves at this point solely with the LMS built designs. In fact, this is not too illogical since, apart from a very few perpetuated pre-group designs, all new tender construction by the LMS was to LMS standard design or the LMS version of the later Midland types. Drawings of the LMS tender plates are given at *Fig. 4*.

In the early LMS period, three distinct situations existed; namely, the building of complete new tenders, the rebuilding of old MR tenders by fitting new tanks to old frames and finally, the fitting of unrebuilt ex-Midland tenders (from withdrawn locomotives) to newly built standard types. If the rebuilt tenders were originally of the Johnson 2,950 or 3,250 gallon variety running upon frames with a 6 ft 6 in + 6 ft 6 in wheelbase, the rebuilt form was all but identical to the new construction but two details betrayed their origin and can readily be noted. The slots in the frames between axleboxes were of different shape to the Fowler LMS standard type while the edges of the frames at the rear end of the tender were curved on the ex-MR variety and straight on the LMS standards. However, certain MR tenders (originally coupled mostly behind 4—4—0 locomotives) which were rebuilt with LMS standard tanks from 1929 onwards, had a longer than 13 ft wheelbase and the rebuilt version was readily identifiable by the wide platform at the rear of the tender tank.

The Fowler LMS standard tender proper had an equally divided 13 ft wheelbase and was of 3,500 gallon capacity. The coal capacity was nominally quoted as 4 tons but this figure is very low and should not be regarded as an exact value — 5½ tons is nearer the mark. Visually, the design was virtually that of the high, flat sided MR tender but the body was shorter — hence the rear platform when LMS tanks were fitted to those old MR frames which had carried high sided Midland bodies. The original batches of the LMS standard type had fixed bulkheads between footplate and coal space but, commencing in 1927, a change was made and the tenders concerned (4235-54) were fitted with auxiliary coal rails and coal doors. These were fitted to 'Royal Scots'. However, the original style of tender was still being constructed and it was

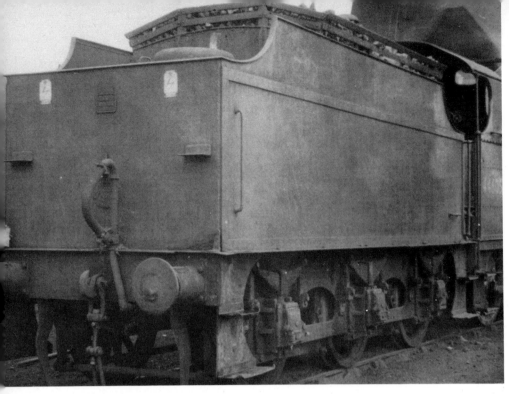

Plate 263 Saltley on 12th July, 1964. A Class 4F 0—6—0 No. 44605 coupled to a Fowler 3,500 gallon tender fitted with coal rails but with the air breather pipes 'inside' the coal space. This is an example of the earlier 'beaded' style of LMS standard tender developed from the Midland style, see Plate 260.

Authors' Collection

not until the final batches of Class 2P 4—4—0s and Class 7F 0—8—0s that coal rails and coal doors became standard for all new construction. In due course, many of the earlier 'bulkhead' tenders were altered and although it was usual to find both coal doors and coal rails fitted, some tenders received coal doors only while a few received coal rails but retained the bulkhead. Personal experience of one of the authors confirms that the tenders without coal doors were far from ideal when used on long distance trains unless the workings allowed time to bring coal forward when stopped. Finally, it should be noted that large numbers of the earlier 'bulkhead' tenders were never altered and remained 'as built' during their lifetime.

Turning now to other details; on the tenders without coal rails, the tank 'breather' pipes were located inside the coal space but when modified with the addition of coal rails, these two pipes should have been, and usually were, placed behind the coal space to the rear of the back bulkhead. There were, of course, examples of tenders where this repositioning had not taken place. To be candid, the positioning of the breather pipes in the coal space was a bit impractical, regardless of whether or not the tender had coal rails, since the coaling of LMS tenders was frequently anything but a precise operation!

Plate 264 The engineman's view! A Fowler 3,500 gallon tender with coal doors but without coal rails. Many of these tenders were built with solid bulkheads which made the task of getting coal forward difficult while the train was in motion, with coal doors one walked through. In this picture can be seen the two lockers for kit and tools, the method of holding the head-lamps when not in use, tender water gauge and the lock on the tool box.

BR LMR

Plate 265 This overhead view of a 3,500 gallon Fowler tender has been included in order to draw the reader's attention to a number of features. Note the coal pick on top of the tool box locker. The dart hooked onto the fire irons handle, the handle of the shovel can be seen on the back of the tender. Note how the coal falls . . . The air breather pipes are not in evidence and must be inside the coal space covered with coal. *A.E. West*

At this point it is probably worth mentioning that a subtle difference in beading detail revealed which tenders fitted with coal rails had originally started life without them. The original design had edge beading on the top edges of the side panelling and this had to be cut away to allow the fitting of coal rails. Of those built with coal rails from new, some had the top beading on the side rather than the extreme edge. It should finally be mentioned that some of the standard Fowler 3,500 gallon tenders were equipped with side doors to close the gap between locomotive and tender. This was a useful feature but nothing like as satisfactory as the doors which were fitted to the later Stanier locomotives in order to fulfil the same purpose.

Mention of Stanier brings us to the final phases of the building of 3,500 gallon tenders. From about the same time as Stanier arrived on the scene, the construction of the Fowler type tender changed to a visibly riveted style without beading — but otherwise unchanged in basic shape and size. These tenders were fitted, for example, to the Stanier 2—6—0s, some of the 'Patriots' and some of the final 2P 4—4—0s and 7F 0—8—0s. These visibly riveted tenders brought the mainstream of construction of the first LMS standard tender to a close; but between these and the later familiar Stanier 4,000 gallon type, there was a short period during 1933-5 when tender construction was somewhat confusing.

Plates 266 & 267 These two plates should be considered together in as much as they illustrate certain variations in design of the final style of Fowler 3,500 gallon tender. **Plate 266** shows the earlier version with the beading 'on top', while in **Plate 267** it is 'on the side'. Most examples of this type of tender when fitted with coal rails were constructed with the air breather pipes outside the coal space but, as can be seen, the application of this instruction was not universal.

Plate 266 BR LMR   Plate 267 Authors' Collection

Plate 268 0—6—0 4F No. 44587 is coupled to one of the ten 3,500 gallon straight sided tenders originally fitted to Class 5XP 4—6—0s of the 'Jubilee' class. Transferred to Class 4Fs built 1936 onwards, some were also found behind 'Patriot' 4—6—0s and Class 8F 2—8—0s. *Authors' Collection*

The building of the first batches of Stanier's taper boilered Class 5XP 4—6—0s coincided with the construction of further tenders of 3,500 gallon capacity to run with them but no good reason can be given why two new designs should have been adopted. Although the first five LMS built 5XPs (5552-6) were coupled to orthodox Fowler type tenders, the next batch of Crewe built engines (5607-16) were given hideously ugly straight sided 3,500 gallon tenders (4564-73) with sides higher than the Fowler type. Meanwhile, the North British built 5XPs (5557-606) were built new with Stanier 4,000 gallon tenders of a new standard type. Crewe then built 50 additional 3,500 gallon tenders for 5517-66 which were basically to the new Stanier pattern but on the shorter Fowler type chassis. Most of these final series 3,500 gallon tenders remained with the 5XPs for the bulk of their time but a few were exchanged in later years.

The first true Stanier tenders were somewhat experimental. Built in 1933 as tenders 9000-2, they were essentially the same shape as the Fowler type but on a longer wheelbase and having a considerably enhanced coal capacity plus 4,000 gallons of water. They were initially fitted to the first two 4—6—2s (6200-1) and 'Royal Scot' No. 6100 for its North American tour. From this style of tender was derived the familiar curved top version soon to become so common. The first of these to appear were those built by North British for locomotives 5557-606 (above), followed by the first Crewe built examples for 4—6—2 No. 6202 and Class 5 4—6—0s Nos. 5001-11.

Although the aforementioned Stanier type 3,500 gallon tenders for locomotives 5617-66 might seem to have been part of the evolutionary process towards the true Stanier tender, in fact the true precursor of the curved top type was the rebuilding in 1933 of tender 3677 (which ran for most of its life behind 4—4—0 compound No. 936) to a curved top style which proved to be a vast improvement on the Fowler type.

Finally, to get this evolutionary period correct, it should just be remarked that in 1935, the original flat sided 4,000 gallon tenders (9000-1) were rebuilt with curved tops and fitted to Class 5 4—6—0s Nos. 5073-4, followed shortly by the rebuilding of tender 9002 in similar fashion for Class 5 No. 5000.

Plate 269 Class 5P5F 4—6—0 No. 5020, the first member of this class to be constructed at Crewe, carrying Livery Code B3 and coupled to a 4,000 gallon Stanier riveted tender with plain axlebox covers. *BR LMR*

Plate 270 4−6−2 No. 6250 *City of Lichfield* in wartime black. Livery Code C22. This broadside view illustrates the arrangement of the Stanier tender when adapted for use with this class in the streamlined condition.   *BR LMR*

Once finalised, the design of the standard Stanier 4,000 gallon tender never changed in all essential details for the remainder of the LMS (and early BR) period. Originally the visibly riveted constructional method was preferred but later on, one or two tenders were built using welding as an experiment and from tender No. 9229, all-welded construction was employed as a standard alternative to the riveted style. There were also tenders built part-welded and part-riveted. J.P. Rowledge has referred to these variations as Mark I (fully or partly riveted) and Mark II (wholly welded) and we shall conform to this definition in the class articles in *Volume III.*

Some few Stanier pattern tenders were also built with somewhat higher sides and coal capacity raised to 10 tons for the various 4−6−2 designs. The first series − Mark III − were riveted and fitted to the 'Princess Royal' Class while Marks IV and V were the two varieties of welded tenders equipped with coal pushers for the streamlined and non-streamlined 'Coronation' Class 4−6−2s respectively. In fact, there were rather more than three variations in the 10 ton tenders and full details will be given in the appropriate section of *Volume III.*

Plate 271 This view shows the tender front of a Stanier 4,000 gallon tender prior to being attached to 4−6−2 No. 6202. The various controls are clearly marked, the tunnel on the left hand side was for fire irons, the locker to the right of the coal doors was for the enginemen's kit.   *Authors' Collection*

Plate 272 An overhead view of a 4,000 gallon Stanier tender coupled to Class 5MT 4−6−0 No. 45253. Note the lifting holes for workshop use, the shape of the coal space and vast improvement in tender design over the older Fowler tenders.   *Authors' Collection*

Plate 273 This view of tender No. 9803 shows a 4,000 gallon tender which was originally streamlined and still retains certain features applicable to these locomotives; rear step ladder and brackets to support the longer sides, see also Plate 270. These tenders were equipped with coal pushers and some of the equipment associated with this unit can be seen on the rear bulkhead.   *Authors' Collection*

Plate 274 This tender was coupled to a Class 2MT 2—6—0 No. 46406 and clearly shows the riveted construction employed on this modern design which was for a locomotive that could be frequently employed upon tender-first running, hence the arrangement for a clear view over the tender at the expense of coal capacity. *Authors' Collection*

Apart from these few 10 ton tenders, the LMS built nothing but the Stanier standard Mark I or II variety for some 12 years until 1946. In this year, the introduction of a new series of 2—6—0s numbered in the 64xx series provided the opportunity to create a new tender of 3,000 gallon and 4 ton coal capacity. These tenders were numbered in a new series 7000-127. The following year, just before the demise of the company as an independent concern, the final LMS standard tender type was introduced for the Ivatt Class 4 2—6—0. These were 3,500 gallon, 4 ton tenders and their numbers ran in sequence immediately following the original 3,500 gallon tenders of the 1930s.

The two Ivatt style tenders, together with the standard Stanier type, continued in production until the final batches of LMS design locomotives were completed early in the BR period. Some of their features, but by no means all, were incorporated in the various BR types which succeeded them.

To conclude this survey, mention should be made of a small number of special tenders built by the LMS:

a) Corridor tender No. 4999, built in 1937 for use with any locomotive under test.

b) Coal weighing tenders 10596 and 10391.

c) Three rebuilt tenders Nos. 2751, 2805 and 2808 which were given flared out upper panels plus coal rails in order to substantially increase the coal capacity. Two (2751, 2805) were used when 4—4—0 No. 1054 and 4—6—0 No. 6113 made their non-stop runs to Edinburgh and Glasgow respectively in 1928. These tenders remained in service with a number of other locomotives. They were Deeley 13' 9" wheelbase tenders and the coal capacity was increased from 7 tons to 8½-9 tons.

There were also a few tenders converted to carry oil fuel tanks in 1926 and after the Second World War. Where details are known of these, mention will be made in the appropriate class chapter(s) of *Volume III*. In this connection it might also be worth mentioning that as far as possible, the chapters dealing with the LMS standard classes will give full details of at least the initial pairings of engine and tender.

PART II
LOCOMOTIVE LIVERIES

The first LNWR locomotive to be painted in the new LMS crimson lake livery was 4—6—0 'Claughton' Class, *Croxteth*, pictured above as No. 5971, Livery Code A2, in 1923.

NRM

Chapter 11 The Standard LMS Liveries

Bearing in mind the high degree of standardisation of locomotive affairs of the LMS Railway, the relative lack of standardisation of locomotive livery is somewhat remarkable. Three major official styles were utilised during the 25 year life of the company. These were supplemented by many minor variations and at no time was one specific 'house' style to be seen concurrently on all the locomotives. Moreover, the number of exceptions to the current officially 'correct' style was always high — especially amongst the pre-group classes.

For railway enthusiasts, the locomotive has always been at the centre of the stage and for this reason there is available more information about locomotive liveries than for many other items of company property. However, and probably because of this very fact, there are more variations to note than in the case of rolling stock or buildings. This has rendered the compilation of an accurate survey doubly difficult and even with rigorous checking, it has not been possible to avoid drawing attention to items which either do not conform or cannot be verified with the degree of accuracy which would have been preferred.

Exceptions apart, however, the livery styles of the LMS locomotive stock can most conveniently be divided into those periods when they were officially 'correct'. Immediately after grouping there was, understandably, no standard livery and engines were turned out in a variety of non-standard styles which are described, where known, in the next chapter and in the chapters devoted to the classes concerned in *Volumes II* and *III*.

The first 'standard' liveries date from mid-1923 and the style then adopted lasted until the close of 1927/early 1928, after which a radical change was introduced which continued with variations until 1939. The Second World War saw no basic changes in specification but events themselves forced numerous changes which are worthy of note. Finally there were the 1946 liveries which, owing to Nationalisation, were not applied to many engines but were to have been standardised had the company continued independent existence. As was the case at grouping, the periods of change-over to the new styles caused quite a number of engines to be painted in non-standard fashion. These, too, are covered in the next chapter or in the appropriate class chapter(s) in *Volumes II* and *III*.

STANDARD LIVERY 1923-1927

Part of Minute 53 of the LMS Rolling Stock Committee meeting of 21st May, 1923, reads as follows:

After consideration it was ordered that, in future, the passenger engines be painted in the crimson lake colour, following the decision in respect of the coaching stock, and that the freight engines be painted black without the lining which has hitherto been adopted.
Ordered also that the Company's engines be not named in future, but that those engines which already bear a name, continue as hitherto.*

The crimson lake livery was, of course, fully lined in yellow with black edging. This basic instruction was amplified by a letter from Horwich Drawing Office on 5th December, 1923, relevant extracts from which are given below:

. . . the following details be carried out on all engines re-painted on and after a date to be fixed later.

(1) *Coat of Arms*
All passenger engines to have the Company's Coat of Arms placed on the panel plate, or bunker side in the case of tank engines.

(2) *LMS Initials*
All goods engines to have the initials LMS without stops, placed on the panel plates in a position corresponding to that occupied by the Coat of Arms on the passenger engines.

(3) *Engine Numbers*
The number of the engine to be placed on the tender, or on the tanks in the case of tank engines, in large figures, transfers in two sizes available . . .

(4) *Engine Numbers on Smokebox Doors*
The number of the engine to be placed on the smokebox door in the form of a cast iron plate . . .

(5) *Builder's Name Plate*
The Builder's plate, if an outside builder, to be retained. For a railway built engine, or an outside maker's engine rebuilt, a small oval brass plate to be fixed to the driving splashers of tender engines and in the most suitable corresponding position on tank engines.

*For subsequent naming policy see page 152.

Plate 275 (Opposite) This view of 'Prince of Wales' Class 4—6—0 No. 5751 illustrates an official view of the pre-1928 red livery when carrying the LMS coat of arms. However, the reader's attention is drawn to the buffers. The line at the base was not used when painted in crimson lake but this picture does not show the line at the buffer end of the housing thus underlining the danger of accepting totally the evidence of pictures depicting locomotives in works grey.   *NRM*

(6)   *Tank Capacity Plate*
All tenders (or tanks in the case of tank engines) to bear a brass plate giving the capacity of the tender (or tank) in gallons. This plate to be . . . fixed on the back of the tender or bunker. Any existing number plates on tenders may remain.

(7)   *Engine Classification Numbers*
The engine classification number to be placed on the cab side, in a conspicuous position about the height of the driver's head; . . . All engines to bear classification numbers.

(8)   *Date of Painting*
The date of painting inside the cab is immaterial.

(9)   *Plate for Driver's Name*
This may be left over until asked for.

(10) *Shed Numbers*
Present practice to continue for the moment.

This directive was approved on 10th December, 1923 and appears to have been given immediate effect. As will be apparent, the livery adopted was, apart from the company markings, all but identical to the former Midland Railway livery. In addition, two or three other minor variations existed during the 1923-7 period which are not mentioned in either of the above quoted documents.

Until the Coat of Arms was available, new and repainted red engines were also given the small letters 'LMS' on cab or bunker side as appropriate (*Plate 276*). This policy stopped for red engines at about the close of 1923 but was continued with the black locomotives until a new cabside transfer emblem was designed. This incorporated the LMS initials in gold on a bright vermilion background with gold edging. At first, this device had cut-out corners but was later changed to a version with rounded corners. Apart from these red panels and vermilion buffer beams, the black locomotives had no other colour relief whatsoever and a detailed livery specification is not necessary. However, the red engines were a little more complex and a detailed description follows.

The Standard Passenger Livery

The crimson lake livery was specified for 'Passenger' engines, which definition was often liberally interpreted and, in consequence, a wide variety of types was painted red. The basic disposition of the body colours was as follows:

Crimson Lake: Boiler and firebox; cabside and front; footplate angle; splasher sides; footstep supports; outside cylinders; tender sides and backs; sides, backs and fronts of side tanks; sides and rear of bunker on tank engines; tender sideframes.

Black: Smokebox; footplate and splasher tops; footplate details; footsteps; tender springs; tender tops; wheels and other ancillary details. Cab roofs were also black except for engines shopped at Derby where cab roofs were painted red.

Vermilion: Buffer beams and shanks.   n.b.   Details of cab interior treatment are given in Chapter 14.

Plate 276   LYR 4—4—0 No. 10163 carrying crimson lake livery, Code A4.   *Real Photographs*

Plate 277 (Above) Ex-MR 4—4—0 No. 335 carrying Livery Code A2. Compare with Plate 276 which has 14″ numbers, No. 335 has 18″ numbers. Note the lining on the frames between the bogie wheels. *Real Photographs*

Plate 278 (Below) This well known photograph of 'Royal Scot' 4—6—0 No. 6126 has been used to illustrate the pre-1928 crimson lake livery as used upon a standard class of locomotives. *BR LMR*

With this lake livery, panel edging was rendered in black and the lining in pale yellow. The yellow shade was intended to be as close a match as possible for the standard gold leaf insignia (see below). The appended official specification issued for the Compound 4—4—0 may be taken as reasonably typical of the lining style adopted for most red engines.

PAINTING AND LINING OF 4—4—0 COMPOUND IMMEDIATELY FOLLOWING FORMATION OF LMS

Engine	Black	— Frames, brakework, smokebox, wheels.		
	Vermilion	— Buffer beam and casings.		
	Red	— All other parts (except motion)		
Tender	Black	— Frame, springs, axleboxes, wheels.		
	Vermilion	— Buffer beam and casings.		
	Red	— All other parts.		
Lining	Engine:	Platform	1″ black	3/8″ yellow
		Footsteps	1¼″ black	½″ yellow
		Panel (Cab)	2¼″ black	½″ yellow
		Cab	1¼″ black	½″ yellow
		Cylinders	1½″ black	½″ yellow
		Boiler (front)	1¼″ black	½″ yellow
		Firebox	1¼″ black	½″ yellow
		Buffer Beam	1″ black	3/8″ yellow
		Buffer Casing	1½″ black	3/8″ yellow
		Tyres		½″ yellow
	Tender:	Side panels:		
		Bottom & Back	2½″ black	½″ yellow
		Top & Front	2¾″ black	½″ yellow
		End panel	2½″ black	½″ yellow
		Frame		½″ yellow
		Footsteps	1¼″ black	½″ yellow

Note: This specification has been copied verbatim and is deficient in odd details. For example, tender sideframes were lined both black and yellow while it was generally more common for the upper part of the cab side to receive narrower yellow lining than the main cab panel. Splasher tops were normally black, not red as might be inferred and there are sundry other deficiencies.

Of course, the precise lining details and dimensions had to be slightly adjusted to suit the various styles of engine to which they were applied. Some general principles were, however, fairly consistently adopted throughout:—

1) Despite the official specification, lining dimensions were normally 2-2½″ black with ½″ yellow inside (larger areas) or ¾-1″ black with 3/8″ yellow inside (smaller areas). The wider dimensions were never used below the footplate level and the narrower ones rarely applied above the footplate.
2) Cab fronts were, normally, unlined.
3) Outside framed engines usually had full lining both at the lower edges and round the apertures of the frames.
4) Intermediate *horizontal* beading was usually black with a yellow line at both top and bottom edges.
5) Intermediate *vertical* beading was usually red without lining.
6) Where flat beading was lined out, the lines always appeared on the edge of the beading itself and not on the adjacent body panel, regardless of the precise beading dimensions. Where engines had simple edge beading only, then the proper lining dimensions were used and all lining appeared on the main body panels.
7) Vacuum pipes, if they crossed buffer beams, were painted and lined to match the buffer beam where they crossed it. Other areas were black.
8) Front buffer beams and shanks were almost always lined as per the specification, but some tender buffer beams, usually those of Deeley and Fowler pattern tenders, were usually given a much wider black edging (c. 3″).
Variations from these general principles were normally fairly consistent within any one class and will be dealt with in the appropriate chapters in later volumes, as will any known exceptions.

Lettering and Numbering — both liveries

The locomotive number was carried in large gold leaf figures on the tender or tank side. These figures were generally 18″ high on tender engines and arranged so that the complete number was central both left to right and top to bottom on the main rectangular part of the side panel, not counting raised or flared upper side panels. Where a vertical beading was present in the centre of the side (e.g. certain types of Johnson Midland tenders) any running number with an odd number of digits was always placed with the extra figure to the rear of the beading in such a way that the beading was midway

Plates 279 & 280 Two Scottish locomotives both carrying crimson lake livery, Code A1. Note the absence of lining on the tender underframes of No. 14768 and the style of a painted name when in LMS livery. On Plate 280 the reader's attention is drawn to the depth of the black on the beading on the splashers. *Both Plates NRM*

between the figures on either side of it. Single digit running numbers on the ex-MR 2—4—0s were also placed to the rear of this central beading. On all locomotives, the horizontal spacing between figures when the 18″ height was used was as follows:

(a) Between the centres of any two '1's, 16″
(b) Between the centre of '1' and any other figure, 20″
(c) Between the centres of any other two figures, 24″

The numbers were applied in gold leaf transfers with black shading to the right and below which increased the height by $7/8''$ and the width by 1″ but it is more convenient to refer to them by their *unshaded* height and this will be the general policy throughout the book. The transfers themselves were of unaltered Midland pattern and, of course, having black shading, appeared as plain gold on all the freight engines. Occasionally, when photographed, the black shading would reflect light in a different way to the plain black of the main body panel and give the appearance that the engine had red shaded numerals. However, red shading was not introduced until 1929 (see page 191) and if it was used prior to this date it was an unofficial variation.

On all running numbers, the transfer figures had the right hand side and lower edges of the gold portion picked out with a fine white 'highlight' line some $1/8''$ wide. This had the effect of making the numbers 'stand out' from the engine in a very striking manner and can sometimes be detected on a very good photograph.

Plate 281 This picture of No. 15103, an ex-Caledonian 0—4—4T, has been included to illustrate Livery Code A3 on a 'non-Midland' locomotive. Note the footstep lining on 15103 compared with the absence of such a line on No. 2024, Plate 282. The reader's attention is drawn to the tankside lining which would suggest that the entire tank top was painted black, together with the entire tank end by the cab.

Stephen Collection — NRM

Several classes of engines, usually tank designs but also some tender classes with smaller than average tender side panels, were given smaller numerals, 14″ high. These were again increased in height when shaded and were styled to match the 18″ variety. When the 14″ numbers were used, the spacings between the figures were reduced to the following values:

(a) Between the centres of any two '1's, 13″
(b) Between the centre of '1' and any other figure, 15″
(c) Between the centres of any other two figures, 19″

Both sizes of numeral are given at *Figure 5* and there was no rigidly applied rule as to which size should be used. The 14″ variety was designed for smaller sized locomotives but there were many exceptions. The detailed coverage of these cases will be found with the individual class chapters in *Volumes II and III*.

From the very end of 1923, the circular Company Coat of Arms was transferred centrally on the main cabside panel of red tender engines, or onto the rear splasher if there was no room on the cabside proper, while it was similarly applied to the centre of the bunker side panel on red tank engines. The device was not strictly a true 'Coat of Arms' but has always been traditionally referred to as such and will be so called in this book. It was nominally 14″ in diameter and although its exact date of introduction is not certain, probably the first recorded example of its use was on Compound No. 1014 on 18th December, 1923. During most of 1923, before supplies of this Coat of Arms were available, company ownership was depicted by small letters 'LMS' on the cabside in gold shaded black to the right and below. The exact size and spacing of these individual letters cannot be ascertained but a good approximation from pictures would give the height as some 4½″ spaced about 18″ between centres. The serifed style of these letters was almost identical to that adopted in much larger form as standard in 1927/8.

This particular variation of company identity was not very common. For the first few months of 1923, no standard liveries had been settled at all and engines were emerging in a wide variety of hybrid styles — even pre-group liveries (see Chapter 12). The small letters 'LMS' were, therefore, only in use for perhaps six months or so. However, it is possible that a higher proportion of the repainted ex-LNWR locomotives got them than did any other group of engines, but this is only because Crewe works stopped repainting for some 12 to 18 months at the time of introduction of the Coat of Arms (see p. 207) and never used it extensively after repainting started again. In fact, Crewe is reported to have repainted only 120 engines before June 1924, when the stoppage took place and it is felt that most of these would have been given the individual letters rather than the Coat of Arms.

Some black engines carried the circular Coat of Arms on the cab or bunker and a few had the individual small letters 'LMS' as described above, but both these variations were somewhat rare. From mid 1924, the normal method of depicting ownership was a vermilion panel, 2′ 9″ x 1′ 0″, on which were the letters 'LMS' in gold with black shading to the right and below. As far as can be ascertained, the letters on this panel were exactly the same style as the aforementioned individual

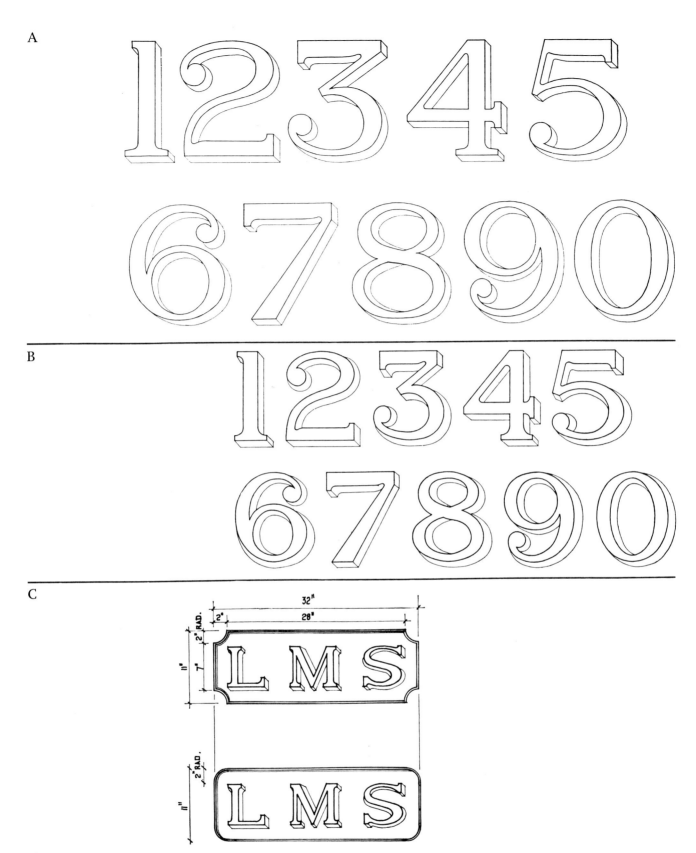

Figure 5

PRE-1928 INSIGNIA

A *18" numerals* These were a pure MR style and were always gold leaf with black shading.

B *14" numerals* These were again a pure MR style and continued in use after the 1927/8 livery change. Until 1929 they were gold leaf with black shading. At this stage, blended red shading (countershading) was introduced and the two versions remained co-existent until 1937/8 when the colour changed to chrome yellow and the shading became exclusively vermilion.

C *Cabside panels* The upper version lasted until about 1926 when it was replaced by the lower version. In both cases, the background was vermilion, the edging and lettering gold leaf and the shading black.

(all drawn by Arthur Whitehead)

Plate 282 Midland 0—6—4T No. 2024 in crimson lake livery, Code A1. This picture illustrates the pre-1928 livery on a Midland locomotive and confirms the absence of footplate lining.

Stephen Collection — NRM

letters and a drawing of the panel is included at *Figure 5*. The panel itself was outlined in gold and had a black line inside the upper and left hand edges.

The original design for this panel had cut out corners, but later the design was slightly altered and given plain rounded corners. It is understood that the reason for this change was a feeling on the part of the Company that the original design was a little old fashioned in appearance and that the round cornered version was more modern. Be that as it may, the original version was the more common although it is reported that Crewe preferred the later version as being somewhat reminiscent of the old LNWR cast cabside numberplate. The cab panel was mounted in a similar position to that of the coat of arms on the red engines but for tank engines with restricted bunker areas, a smaller version, some two thirds the size, was devised. This is also believed to have been a transfer although no official record of it has been traced.

The position of the Company markings (coat of arms or red panel) did vary a little on some classes of engine which could not conform to the cabside/bunker side arrangement. Generalisation is difficult but one of the main variations was in the case of ex-MR and ex-LNWR saddle tanks where the panel was affixed to the lower part of the saddle and the number was placed on the cabside panel, this being standard ex-MR practice. However, this was by no means universal since the pre-group saddle tanks from other companies — e.g. LYR and CR — often had restricted areas of cabside and the running number appeared on the saddle even though it was often difficult to see in this position.

All engines were, or rather should have been, fitted with cast iron smokebox numberplates of Midland pattern although by the middle thirties, except for the standard locomotives and, of course, the ex-MR ones, the bulk of them were running without them (*Figs. 6-7*). The Official agreement to dispense with smokebox plates did not, however, take place until February 1928 when it was agreed that with the change in the position of the running number to the engine at that time, there was no longer any need for the numberplates on Western, Central or Northern Division engines. It is highly probable, therefore, that many non-Midland engines (especially ex-LNWR engines) were never given smokebox plates at all unless repainted during 1923-7. They were to be continued on the Midland Division where roundhouses predominated and it is an interesting fact that whenever the Midland Division received an engine without a smokebox plate, it was usual to chalk or handpaint its number on the smokebox for ease of identification on the shed. Most authorities are agreed that it was rare to see a Scottish (and almost unknown to see an ex-LNWR) locomotive with a numberplate by the time of the Second World War, although a few ex-LYR engines did keep them after repainting in the thirties. Needless to say, all standard designs received front numberplates which were never *deliberately* removed.

When fitted, the numberplates carried raised figures, some 4¼″ high, of Midland style, the plate itself being black and the numbers generally bright metal. Many engines had these figures painted white in later years, often with a coloured backing on the plate itself — usually done at the sheds. The plates varied in length according to the number of digits to be carried and these dimensions are given in *Figure 6*.

Mention should also be made of the adoption by the LMS in 1923 of the old Midland Railway motive power classification scheme by bringing all non-Midland engines into line with the principle. This, as it did when extended to the whole of British Railways in 1948, produced some decided anomalies like ranking the ex-LNWR 'Georges' as no better than a

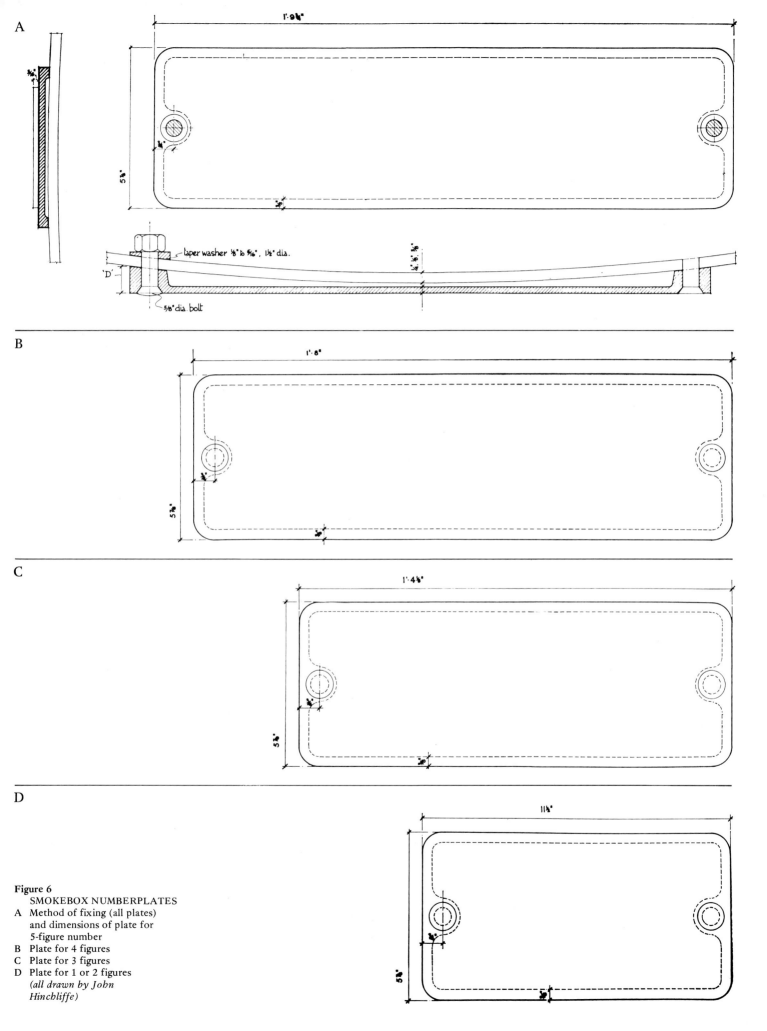

A

1'·9¼"

5⅞"

taper washer ⅛" to 5/16", 1½" dia.

'D'

⅝" dia. bolt

B

1'·8"

5⅞"

C

1'·4⅛"

5⅞"

D

11½"

5⅞"

Figure 6
SMOKEBOX NUMBERPLATES
A Method of fixing (all plates)
 and dimensions of plate for
 5-figure number
B Plate for 4 figures
C Plate for 3 figures
D Plate for 1 or 2 figures
 *(all drawn by John
 Hinchliffe)*

Figure 7
SMOKEBOX FIGURES
A Midland pattern, used
  1923-35 and again from
  about 1938 onwards
B 1936 pattern, used 1936/7
  and to a limited extent
  afterwards
  (Drawings, both to same
  scale, by:
  a Arthur Whitehead
  b John Hinchliffe)

Plates 283 & 284 These two pictures illustrate the pre-1928 livery with 18″ numbers. **Plate 283** depicts Livery Code C3 with the small 'LMS' and **Plate 284** shows the 'cut out' corner cabside panel − Livery Code C1.

Plate 283 Real Photographs, Plate 284 BR LMR

Johnson 'Belpaire' but was, nevertheless, applied throughout the system and the power classification number was applied, or should have been, to the cabsides of all engines.

The Midland used raised brass numbers for this task and the original idea was to standardise these for all engines but this was changed in January 1924 when gold leaf transfers with black shading were specified instead (*Fig. 8*). However, the ex-MR engines retained their raised brass numbers which were also applied to some of the new LMS standard Compounds as well (up to 1080 − probably as far as 1084). These numbers were only replaced by transfers or painted figures if they became lost or damaged and many survived with the engines until final scrapping long after Nationalisation. Oddly enough, Midland tank engines never received raised brass figures and were consequently, after 1922, given transfer or painted figures. In fact, Midland tank engines were never classified for power and on the LMS, it was only the occasional tank engine which received power class markings before 1928. It will, of course, be recalled that during this period, the LMS used a power class number *only*, the more familiar letter suffix coming after 1927.

When applied to the engine, the classification number was rendered in similar style to the running number but very much smaller − some 2¼″ over shading. This was, when possible, placed midway between the cabside cutaway and the front edge of the cabside but this position was somewhat variable on the standard classes, and cannot be more precisely specified beyond repeating the official edict that it was to be placed in a conspicuous position at about the height of the driver's head. This system of marking was carried forward to the new 1928 liveries with the addition of the letter suffix from April 1928 and for the majority of *non*-Midland engines, this was the first time these markings were, in fact, applied.

Plate 285 Ex-Midland Railway Kirtley 0−6−0 No. 2842 displays Livery Code C4 with the 'cut out' corner cabside panel.

Stephen Collection − NRM

Figure 8
POWER CLASSIFICATION
MARKINGS — ALL PERIODS

A MR pattern raised brass
   figures — ex-MR locomotives
   only

B Scroll pattern transfer
   figures — coloured to match
   main insignia of locomotive.

C Serif pattern letters —
   coloured to match main
   insignia
   *(all above drawn by Arthur
   Whitehead)*

D 1936 pattern sans-serif
   figures — coloured to match
   main insignia. Note the
   absence of figure '0'

E 1936 pattern sans serif
   letters — coloured to match
   main insignia
   *(D and E drawn by John
   Hinchliffe)*
   All drawn to a common
   scale

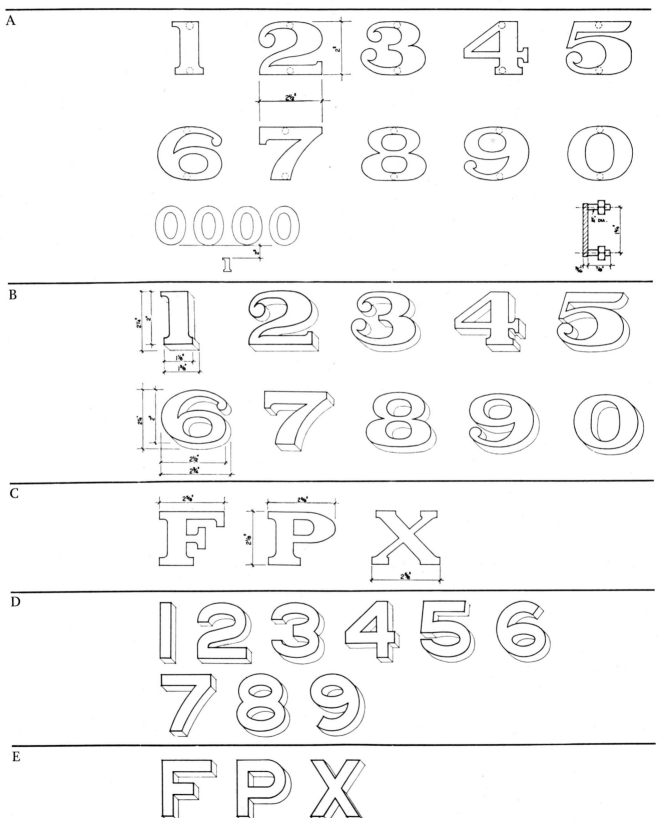

Plate 286 (Above) Ex-LNWR 0—6—0 No. 8208 is shown carrying Livery Code C5 and the less common round cabside panel can be seen. Note the smokebox door numberplate, later to be removed.

Real Photographs

Plate 287 This close up picture of 0—6—0 2F No. 3229 illustrates Livery Code C5 and the 'round corner' cabside panel can be seen. On the original print the black shading to the gold transfers, visible on the black locomotive, is clearly evident.

BR LMR

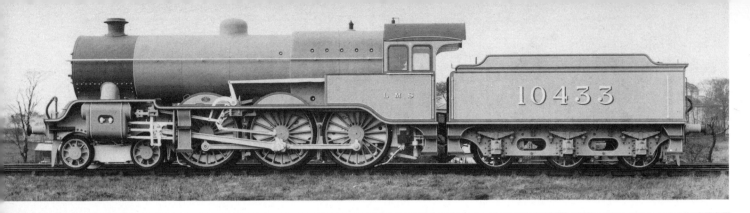

Plates 288-295 These eight pictures, illustrating locomotives in works grey livery, have been included to show the different works interpretation of the crimson lake livery as used upon certain classes of locomotives. However, the reader's attention is drawn to the fact that, notwithstanding the lavish treatment accorded to locomotives finished in this manner, the same classes when painted in crimson lake were not always painted in exactly the identical style, and so caution must be exercised when using works grey locomotive pictures as a guide to painting and lining models.

All photographs BR LMR and NRM

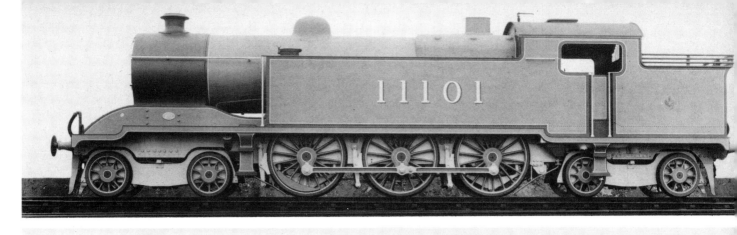

◄ **Plate 288**   Ex-LYR 4—6—0 No. 10433, Livery Code A2.
◄ **Plate 289**   Ex-LYR 4—6—0 No. 10451, Livery Code A1.
◄ **Plate 290**   Ex-FR 4—4—0 No. 10187, Livery Code A1.
◄ **Plate 291**   Ex-MR 4—4—0 No. 1014, Livery Code A1.

Plate 292   Ex-FR 4—6—4T No. 11101, Livery Code A1.
Plate 293   Ex-LYR 2—4—2T No. 10919, Livery Code A1.
Plate 294   Ex-LNWR 4—6—0 No. 5999, Livery Code A8.
Plate 295   Standard 4—6—0 Class 5XP No. 5706, Livery Code A6.

STANDARD LIVERY 1928-1946

In late 1927, a decision was made to place the engine number on the locomotive itself in the case of tender engines and on the bunker side of tank locomotives. The CME's decision to make the change was effected on 15th December, 1927 when new transfers were also issued in 'imitation gold with black shading' but since the first repainted locomotives were not really in evidence until the following year, the new style has, by long tradition, always been referred to as the 1928 livery. Apart from the odd black example painted experimentally during late 1927, the first correctly liveried locomotive in the new style was probably LMS standard Compound 4—4—0 No. 1121.

There is a common but, it is felt, erroneous and rather misleading belief that the change was a result of awkwardness on the part of the non-Midland constituents of the LMS, particularly Crewe, who wanted to change the almost completely pure 'Midland' look which was evident during the first troubled years of the Company. This, however, does not seem very likely. None of the works, aside from Crewe, showed any real reluctance to use the new livery in 1923 as is witnessed by the very large number of engines of non-Midland origin which were painted red during the early years. Especially was this so in Scotland although this might be explained by the fact that the chosen livery was alien to all. One shudders to think what might have happened at Kilmarnock for example if the chosen LMS livery had been Caledonian Blue! Speculation aside, the radical change in style was necessary for less romantic reasons than some have suggested and was brought about to achieve three objectives:

(a) To reduce expenditure by cutting the number of engines carrying the full red livery which was expensive both to apply and maintain.

(b) To increase the flexibility of tender engine working by removing the running number to the engine itself, thereby enabling tenders to be exchanged between engines more easily if need be — see also Chapter 10.

(c) To enable engines and tenders to be numbered separately. The general application of this policy to the whole system dates from 16th February, 1928, it hitherto having been confined to those parts of the Company which had numbered tenders before grouping — see Chapter 10.

It seems very clear that there were considerable difficulties on the non-Midland parts of the system as a result of having the running number on the tender. Especially was this true at Crewe works where repainting and renumbering ceased for about a year or so from mid-1924. As already noted, the LNWR had based its supply of tenders on the assumption that locomotives took longer to pass through shops for repairs than did the tenders. No tender was allocated to a specific engine, beyond the use of a specific type for each class and, as a result, black engines were seen with red tenders and vice versa while the number on engine and tender frequently did not agree. One attempt made to alleviate this problem was by providing the odd tender with a frame into which could be fitted detachable number boards — rather after the fashion of a church hymn-board — but it does not seem to have been widespread. There was undoubtedly a certain amount of 'anti-Midland' feeling at Crewe but there was, equally, unquestionable difficulty in working the system of tender numerals. Just which of these two factors was the more dominant is difficult to assess at this distance in time and may well depend on where one's prime allegiances rest but, as already mentioned, Crewe had only renumbered some 120 engines by mid-1924 at which time all activity ceased for a year or more. So chaotic did things ultimately become — according to one source it bordered on internecine war at Euston — that firm action had to be taken and, as a result, many ex-LNWR engines were renumbered at the sheds themselves. This often took the form of merely removing the cast LNWR numberplate and painting the vacant space with the new number.

The 1928 change in style resulted in the longest lasting of the main LMS liveries — in fact, many locomotives bore this type of insignia until after Nationalisation. At the same time, there were many more detail variations within the style than in 1923-27. The reasons for these variations are a little obscure and may have resulted from different interpretations of the official specification at different works — Derby's edicts did not always get as fully observed as the ex-Midland supporters would have liked. At the same time, there were only three official liveries and almost all variations were to be found in the size and shape of locomotive insignia — particularly numbering. In order to make matters a little less confusing, most of these sundry variations will not be considered until the next chapter.

The Standard Express Passenger Livery

The crimson lake livery was now confined to certain specific classes of engine and the colour and lining details remained exactly as specified for the 1923-7 period (page 170).

As with the 1923-7 livery, there were variations within the layout of the yellow lining occasioned by the differing shapes of the red engines concerned. Fairly detailed specifications for the 'Royal Scot' and 'Princess Royal' Class locomotives have survived and are appended below. They are believed to be reasonably accurate for all red engines. Photographic evidence supports this view and the only noticeable variation was in the case of Stanier pattern cabs where the

◀ **Plate 296** 4—6—0 Class 5XP No. 5966, later to become No. 5512 *Bunsen*, in works grey, depicts exactly the crimson lake livery, Code A6.   *NRM*

lining went to the full height of the cabside at front and rear edges and was not applied along the upper edge, except for a batch of new 'Jubilee' Class 4—6—0s built by outside contractors. This variation only lasted until the first full repaint. During the period under review and certainly before 1935, the yellow lining colour was changed from the pale shade of the 1923 livery to a darker but brighter chrome yellow hue. Neither Derby nor Crewe can give an exact date for the change.

LINING SPECIFICATION FOR LOCOMOTIVE No. 6100 IN LMS LIVERY

Lettering

6100	L.M.S.
4' 2¾"	10' 9½"
Numbers 10" deep	Letters 14" deep
Classification numbers 2³/8" deep	

Lining	*Black*	*Yellow*
Platform angle	1"	3/8"
Panel	2¼"	½"
Rear footstep	1¼"	½"
Cab sides	1¼"	½"
Line just above panel	—	½"
Cylinders	1½"	½"
Front footstep	1"	½"
Splasher and nameplate support	1¼"	½"
Firebox immediately in front of cab angle	1¼"	½"
Front end of barrel, immediately behind smokebox	1¼"	½"
Buffer		3/8" wide yellow line, 2½" from buffer casing.
Buffer beam — measured from bottom edge	Black 1", yellow 3/8", bright red 1' 0¼", yellow 3/8", black 1".	

Note: The lining on the buffer beam was applied all round but the measurements given above are to allow for the fact that on these engines there was a narrow band of crimson above the buffer beam below the footplate.

Deflector Plates	All black

Tender

Sides	2½" black from beading bottom and back
	2¾" black from beading top and front
End	2½" black and ½" yellow

The date of this specification is not known but from the mention of deflector plates can be deduced later than 1931. It does, however, raise a few problems which must, presumably, remain unanswered. Firstly, no mention is made of the ends of the buffers being black and yet this feature was present on almost every red engine as far as photographic evidence indicates. Secondly, the use of 10" figures was very rare on this class and no example has been located of any 'Royal Scot', much less 6100, carrying 10" scroll type figures *after* fitting with smoke deflectors. The spacing of the 'LMS' on the tender side is much wider than the known value for Fowler tenders if it refers to this type while if it refers to the wide tender which 6100 took to America, the engine should have 14" numbers. In addition, the specification implies a lack of yellow lining on the tender side which is not in accord with any known picture of a red Fowler tender. The spacing could refer to the time when the engine had a Stanier tender but again — why no mention of the tender side yellow lining? If it does refer to the time when the locomotive had a Stanier tender, which is felt most probable, then the size of the insignia would indicate the 1936 block style — see page 191. However, 6100 is not thought to have been one of the few 'Scots' given this style so there is a certain amount of mystery about it all.

The specification does not define the red areas but, on the other hand it does give accurate lining detail. The term 'cab angle' refers to the angle iron at the junction between cab front and firebox sheets.

Plates 297 & 298 (Opposite) Both these locomotives depict Livery Code A6; however, there are ▶ differences of a subtle nature. **Plate 297** shows 'Princess Royal' Class 4—6—2 No. 6205 *Princess Victoria*. This locomotive, built at Crewe, can perhaps be considered as being the definitive Crewe version, whereas 'Silver Jubilee' Class 4—6—0 No. 5564, built by the North British Locomotive Co Ltd, differs. There is no black edging to the buffer housing compared with 6205 and the lining on the cabsides has been returned along the top towards the windows on the 'Jubilee' but not on *Princess Victoria*. Note also the bright metalwork finish of this period. *Both BR LMR*

PAINTING AND LINING OF 'PRINCESS ROYAL' CLASS 4–6–2 LOCOMOTIVE c. 1933

Engine   Painted red with the exception of the smokebox which is painted black. Lining details as follows:

Running angle:	1″ black line along bottom edge and ³/8″ line adjacent to it.
First lagging belt (smokebox):	Painted black with a ³/8″ yellow line running adjacent to it on the clothing.
Firebox lagging belt (at cab):	2″ black line and ³/8″ yellow line adjacent to it.
Cab side:	2¼″ black line running down both sides and along bottom edge and ³/8″ yellow line adjacent to it on the inside. The engine numbers are central on the cabside and the horizontal centre line of the numbers is 22″ from the platform plate. Total width of numbers — 44″ and the size of the latter is 12″.
Splashers:	Periphery 1″ black line and adjacent to it a ³/8″ line on the inside.
Buffer beam:	Red.

Tender   Painted red with 2¼″ black line all round side and back plates and ½″ yellow line adjacent to it on the inside. Other details as follows:

Frame holes:	1″ black line all round and ½″ yellow line on the outside.
Bottom of frame:	1″ black line with ½″ yellow on the inside.
Footsteps:	1″ black line on sides and bottom and ½″ yellow line on inside.
Buffer beam:	Red.

The letters 'LMS' are painted on the tender tank. The letter 'M' coincides with the centre line of the intermediate wheel. The distances from the centre of the 'M' to the centre line of the 'L' and 'S' are 5′ and 4′ 9″ respectively. The letters are placed 2′ 6″ from the bottom of the tank, i.e. to the bottom of the letters.

Note: As with the 'Royal Scot' specification, the above details are quoted verbatim and are again deficient in certain details. No mention is made of buffer beam lining, nor of the shade of red for the buffer beam (in fact vermilion). The engine seemed to have ³/8″ lining throughout whereas the tender had ½″ throughout. It was much more common in fact for the ³/8″ lining to be confined to areas below the footplate with ½″ lining above the footplate. Finally, no mention is made of the engine footsteps nor the nameplate. The footsteps were lined out and the nameplate was finished with polished brass letters and surrounds against a black painted background — this being standard LMS practice. The reference to 'painted' letters on the tender was probably a misprint.

From mid-1932, bright metal finish was specified for motion components, tyres, buffer heads, cylinder ends etc., but this rarely remained obvious when the engines had been in service for any length of time. Bright metal was most in evidence on new engines although, except for the tyres, it was also specified for repaints.

The painted yellow line around the wheels of earlier red engines was discontinued in late 1933 although one member of the paint staff at Derby works informed the authors that the compounds continued to receive this feature until the Second World War. As these were the only crimson lake locomotives regularly shopped at Derby after 1927, this assertion is highly probable and has been confirmed by other observers. No official record of this exception has been located.

Lettering and numbering was applied in one of the many permutations to be described and was generally gold with black shading although many engines in the middle and later thirties received red shaded insignia.

Classes officially allocated this livery were as follows: non-streamlined 4—6—2s, 'Royal Scots', 'Patriots', 'Jubilees', 'Claughtons', Hughes LYR type 4—6—0s and compounds. A few members of other classes also received the red livery during the transition period in the late 1920s — see next chapter and the appropriate class chapters.

The most striking exceptions to the 1928 standard liveries were to be found on the streamlined 'Coronation' Class 4—6—2s and on Class 5XP 4—6—0 No. 5552 *Silver Jubilee*. Details of these locomotives will be given in the appropriate class chapters. In addition, mention ought to be made of the fact that the first five non-streamlined 'Coronation' Class 4—6—2s (6230-4) were given gold lining with vermilion edging rather than the standard yellow lining given to all other red engines. This specification is given in full in *Volume III*.

The Standard Mixed Traffic Livery

Sometimes referred to as the *Intermediate Passenger Livery*, this was an entirely new style introduced in place of red for those classes not allocated purely as goods engines and which did not retain the crimson lake colour. When the decision was made not to perpetuate red for more than a few classes, a lined out black livery was sought and, not surprisingly, thoughts turned to the possibility of re-introducing the old LNWR livery. In fact, Class 2P No. 534 was inspected in full LNWR livery on 2nd March, 1928 but, according to first hand information, the practice was not continued because of the time taken to apply the lining. It seems rather odd that in the even more stringent times after Nationalisation this aspect seems not to have been a consideration. At all events, the livery finally adopted in 1928 was the familiar black finish with single red lining.

It is difficult to state which classes had the livery but the majority of the red engines of 1923-27 that were not withdrawn before repainting should have received it, together with the new mixed traffic classes. Little has survived in the way of a basic specification, but an official picture of Class 2P 4—4—0 No. 563 was issued as a guide for the red lining.

The whole engine — and tender if applicable — was finished in *varnished black*. Lining was vermilion but, as with the red livery before 1928, such was the variety of engines given this livery that it is impossible to give an exact specification. The general principle was to apply a single red line wherever a yellow one would have been placed had the engine been crimson. After a certain amount of early indecision, the dimension of the red line was finally settled at $3/8''$ thick for all areas except the boiler bands which had $½''$ lining. Buffer beams had a 1" black border only and tender side-frames and footstep plates were unlined. Vacuum pipe standards were generally painted to match the buffer beams if they crossed it. The footplate edging and outside cylinders were generally lined on all tender engines but not on standard and ex-MR tank engines — at least as far as pictures indicate. Most non-Midland tank engine classes had lined footplates and where this is not so, the fact is mentioned in the class chapters, but absence of footplate lining was a distinctive feature of the standard series of tank engines introduced during the period. Panels were lined round the edge as for the red livery but the red lining usually had rounded corners on LMS standard and ex-MR tank engines. This 'rounding off' may have been a later change in policy, but most pictures show it to be present. Wheels were unlined with this livery, as were tender side-frames.

The styles and sizes of insignia used with the lined black livery are given below and the insignia were most typically red shaded. Quite a number of engines had unshaded gold insignia (actually black shaded transfers) during the first few years of the style but this was less common.

Plate 299 This picture of standard Class 2P 4—4—0 No. 563 was the official picture issued by Derby to other works as a guide for the red lining to be used on those locomotives entitled to this style. This picture is in works grey, new locomotives were finished in Livery Code B3/B6.

BR LMR

Plates 300 & 301 Both these pictures depict locomotives finished in red-lined black livery using gold/black shaded transfers which on a black locomotive gave a plain gold appearance. On ex-CR 4—4—0 No. 14498 (**Plate 300**) the offset LMS on the tender is visible and the locomotive is incorrectly classified P4, its Livery Code is B5. **Plate 301** depicts standard 2—6—0 Class 5P4F No. 13112. Note the all red vermilion buffer beam and absence of a black band on the end of the buffer housing. Livery Code B5.   *Both pictures BR LMR*

The Standard Goods Livery

The goods livery remained unlined black but exhibited the same bewildering variety of number sizes and styles as the other two styles. Many engines which could have had the mixed traffic livery were turned out in plain black and it was essentially the goods livery which became the standard for all repainted engines shortly after the start of the Second World War. With the goods livery, lettering and numbering was executed in plain gold, gold shaded red, yellow shaded red or plain yellow (see below). The latter style was particularly evident at Crewe but became widespread everywhere during the war, being frequently hand-applied over the older transfers.

Plate 302 Class 4 0—6—0 No. 4429 ex works on 30th October, 1928 is believed to be the first locomotive to be built at Derby to carry the new livery for freight locomotives. Note that it is still Class 4 but shortly after this picture was taken this class was classified as 4F.   *BR LMR*

Lettering and Numbering — all liveries

Company ownership was now depicted by large letters 'LMS' which were placed on tender or tank side, generally in the place previously occupied by the pre-1928 large running numbers. The running number was similarly transposed to cab or bunker side.

Smokebox numberplate design was unchanged but, as stated above, only the standard classes and ex-Midland locomotives received front numberplates as a matter of policy after 1927. Most of the numberplates fitted to other classes before 1928 were subsequently removed but a few did remain in position on several different types of engine. These are mentioned, where known, in subsequent chapters.

Power classification markings continued to be as previously described (page 177), styled and coloured to match the insignia of the engine but with the addition of a 'P' or 'F' suffix as appropriate (*Fig. 8*). The ex-MR engines retained their existing raised brass figures for the most part and only the 'P' or 'F' was applied to these engines. This gave them a rather untidy appearance.

LMS locomotive insignia design went through a number of permutations during the 1930s and it is this aspect which makes most difficult the rationalisation of LMS livery styles.

The initial insignia specified for the new 1928 livery on 15th December, 1927 was of scroll and serif face coloured exactly as for the Midland styled characters of 1923-7 (i.e. gold with black shading). Letters were to be 14″ high and figures 10″ high. On 20th April, 1928, it was decided to adopt three sizes of figure — 10″, 12″ and 14″, the policy being to utilise the largest size which would conveniently fit the engine. The 14″ figures were to continue to be of the old MR style but the new 10″ and 12″ heights were provided in a new and somewhat coarser shape (*Fig. 9*). Instructions were given that the new characters (including shading) were to be painted on the engine until transfers were available. The most commonly adopted base colour for such handpainted characters tended to be the pale yellow lining shade used on red engines and Crewe continued to follow this practice on freight classes for many years after transfers were available. Crewe further complicated matters by handpainting the 14″ high numerals in the new 1928 shape rather than the specified MR style. Thus, even before the end of 1928, four types of locomotive cabside numeral were to be seen (14″ Midland, 14″ standard, 12″ standard and 10″ standard). The resultant untidiness, allied with the dropping of the red livery for many classes, did not always please contemporary enthusiasts!

Plates 303 & 304 Both these locomotives are carrying 14″ gold numerals with black shading and these pictures have been selected to show the different appearance when used on red and black locomotives. On **Plate 303**, an ex-CR 4—6—2T No. 15351, the plain gold appearance on a black locomotive contrasts with the black shading evident when used on a red locomotive, No. 6170 *British Legion*, **Plate 304**. Livery Codes: 15351, Code B7; 6170, Code A7.

BR LMR

Figure 9
POST-1927 INSIGNIA

A *14″ letters* Utilised 1927-47. Depending on the class to which fitted, these characters were applied in the following colours: gold shaded black, gold with blended red shading, gold with plain red shading, plain gold, plain 'straw', plain yellow, yellow with red shading

B *12″ Standard numerals* Utilised 1928-47. Colours as for LMS

C *10″ Standard numerals* Utilised 1928-47. Colours as for LMS
(all drawn by Arthur Whitehead)

Plate 305 This picture of ex-LNWR 0–8–0 No. 9453 at Crewe South on 19th April, 1936 displays a perfect example of Crewe's finish for this class of locomotive. Livery Code C18.

L. Hanson

Plate 306 This picture of a standard 0–6–0T No. 16697 illustrates the problem of being totally accurate in defining livery. This locomotive built by outside contractors could be hand-painted C16, or gold transfers C13.

BR LMR

Plate 307 (Below) Ex-MR Class 1P 0–4–4T No. 1240 is equipped to work motor trains. In this picture it displays Livery Code B3 and the countershading can clearly be seen on these red shaded transfers. *BR LMR*

On 17th June, 1929, when gilt transfers were available, it was decided that future supplies would be supplied shaded vermilion at the right hand side and glazed lake on the undersides. The object of this change was to improve the appearance of the insignia and the change-over was to be 'as soon as possible'. These 'countershaded' transfers were provided in all three numeral heights and were very attractive in appearance. The instruction to stock them did not, however, clarify which classes should receive them so the mixture continued as before.

Almost exactly a year later (18th June, 1930), some order was produced from the incipient chaos by defining the appropriate insignia for each of the three official liveries, viz.:

Crimson Lake engines	—	black shaded transfers as hitherto.
Lined Black engines	—	the new red shaded transfers.
Plain Black engines	—	black shaded transfers as hitherto which continued to give the appearance of unshaded insignia.

From this date, although mistakes did occur, most locomotives tended to conform to this ruling. Known exceptions are listed in the class articles. Crewe works, however, continued to pursue its semi-independent line with plain black engines, particularly ex-LNWR types, and gave most of them handpainted insignia in the pale yellow lining colour without shading.

By the mid-1930s, things were beginning to look reasonably homogeneous, albeit with some regional variations. For example, St Rollox works frequently used black shaded transfers on lined black engines and tended to favour 14″ figures where Derby might prefer the 12″ height (e.g. Compounds and 'Crabs'). In general, however, the various classes had settled down quite well in their appointed styles. This happy position was not to last long.

On 15th February, 1936, a further change was initiated. A new style of sans serif insignia was devised with 14″ 'LMS' as before but with only one size of figure, namely 10″ (*Fig. 10*). These new characters were to be provided in gilt with the same shading policy as defined in June 1930 (above) although the countershading of the red shaded transfers gave way to plain red shading. However, instructions were also issued on this occasion that the block style insignia were to be confined to new engines only, until existing stocks of scroll/serif transfers had been used up on *repainted* locomotives.

Plate 308   Standard Compound 4—4—0 No. 1099 displays the experimental 1936 style which, as far as the authors know, was not put upon any other locomotive in this exact form but appeared as shown in Plates 309 & 310.   *BR LMR*

Plate 309   4—6—0 Class 5XP 'Patriot' No. 5502 *Royal Naval Division* displays a perfectly correct example of the 1936 block style when applied to crimson lake locomotives. Livery Code A12.   *BR LMR*

Figure 10

1936 SANS SERIF INSIGNIA

A *14″ letters* Utilised 1936/7. Supplied in two styles only, either gold with red shading or plain gold. Originally gold with black shading was intended for red engines but only one example of this style has been located (Plate 310)

B *10″ numerals* Utilised 1936/7. Colour details as for LMS *Note:* This style of insignia was substantially the same as that used on the fully lined out streamliners

On the streamliners, the silver or gold characters (depending on the colour of the engine) were edged in dark blue or black as appropriate *(all drawn by John Hinchliffe)*

A

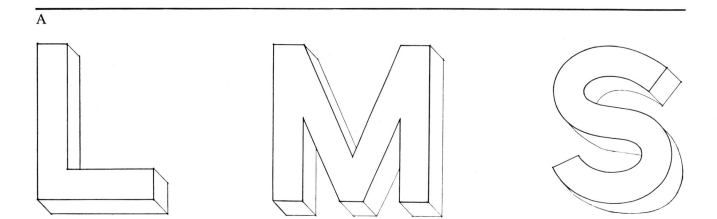

B

Additional complication was provided in June 1936 by a decision to standardise vermilion shading for *all* engines given the new transfers — again with a proviso that existing black shaded new style transfers were to be used up — this time on *non-standard* engines!

It is hardly surprising to relate that, contrary to these edicts, new freight engines appeared with black shaded 1936 insignia (Class 8F 2—8—0s) while some pre-group locomotives were given red shaded 1936 transfers! It should also be mentioned that many locomotives given the 1936 insignia were also fitted with matching sans-serif smokebox number-plates, but not exclusively so. Most of these engines were new machines but some older locomotives were also given replacement block style numberplates.

Plate 310 4—4—0 Standard Compound No. 1094 displays the prototype 1936 block style of gold shaded black, future use of this style was shaded red. This picture has been selected to illustrate the different widths of lining employed.

BR LMR

Plate 311 This picture displays the 1936 livery in probably its most common form, some 227 were built new using this style and others were repainted in this form. This picture also displays the 60″ spacing used on the majority of Stanier 4,000 gallon tenders. Livery Code B11.

BR LMR

The 1936 style was not a universal success and by October 1937, the company had ordered that the 'old type transfers' (i.e. scroll/serif including all three numeral heights) were to continue to be ordered until the new style had been settled. In fact the company completely reverted to the scroll and serif face from late 1937 onwards. Supplies of 1936 transfers were ordered to be used up but this does not seem to have had much effect. However, many locomotives continued to receive the sans-serif front number plates after the reversion to the older insignia style. This may well have been purely a Derby trait since Derby never reverted to the MR style plate. Perversely, Crewe did!

The return to scroll and serif transfers was accompanied by yet another change of insignia colour. By 1937/8, the cost of gold leaf transfers was, presumably, becoming too high so from this date, chrome yellow was substituted as the base colour. These chrome yellow transfers were a much brighter shade than the 1928 yellow painted figures (above) and, in fact, matched the darker yellow lining shade recently adopted for red engines. Furthermore they had bright vermilion shading to the right and below rather than the blended red shading of the 1929 gold transfers. The company ruled that the new red shaded yellow transfers, which were supplied in all three numeral heights, were to be used with all three basic liveries.

To complete the confusion it seems fairly clear that there were also supplied some gold transfers in scroll/serif style with plain red shading! These were given to the non-streamlined 'Coronation' Class 4–6–2s (6230-4) and were extensively employed at St Rollox.

The red shaded chrome yellow transfers remained standard until after the war but wartime 'utility' repainting tended to confine the use of transfers mainly to new engines. It became common policy on most of the existing stock for insignia to be handpainted over the outline of the old transfers. For this purpose a bright yellow paint of almost orange hue was provided, even darker than the yellow transfers. This paint was often applied at the sheds and not infrequently resulted in some rather messy-looking engines. Needless to say, such wartime handpainting did not incorporate shading.

By 1946, examples of most of the above mentioned styles could be seen and the result was, to say the least, more than a little untidy. Moreover, although officially superseded by the 1946 livery and insignia, the older scroll and serif characters in all their variations continued to be seen and used until well after 1947. Many engines initially received their BR numbers in LMS style characters.

Plates 312 & 313 Both these locomotives are carrying 12″ yellow shaded red transfers. **Plate 312** is an ex-MR 2F 0–6–0 No. 22940, Livery Code C22. **Plate 313** is a 'Silver Jubilee' Class 5XP 4–6–0 No. 5616 *Malta G.C.* photographed on 11th November, 1943.
Plate 312 L. Hanson
Plate 313 BR LMR

Insignia Spacing

With all variations of the 1928-46 insignia, numeral spacing was fairly consistent, there normally being some 2-3″ space between each figure. The spacing between the letter centres varied considerably but the following summary is believed to be generally accurate:

(a) *60″ spacing* — confined to Stanier pattern curved top tenders. In many cases the actual spacing varied between 57″ and 60″ between centres.

(b) *53″ spacing* — the standard spacing on Deeley and Fowler type tenders and on the larger pre-group tank engine designs. It was also widely used on Scottish pre-group tender engines and by Horwich works on many tender engines.

(c) *40″ spacing* — again a standard spacing for many smaller tenders and for all the range of standard 2—6—4 and 2—6—2 tank engines of Fowler, Stanier or Fairburn design. It was also used extensively on Fowler type tenders and almost without exception on tenders of ex-LNWR design.

(d) *27″ and smaller spacing* — this variation was much less in evidence, being generally confined to smaller tank engines and the Garratts. It was quite common on ex-CR tank engines.

In passing, it might be interesting to note that only the last of the four spacings quoted is based on photographic measurement, the rest being from livery drawings or specification. Of the three larger variations, 40″ was probably used more than either of the others but this can never be absolutely confirmed. When used instead of 53″ spacing on Fowler tenders, for example, there appears to have been no set pattern; except to remark that Crewe works seems to have favoured 40″ spacing for *all* except Stanier tenders.

The siting of the letters on the tender or tank side was also rather variable. In the absence of any complicating factors, they were placed with the 'M' centrally over the middle axlebox of the tender — or midway between the centre pair of axles of an eight wheel tender — and were placed midway or slightly above the mid point between top and bottom horizontals of the purely rectangular part of the tender side sheets, ignoring flared or raised upper portions. When applied

Plate 314 (Upper) Ex-CR 4—6—0 No. 14800 carrying 'P5' classification displays Livery Code B7, gold shaded transfers on a black locomotive. Note the 53″ tender spacing centred on the tankside but not centred over the wheels.

BR LMR

Plate 315 (Lower) Ex-FR 3F 0—6—0 No. 12501 displays Livery Code C14 — 12″ gold shaded black transfers on a black locomotive. The 'LMS' at 53″ centres is central on the tankside and the 'M' is over the centre axlebox.

Real Photographs

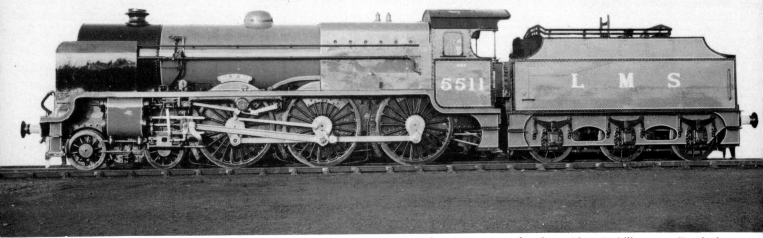

Plates 316 & 317 These two pictures show that there was not a consistent treatment for rivets. **Plate 316** illustrates 'Patriot' Class 5XP No. 5511 *Isle of Man* in Livery Code A11 — very rare indeed. 53″ centres for the 'LMS' with the 'M' over the middle axlebox despite rivets. 'Silver Jubilee' Class 5XP No. 5552 in **Plate 317** is carrying Livery Code A6 with 40″ spacing and with the 'LMS' offset to avoid the rivets. This picture also displays the treatment given to these high sided tenders when in crimson lake livery.

Both BR LMR

Plate 318 Ex-LNWR 0−6−2T No. 6900 displays Livery Code B3 with 40″ spacing to the LMS. Note the rounded panels of the lining, unusual for this class of locomotive.

BR LMR

to tank sides, they were, as far as possible, central left to right and top to bottom on the main panel. The known exceptions to this general rule are as follows:

(a) *Stanier 4,000 gallon tenders with curved top* — as described above but with the lowest edge of the letters, not counting shading, 2' 6" above the upper surface of the tender footplate.

(b) *Johnson Midland pattern tenders* — as described above but with two letters always to the *rear* of the vertical centre beading. The 'M' was placed as close to this beading as possible and a generally accurate value would be to take its centre as being some 9" to the rear of the beading. 40" spacing was well nigh universal on these tenders except for those with no beading which often had 53" spacing with the 'M' above the centre axle.

(c) *LNWR and Caledonian type tenders* — The vast majority of tenders originating from these companies were constructed in such a way that the vertical centre line of the main rectangular part of the side was slightly to the rear of the centre axlebox. The 'M' was placed on this centre line which had the effect of offsetting the 'LMS' so that the *cab end* of the 'M' was centred over the axlebox — ie. the letter was offset some 6"-7" to the rear. This practice may have been followed for other similar pre-group tenders although most ex-LYR, GSWR and HR tenders were not of this type and had the 'M' over the centre axlebox.

(d) *Fowler, Stanier and Fairburn 2–6–2/2–6–4Ts* — The position of the letters on these engines was complicated by the irregular shape of the tank side but, in general, seems to have followed the following scheme:

2–6–2T The horizontal centre line of the letters was a little above the mid-point between the extreme top and bottom edges of the tank (about 1-2"). The 'M' was some 6" forward of the mid-point between the drop in the footplate below the tank and the front edge of the cab door opening. Some of the Fowler engines had the 'M' at this point when originally numbered in the 15xxx series prior to 1934.

2–6–4T The top to bottom spacing was as for the 2–6–2T but the centre of the 'M' was more variable, being about 4' 0" ahead of the cab front on the taper boiler tanks and some 6"-9" less than this on the Fowlers.

On each type of tank, 40" spacing was normal.

It is not possible to give any simple analysis of the sizes and positioning of the engine running numbers after 1927. Official policy was to use the largest size of figure which would fit the available space on the engine, but regardless of height, if there was room on the engine, it was usual to space a four figure number so that the extreme width of the panel

Plate 319 Ex-Cr 2F 0–6–0T No. 16163 displays Livery Code C21 with 27" spacing.   *BR LMR*

was 50-51″; while lateral spacing of other than four figure numbers was arranged to suit the number of digits or merely to get it onto the available space. The number was located midway between the footplate and the cabside window or in the middle of the cabside panel if present. Sometimes it was placed wherever it would fit without impinging on beading, etc., and on certain classes it migrated to most odd locations. Many ex-GSWR engines had the numbers high up on the cabside while the ex-MR Kirtley 2–4–0 designs after being renumbered on to the duplicate list often had to do with tiny hand painted numbers, there being so little space available. On tank engines, the horizontal centre line of the numbers was, wherever possible, at the same level as that of the 'LMS' but, of course, some classes of engine (particularly saddle tanks) could not be thus treated.

Of the three heights of number there was again little uniformity in spite of the edict to use the largest size possible. In general Derby followed the principle throughout although other works were less rigid in their interpretations. The 12″ was probably the most commonly used size for the red engines and the 14″ on the lined black but much may have depended on what was in stock at the time of shopping. When it came to the style of number, pictorial evidence suggests that Crewe made little use of the Midland type figures until the later 1930s while Derby used them as often as possible. Horwich and St Rollox developed variations of their own with each showing a slight preference for the Midland pattern.

Plates 320 & 321 These two plates provide the opportunity to consider the detail differences between the Stanier and Fairburn 2–6–4Ts. **Plate 320** No. 2537 is in Livery Code B4. Note the bright metal finish of a pre-war locomotive. **Plate 321** displays Livery Code C23 and by now the 'LMS' has been moved forward on the tankside and the numbers closed up.
Both pictures BR LMR

THE 1946 STANDARD LIVERY

In March 1946, two engines were given experimental 'blue/grey' livery (Class 7P 4—6—2 No. 6234 and Class 5XP 4—6—0 No. 5573) and one was repainted in a modified form of the traditional crimson livery (Class 5XP 4—6—0 No. 5594). These schemes seem to have been 'try-outs' for a new standard post-war livery but neither seems to have been pressed very hard since later the same year the LMS adopted as standard a very austere livery with matching insignia. All engines were to be black and, except for the principal express passenger classes, no lining was to be applied.

The ghost of Richard Moon may have laughed at the final eclipse of Midland Lake as a railway colour but for the enthusiast, starved for six years of much to enthuse over, it must have seemed a retrograde step; moreover, Sir William Wood in the LMS Staff magazine felt it necessary to explain why the rather uninspiring scheme had been chosen. Fortunately, there was some consolation in the decision to line out the main passenger classes in a new way, although it is reported that even this mild amount of colour would not have been approved without a certain amount of pressure from influential men who wished to see 'a bit of Lake' on the engines again in spite of the need for economy. The original specification for this lined out livery has survived in full and is, therefore, quoted complete.

PAINTING AND LINING OF LMS EXPRESS PASSENGER LOCOMOTIVES — 1946

Body Colour:	Black — glossy finish
Running plate angle — except below the cab:	Lined 2½″ maroon band in centre with ³/8″ straw line adjoining top and bottom and ³/8″ black line top and bottom outside.
Cylinder and steam chest casing:	
Leading edge:	½″ black, ³/8″ straw, 1¼″ maroon, ³/8″ straw
Trailing edge:	³/8″ straw, 1¼″ maroon, ³/8″ straw, ½″ black (outer edge).
	(*Note: This lining was vertical only.*)
Cab:	Lined sides and bottom only with 2½″ maroon line outside and ³/8″ straw line adjoining on inside.
Tender:	Lined all round (top, bottom and sides) with 2½″ maroon line outside and ³/8″ straw line adjoining inside. (The beading strip round the top edges of sides and back was black while on Fowler pattern tenders the beading separating upper/lower tender side panels was also maroon with straw edging.)
Wheel rims and centre:	Black.
Motion and cylinder/steam chest covers:	Bright steel
	(*Note: This was sometimes applied to tyres as well.*)
Buffer beams/casings:	Vermilion.
Nameplate on engine:	Straw borders and letters — maroon background.
Letters on tender side:	Gill Sans type (no serifs) — straw colour lined maroon all round leaving straw margin outside — unshaded.
	14″ letters, centre line of 'M' coincides with centre line of middle wheel of tender.
	Centre of 'M' to centre of 'L' — 5′ 3″
	Centre of 'M' to centre of 'S' — 5′ 0″
	Bottom of letters to top of footplate — 2′ 6″
	(*Note: This dimension was usually reduced to about 2′ 0″ on Fowler pattern tenders.*)
Running number:	Gill Sans type as for 'LMS' — unshaded.
	12″ numerals, total width for four figures to be 50″.
	Bottom of figures to bottom of cabside — 2′ 6″
	(*Note: This dimension was sometimes reduced if the engine ran with a Fowler tender — e.g. the unrebuilt 'Patriot' Class.*)

Note: The power classification numbers were placed centrally below the running number and rendered in the same style of lettering — including the thin maroon line near the edge. Sizes are not given but they were about 2½″ high placed some 3″ below the number of the engine.

This specification although official is not in accordance with observed fact, for most pictures of this livery show lining to have been applied to boiler and firebox as well. This took the form of a maroon band edged on both sides with a ³/8″ straw line and was applied to the front and rear boiler bands and the firebox band at the cab angle. The explanation would seem to be that this boiler lining was a later addition since the first few repaints did have unlined boilers. These early repaints often had unlined insignia too, and on several of the 'Coronation' Pacifics, the letters and numbers were set rather lower than the 2′ 6″ dimension quoted and with the 'LMS' rather closer spaced on the tender.

The design of the numbers and letters is depicted at *Figure 11* and it should be mentioned at this stage that the official drawings show smaller heights than those quoted above. As far as can be ascertained from pictorial evidence, the larger variety was the size generally used, the smaller ones being confined to the new Ivatt Class 2 engines of 2—6—0 and 2—6—2T arrangement. These smaller letters and numbers were 12½″ and 10″ respectively. Despite the official designation, the 1946 numbers and letters were, although sans serif, not a particularly good reproduction of Eric Gill's shape and why they were ever referred to as Gill Sans is not known. Some of the early 1946 repaints with the unlined insignia seem to have received a slightly different shape of number (e.g. 'Jubilee' No. 5728 which was given 10″ figures in the middle of the cabside) which may, subsequently have been replaced by the more common shape.

The drawings for the 1946 insignia suggest that transfers were envisaged but all observations confirm that the letters and figures were hand applied. Moreover, reliable contemporary observers state that the extreme outer edge of the straw characters sometimes carried a fine maroon line — in other words, straw and black did not meet. This subtle feature would not register on a black and white photograph and it is doubtful if even the rare colour pictures would reveal the outer maroon edging.

Figure 11
1946 INSIGNIA

A *12½″ letters* Utilised 1946/7. The base colour was the 1946 shade of 'straw' (almost off-white), the inset edging being maroon. The most common height was, in fact, 14″ although no drawings of this version have been located. As far as has been ascertained, they were an exact proportionate enlargement of the version drawn

B *10″ numerals* Utilised 1946/7. Colours as for LMS. The common height was 12″, again believed to have been an exact proportionate enlargement of the version drawn

Notes: 1. Initially (early 1946), these characters were applied *without* the maroon edging

2. Power classification drawings for this style of insignia have not been located. The figures seem to have been identical to the running numbers in style and about 2½″ high.

(all drawn by Arthur Whitehead)

A

B

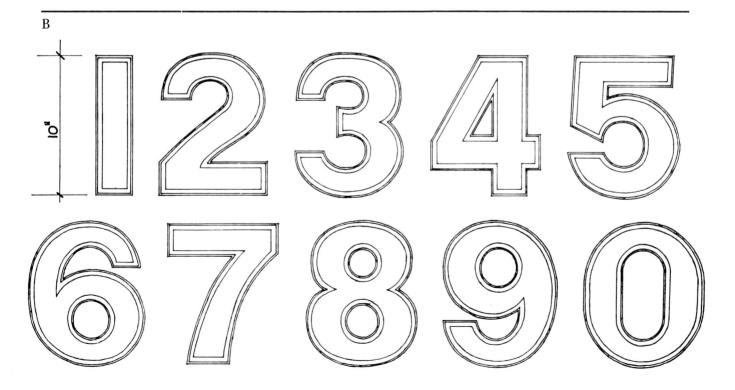

The exact date of introduction of the 1946 livery is not known but it would seem that the first engines with unlined boilers but otherwise correct livery, were emerging around April/May 1946 while the full boiler lining came into use about July 1946. This lined out version of the 1946 livery was, when clean, most attractive. The pity is that it was not more widely applied, being confined exclusively to 4—6—2s, 'Royal Scots', 'Patriots' and 'Jubilees'. Not all the entitled engines received it before the end of 1947 so again it is best to accept only photographic evidence to determine which did carry it.

All other engines were to be turned out in plain black with unlined vermilion buffer beams. No distinction was made between goods and mixed traffic engines and the style of lettering and numbering was the same as for the passenger livery. As with the lined engines, most if not all classes, other than the above mentioned Ivatt engines, received the larger characters and it is again possible that one or two engines received plain unlined insignia but no examples have been located. In some respects, the 1946 livery on an unlined engine is difficult to distinguish on an undated poor quality picture from the 1936 block style and the best guide to its identification, if the lining at the edge of the figures cannot be seen, is the position of the number on the cabside — see below.

One or two interesting points are worth mentioning in connection with the 1946 livery. For the first time since 1883, Midland Red was dropped out of the livery book and became maroon (for coaches too). This change in nomenclature may well account for the oft repeated error of describing LMS engines as maroon when referring to *pre*-war days. It should also be noted that the shade of lettering and lining was changed from yellow to straw — a pale creamy yellow quite unlike the chrome shade of yellow which had been used for almost a decade. As far as is known, this 1946 livery specification was the first occasion on which the colour 'straw' was *officially* used but it was somewhat paler than the pre-1935 lining colour which had often been unofficially called 'straw'. Finally, the position of letters and running numbers was changed, albeit only slightly. On Stanier engines the positions were as recorded above which had the effect of placing the number much nearer to the cab windows, but on the three classes of Ivatt engines introduced during 1946 and 1947, the details of insignia placing were as follows:

> *Ivatt 2—6—2 Tanks Class 2 (12xx):* The smaller insignia were used and the number was midway between the lower edge of the cabside windows and the bottom of the cabside. The centre line of the 'M' was some 9″ ahead of the middle driving wheel axle and the lower edge of the letters was level with the lower edge of the numbers.

> *Ivatt 2—6—0 Locos. Class 2 (64xx):* Smaller insignia, lower edge of running number some 24″ above the lower edge of the cabside, lower edge of letters some 21″ above lower edge of tender side, 'M' over centre axlebox.

> *Ivatt 2—6—0 Locos. Class 4 (3xxx):* Larger insignia, running number in centre of cabside with tender detail as per 64xx Class. Only three were finished in time to receive LMS livery and incredible though it may seem, the first one (3000) did not conform and had the number just below the cab window.

It is not possible to give details of the methods adopted for other engines since so very few received the style apart from the express types. Of the pre-Ivatt designs, only the Stanier Class 5s and Fairburn 2—6—4Ts seem to have been given it at all, although the high up number position which was adopted with this style on tender engines was also used with the earlier scroll and serif insignia. This location for running numbers, mainly on Stanier tender engines had, in fact, been introduced somewhat earlier than the 1946 livery and was first used on the 'Coronation' Class (except for 6230-4). When these engines were painted black, they received scroll type insignia in the same position as the block style markings which the striped streamliners had carried in their earlier days but the general adoption of the higher position does not seem to have been used for other classes until about the end of the war. Several 'Jubilees', e.g. 5737, have come to light with red liveries but high up numbers and these are presumed to be late wartime or early post-war repaints which retained the pre-war livery — i.e. patch painted only.

Plate 325 This picture of Ivatt 2—6—0 Class 2F No. 6400 displays the 1946 Livery Code C27. Although in workshop grey the position of the insignia was unchanged when the locomotives were painted black. *BR LMR*

◄**Plate 324 (Opposite)** This picture of Class 5 4—6—0 No. 4768 depicts the 1946 insignia upon an unlined black locomotive, although in this instance 4768 is in workshop grey. *BR LMR*

Plate 326 This close up of 'Silver Jubilee' Class 5XP 4—6—0 No. 5739 *Ulster* carrying Livery Code B12 clearly shows the method of lining a Stanier 4,000 gallon tender. *BR LMR*

TABLE 10. LMS LOCOMOTIVE LIVERY KEY LIST

Crimson Lake Livery variations

A1	Pre-1928 standard,	18" figures,	LMS Coat of Arms
A2	"	"	Individual Letters 'LMS'
A3	"	14" figures,	LMS Coat of Arms
A4	"	"	Individual Letters 'LMS'
A5	Post-1927 standard,	Gold/Black insignia,	10" numerals
A6	"	"	12" "
A7	"	"	14" " (Midland pattern)
A8	"	Straw/Black insignia,	10" "
A9	"	"	12" "
A10	"	"	14" " (Standard pattern)
A11	"	Gold/Red insignia	12"
A12	"	"	1936 pattern
A13	"	Yellow/Red insignia	10" numerals
A14	"	"	12" "
A15	"	"	14" " (Midland pattern)

Lined Black Livery variations

B1	Lined Black livery, Horwich/St Rollox style, 18" Midland figures		
B2	Post-1927 standard,	Gold/Red insignia,	10" numerals
B3	"	"	12" "
B4	"	"	14" " (Midland pattern)
B5	"	Gold/Black insignia	10" "
B6	"	"	12" "
B7	"	"	14" " (Midland pattern)
B8	"	Yellow/Red insignia	10" "
B9	"	"	12" "
B10	"	"	14" " (Midland pattern)
B11	"	Gold/Red insignia	1936 pattern
B12	1946 standard livery — full lining style		
B13	"	simpler original lining style	

Plain Black Livery variations

C1	Pre-1928 standard,	18" figures,	Standard cab/bunker panel
C2	"	"	Round cornered cab/bunker panel
C3	"	"	Individual Letters 'LMS'
C4	"	14" figures,	Standard cab/bunker panel
C5	"	"	Round cornered cab/bunker panel
C6	"	"	Individual Letters 'LMS'
C7	Crewe 'hybrid' style,	18" figures,	LMS Coat of Arms
C8	"	14" "	(Midland pattern), LMS Coat of Arms
C9	"	14" "	(Standard pattern — straw), LMS Coat of Arms
C10	"	18" "	Individual Letters 'LMS'
C11	"	14" "	(Midland pattern), Individual Letters 'LMS'
C12	"	14" "	(Standard pattern), Individual Letters 'LMS'
C13	Post-1927 standard	Gold/Black insignia,	10" numerals
C14	"	"	12" "
C15	"	"	14" " (Midland pattern)
C16	"	Plain Straw insignia,	10" "
C17	"	"	12" "
C18	"	"	14" " (Standard pattern)
C19	"	Gold/Red insignia,	1936 pattern
C20	"	Gold/Black insignia,	"
C21	"	Yellow/Red insignia,	10" numerals
C22	"	"	12" "
C23	"	"	14" " (Midland pattern)
C24	"	Plain Yellow insignia,	10" numerals
C25	"	"	12" "
C26	"	"	14" " (Midland pattern)
C27	1946 standard insignia — smaller size		
C28	"	— larger size	

Footnote   *The above key list should adequately define the vast majority of liveries applied during LMS days with the exception of letter spacing in the post-1927 period. This will be specified in the individual class chapters, as will all known variations not tabulated above.*

Chapter 12   Variations from the Standard Liveries

During 1923-47, certain LMS engines ran in a variety of miscellaneous and non-standard liveries. Some of these were confined to one particular works but others affected the whole company. In analysing these variations, some repetition of ground covered elsewhere is inevitable but this seems preferable to covering the pages with a series of cross-references. For convenience, the sundry variations have been grouped under individual headings.

EARLY POST-GROUPING ACTIVITIES

Once chosen, the 1923-7 livery quickly became very widespread and, because of its relatively short life, it did not develop anything like the number of variations which its successor was to do. It undoubtedly played a major part in the 'Midlandisation' of the LMS and, because of its widespread application, many engines carried it well into the 1930s before being repainted. Some engines, indeed, carried it until the Second World War and not a few engines were noted in Scotland in the style during 1938/9. Derby works is reported to have put it onto some repainted engines during 1938. The latest known date of an engine running in this livery which has been personally verified is January 1944 (ex-CR 0–6–0T No. 16253).

The 1923-7 livery was perpetuated in modified form on some classes of tank engines during the 1930s, particularly by Crewe, St Rollox and Horwich but in order to maintain a reasonably chronological treatment, these will be considered later in the chapter.

The main non-standard styles during the period of the 1923 livery were, of course, to be seen during the immediate post-grouping years and it is a great pity that more details have not survived. In the survey which follows, no guarantee can be given that the information is complete but it is reasonably comprehensive and, hopefully, will prove of interest.

Midland Division (Ex-MR, N. Staffs., SMJ; Number series 1-4999)

The bulk of engines in the Midland Division retained their pre-group numbers and being of Midland origin, their liveries too. There being less need to repaint ex-MR engines, it is conceivable that, pro rata, fewer of them received *new* LMS liveries than the other divisions. However, there are a few aspects worth noting.

Initially, newly painted ex-MR engines were turned out without 'MR' on the buffer beams and with no Company markings at all — e.g. 2–4–0 No. 76. Very few seem to have been given the small individual letters 'LMS' and most of them probably ran in anonymous form until the introduction of the Coat of Arms and the red panel. This is not really surprising since many types of ex-MR engines (outside framed 2–4–0s, 0–6–0s, all 0–4–0Ts, 0–4–4Ts and 0–6–0Ts) ran without the Coat of Arms in MR days. One interesting batch of engines, however, was that of 10 Tilbury 4–4–2 tanks (2110-19), the first eight of which were initially turned out with 'MR' on the buffer beams and the Midland Coat of Arms on the cab end of the tanks — but in 1923! Only 2118/19 of this batch were lettered 'LMS' from new.

It would further seem that on most of the ex-MR 4–4–0 engines, Derby continued to paint the engine side-frames in red and line the edges in black/yellow for a few years after grouping. This was a pure MR practice and is not thought to have been applied to any other classes of engine or in any other division. Evidence is a little fragmentary and it is not known even if the practice was universally employed at Derby during this period (c. 1923-6).

Derby also continued the ex-MR practice of lining out the upper edge of the spectacle plates of many red engines during this same few years after grouping. This took the form of continuing the black/yellow line at the upper edge of the cabside round onto the spectacle plate without a break, continuing the lines across the engine to the other cabside. Generalisation is not possible but it is believed to have been a technique confined to those engines with the older type of Johnson cab (e.g. the original Johnson 4–4–0, all 2–4–0 and most 4–2–2 engines, most 0–4–4Ts). Engines with the later Johnson cabs (e.g. the 'Belpaires') and 4–4–0s with Deeley cabs generally had plain cab fronts as did most of the 0–6–4Ts, although the odd exception to this cannot be ruled out.

It is also reliably reported that some of the MR and early Midland Division black engines were a 'grey' black rather than the 'blackberry' black of the LNWR and did not have a full gloss finish. If not cleaned, this paint went absolutely matt and looked dark grey. If cleaned with oil it apparently looked rather like an ordinary black engine which had lost its shine. The practice seems to have been confined to Derby.

The ex-North Staffordshire engines, when renumbered into the Midland Division series, were, apparently, renumbered and in many cases repainted quite quickly. Before the standard styles were settled, Stoke works repainted engines using the small and rather florid style of N. Staffs. Scroll numeral in the N. Staffs. position with the engine unlined and this treatment was also applied to some ex-LNWR engines which were shopped at Stoke (e.g. 0–8–0 No. 9001). The two Leek and Manifold engines also had an interesting history after grouping. The LMS gave them both the fully lined out crimson livery with red backgrounds to name, number and builder's plates. No. 1 *E.R. Calthrop* kept the builder's plate on the bunker and had no Coat of Arms, while No. 2, *J.B. Earle* had the LMS Coat of Arms but no builder's plate. At the end of the 1920s, both became unlined black (still with red plates) but No. 2's builder's plate was not restored. Neither engine was fitted with MR style smokebox numberplates and all the other plates continued to carry the original Company name.

Plate 327 Ex-NSR 0–6–0 No. 2320 displays a small, rather florid style of transfer used in 1923 before Midland style transfers became available at Stoke. *Real Photographs*

Plate 329 Ex-LNWR 2–4–2T ▶ No. 6710 in LNWR black, the only lining visible is on the buffer beam. The original LNWR numberplate has been removed and the new LMS number has been stencilled in its place.
Real Photographs

The ex-N. Staffs. engines which received the full crimson livery were as follows: 0–4–4Ts, 2–4–2Ts, 0–6–4Ts, 4–4–2Ts, 2–4–0Ts, 4–4–0s (only one of the 4–4–0s is confirmed as ever becoming black and that was not until after it had been renumbered 5413 at a later date).

Western Division (Ex-LNWR, Wirral: Number series 5000-9999)

The Western Division was not particularly quick off the mark with repainting or renumbering, probably due to the difficulties of the tender numbering system and the general anti-Derby feeling at the time (see p. 207) and in consequence, many ex-LNWR engines remained unaltered for some time.

Immediately after grouping, several new engines (and repaints) were given the full LNWR lined out livery with block letters 'LMS' on the tank sides, about the same height as the LNWR numberplate which was retained. The letters 'LMS' were probably in gold leaf and were red shaded. Confirmed examples include the following: 4–6–2Ts Nos. 2384 (later 6995) and 316 (6988); 4–4–2Ts Nos. 1572 (later 6805) and 1305 (6784); 0–8–4Ts Nos. 380 (7930) and 739 (7937).

These latter 0–8–4T engines were particularly interesting as being the last new design of LNWR engine although not built until after 1922. Although not confirmed photographically, another four were scheduled to have the above livery

Plate 328 The largest LNWR passenger tanks were the 4–6–2Ts, sometimes referred to as 'Prince of Wales' tanks, and this picture of LNWR No. 316 is interesting in that it has full LNWR livery except for a non-standard 'LMS' on the tank sides. No. 316 later became LMS No. 6988. *Real Photographs*

(LNWR Nos. 256, 731, 1908, 1956) but the last two were turned out without finishing coat. These four became LMS 7935-6/8-9 respectively. At the turn of 1923/4, a batch of six more (LMS Nos. 7943-8) were given the full crimson livery, with small letters 'LMS' rather than the Coat of Arms and were sent to Abergavenny. Finally, in early 1924, No. 7957 was reported as appearing in white livery, details unknown, with wording to the effect that it was the 5,639th engine to be built at Crewe!

Of the other LNWR classes, the first red engine of all was 'Claughton' No. 5971 (ex-2511 *Croxteth*) with small letters 'LMS' on the cabside, closely followed by two 'Precursors' 5290 and 5309 (ex-310 and 2578) and 'Jumbo' 2—4—0 No. 5050 (ex-860). However, red engines were not very common during the first year or two and it was not until the Spring of 1924 that the first ex-LNWR engine was turned out in the correct red livery with the Coat of Arms (4—6—2T No. 6956 — ex-217). The pioneer 'Prince of Wales' Class 4—6—0 No. 5600 (ex-819) was also an early correct style red repaint and ran for a short time in late 1924 with its new number but no nameplates. This was because the name had been applied (temporarily) to the new 5845. It is thought that new plates were made for 5845 on this occasion. In the meantime, several passenger engines had been turned out in unlined black including 'Jumbos' 5039, 5080 and 5108.

It was about this time (mid 1924) that most repainting and renumbering of ex-LNWR engines stopped at Crewe 'for purely domestic reasons' and it was not until early 1926 that general renumbering started again after a particularly acrimonious period of Crewe/Derby relationships which, apparently, had spread to Euston itself. In fairness to Crewe, however, it should be pointed out that the works itself was being reconstructed during this period and engines repaired there were not repainted. It appears that the advent of the LMS standard Compounds on the Western Division was basically responsible for a return to renumbering since these engines had been given numbers which clashed with the 'native' stock. Instructions to sheds to renumber ex-LNWR engines as soon as possible were sent out and this was effected by removing the cast numberplates and painting the new number in the vacant spaces. This reversion to Ramsbottom practice was generally done in small yellow figures and confirmed examples are 'Claughtons' 5901 and 5906 (ex-1161 and 1159), 'Precursors' 5194, 5199 and 5200 (ex-1117, 1104 and 1111) and 2—4—2T No. 6664 (ex-1150).

Once the conflict with the Compound numbering had been resolved, renumbering seems to have continued in earnest but the number of red engines only slowly increased, considerable numbers of tender engines being simply given plain black finish, often with cabside Coat of Arms and smokebox numberplates but without tender numerals. Tank engines were also frequently given plain black finish with the Coat of Arms and large tank side numbers. These black engines often

Plates 330 & 331 The problem when carrying the locomotive number on the tender and smokebox door and the need to exchange tenders is shown in **Plate 330** and one attempt to resolve this was made when 'Prince of Wales' Class 4–6–0 No. 5788 was equipped with detachable numberplates on the tenderside. The authors believe this was the only locomotive so equipped in this style. Livery Code is basically A2. **Plate 331** shows a red locomotive, ex-LNWR 'Precursor' No. 5290 *Achilles* coupled to a black tender from an 0–8–0, No. 9229.

Both Real Photographs

retained their LNWR style buffer beam lining which had black edging and a thin black line in rectangular form with rounded corners set between the buffers, together with black ends to the buffer shanks. This latter feature was, incidentally, a standard Crewe practice for all steam locomotives right up to the late steam days of BR, Crewe being of the opinion that black ends to the buffer shanks looked neater and showed the grease from the buffer less than an all red shank would do. Reverting to the plain black livery of the middle twenties, it is conceivable that this style was the forerunner of the Crewe hybrid livery (p. 214), which continued for many engines after the introduction of the 1928 numerals.

Such was the confusion that, as one correspondent put it: '. . . when some goods engines appeared with their numbers on the cabside towards the end of 1927, it did not seem particularly remarkable . . .' In spite of all this delay, full LNWR livery *as such* was causing comment by the time the 1928 livery was announced and probably one of the last engines to retain it with full lining was 2–4–0 No. 862 *Balmoral* (in August 1928).

The Wirral stock seems to have escaped much comment in the contemporary press and the only well recorded example is 2–4–2T No. 6762 which was, in fact an LYR design of engine and received the full red livery with Coat of Arms, early in 1924. It is fairly certain that the only two other ex-Wirral engines to receive LMS numbers were 2–4–2T No. 6761 and 0–4–4T No. 6776, although there may have been others.

Central Division (Ex-LYR, Furness M&C, C&W; Number series 10000-12999)

There does not seem to have been as strong a resistance to the new livery in the Central Division as there was at Crewe and progress in renumbering and repainting was steady if not spectacular. There is, however, evidence that there was a slight shortage of big passenger engine power on the old LYR section and many engines were put in service with the new numbers but incorrect livery.

As at Crewe there were one or two hybrids and 4–6–0s Nos. 1659-64 when new were given LYR type numberplates (lettered 'LNWR') with 'LM&SR' on the tender in, according to Eric Mason, 'large and ugly yellow letters'. The engines themselves were in battleship grey. A further 19 Hughes 4–6–0s were put in service in dull black at the end of 1924 with

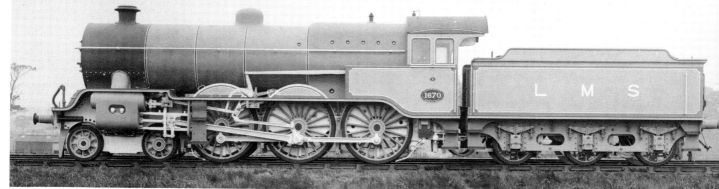

Plate 332 This picture of an ex-LYR 4—6—0 No. 1670, which became LMS 10441 was taken early in 1923 and shows LYR 'works grey livery' with a block style 'LMS' on the tender. There is no evidence to suggest that any locomotives ever ran in this condition. *NRM*

Plate 333 This view of ex-LYR 4—6—0 No. 10473 shows the small stencilled number used by the Central Division prior to the adoption of the standard Midland styles. *NRM*

small yellow numerals just below the cab window (10455-73). This treatment was, presumably, to get them in service quickly and is believed to have been scheduled for the whole batch of 20 engines which were built (i.e. including 10474). However, this last engine was finished in the red livery, possibly because it was scheduled to and did appear at the Stockton and Darlington Centenary in July 1925. Previous to this, very few Hughes 4—6—0s had appeared in red, the only confirmed example being 10447 (with cabside letters) which was the first *new* Hughes 4—6—0 to be red and was turned out thus in late 1923, being made the subject of a colour plate illustrating the correct LMS passenger livery. Other than this and 10474, probably one of the first of the true LYR 4—6—0s (i.e. built pre-1923) to get the red livery was 10426 (late 1924/early 1925).

The Hughes 4—6—4Ts were also put in service during the first two years after grouping but only 11114 was red at the end of 1924 probably because it was on exhibition at Wembley. No. 11111 later became red but many ran in black all the time, with large 18" numbers and no company markings. One or two Aspinall 4—4—2s also ran in black livery rather than red and of these 10302 is known to have had the Coat of Arms and 14" tender numerals. One of the first, if not *the* first LYR engine to get a red livery was 4—4—0 No. 10163 which received the livery with cabside letters in mid 1923.

The Furness Section seemed to have most of the repainting and renumbering completed by the end of 1924, and amongst the earlier examples were 0—6—0s Nos. 12480 (previously No. 3), 12505 (24), the former, oddly, in red livery and 4—4—0 No. 10185 (ex-130) in red, all these being late 1923/early 1924. Of the smaller companies, little evidence has survived but two Maryport and Carlisle 0—4—2s were given red livery with 14" tender numbers (10011 and 10013) and two Cleator and Workington Peckett 0—6—0STs (11564 and 11566) were given the correct freight livery with 14" numbers on the saddle, 11564 having the individual letters 'LMS' rather than the correct red panel.

Plate 334 Some locomotives were incorrectly numbered but this is the only example known to the authors of a locomotive with a missing number, which was '6'. No. 17906 was an ex-CR 4—6—0 of the McIntosh '179' Class.   *Photomatic*

Northern Division (CR, GSWR & HR; Number series 14000 upwards)

All contemporary observers are agreed that the Scottish constituents were particularly speedy in using the new livery. However, it does seem that, for the most part, all the Scottish works waited until the livery style was settled at the end of 1923 before starting to use it and it has been found possible to confirm only one example of a Scottish engine carrying individual cabside letters of the late 1923 style (ex-GSWR 4—6—4T No. 15402), although there may have been a few more. However, in early 1924, engines and carriages were reported as still being turned out of Lochgorm painted green and lettered 'Highland Railway' and examples were noted in this northern outpost of ex-MR stock, newly lettered 'LMS' carrying a board on the end reading 'On loan to the Highland Railway'!

However, once the repainting started, the Scottish works followed the book very closely, although seeming to make little use of 14″ figures even on small engines; and by 1927, very little evidence was to be seen of pre-group livery north of the border. A possible explanation of this remarkable consistency in Scotland might be the reported keenness of the Northern Division to get things right. It is reported that the first red *Perth* repaint (ex-CR 959 — LMS 14803) was given fully lined boiler bands by mistake and was almost immediately repainted properly — the error having caused something of a furore! This Division seemed slightly more prone to shop mixed traffic engines in black than was the case in England and the 'Jones Goods' and certain ex-CR 4—6—0s never received red livery which might just have been permissible for them, especially since one or two 'Jones Goods' later received the post-1927 intermediate livery.

Many Scottish passenger classes had names painted on the splasher, particularly HR engines, but after grouping, this practice was discontinued on the ex-CR classes. Thus the famous *Cardean* lost its name when it became red.

The ex-HR engines continued to be named and although evidence is not very good as to the colour of the characters, they are believed to have received painted names in the same colour scheme as the locomotive insignia (i.e. gold with black shading before 1928 and gold with red shading after 1927). Pale yellow cannot, however, be ruled out as a base colour — even with shading. The name was generally painted in a curve to match the driving wheel splasher (or straight in the case of the ex-HR 'Castles' and 'Clans') and was usually rendered in small serif style characters (c. 3-4″ high). There were one or two exceptions (e.g. *Loch Naver*) and a few engines received sans serif names. Generalisation is not possible and photographic evidence is the only conclusive answer to each individual named engine.

Of those engines which retained full pre-group livery, amongst the longest lasting were probably ex-CR 4—4—0T No. 7, still blue in August 1928 and ex-HR 'Castle' No. 43, still in green in December 1928. Another interesting oddity is that after the 1927/8 livery change, 4—4—0 No. 14437 was newly shopped in red after at least one of its sisters had been given the new lined black livery, this being in June 1928. Several Scottish engines remained red long after their English counterparts had succumbed to the black livery and ex-HR 4—4—0s 14380 and 14390 were still red in 1937. 'Jones Goods' No. 17920 was also interesting in retaining a genuine pre-1928 livery (i.e. not a 1930s repaint) for 10 years or more, being withdrawn in 1937, still carrying the style; while perhaps the oddest one of all was another 'Jones Goods', 17926, which returned from overhaul in 1938 with its wheels painted green, lined out in white, presumably off the preserved HR 103! However, this is rather outside the immediate post-group period.

EARLY USE OF THE 1928 LIVERY

The exact date when the 1923 style of livery was abandoned is somewhat conjectural. The changed style seems to have arrived without any great flourish but, as far as can be ascertained, it probably originated in October 1927 with a drawing in the paintshop at Derby works showing engines with 'LMS' on tender or tank side and numbers on cab or bunker.

The change took place at an interesting period of LMS locomotive history when the Fowler 2—6—4 tanks were first being put into service and these engines were probably the first complete class to receive the style, No. 2300 entering traffic in December 1927. The change took place during the building of the vast army of Class 4Fs and with these engines, 4435 was probably the last example to receive the early style of livery. Crewe was also quick off the mark with the 'Crab' 2—6—0s. The first 100 of these were mostly in red livery and it is generally understood that the change in insignia took place after 13097, the last two certainly having the new style (13098/9). It is also probable that some of these engines were given the new style without a repaint, thus remaining red and one certain example is 13036.

The rather 'hit or miss' nature of the early phase of this livery, together with its changed basic style, caused a certain amount of caustic comment in the contemporary press:

> The new colouring of the LM&S (passenger engines) is anything but pleasing. For many years it was characteristic of the MR to have a passenger train locomotive and carriages painted to match and now to see smart red trains hauled by dull black engines is not up to popular standards.
>
> The numbers are being taken off as fast as they can, whether repainted or not . . . but whether the engines have had their numbers painted in or not, the tenders are being changed about anyhow so that the large number on the tender is no longer an indication of the engine number. So far, they do not appear to have transfers so that there is considerable variety in the size and pattern of the numbers painted on the engines.
>
> *Locomotive Magazine 1928*

Plate 335 This picture of a Highland 4—6—0 'Castle' Class No. 14687 *Brahan Castle* illustrates a crimson lake locomotive carrying the 1928 insignia style, Livery Code A5 or A8. In the post-1928 period this class should have been painted black with red lining. *BR LMR*

Plate 336 The first members of the Fowler 2—6—4Ts were classified 3 and painted in crimson lake. This picture of No. 2300 in Livery Code A5 displays their early condition. *BR LMR*

Plate 337 Ex-LNWR 'Claughton' Class 4—6—0 No. 5923
Sir Guy Calthrop in black, Livery Code C16 plus LNWR
lining on the tender.   *Stephen Collection – NRM*

Plate 338 Ex-SDJR locomotives in blue with hand-painted
LMS letters and numbers in a 'Highbridge style', locally
painted following the absorption of the SDJR in 1930.
H.C. Casserley

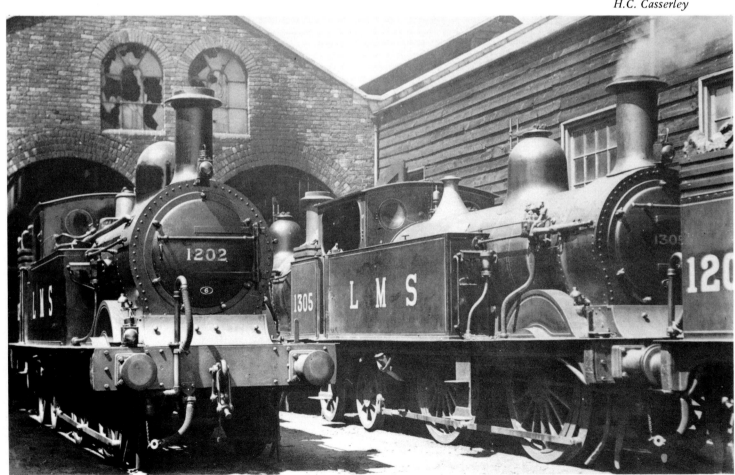

However, as has been noted, even after transfers were available, there were still three sizes, two styles and the many colour schemes to contend with so maybe the complaints continued. One could not always be sure that the numbers and letters were the same colour.

It was, of course, the passenger engines which underwent the most striking change in appearance and there was considerable confusion at first as to which classes should remain red. On 7th February, 1928, the only classes mentioned by the CME as continuing red were 'Royal Scots', 'Claughtons', Hughes 4—6—0, 'Prince of Wales' 4—6—0 and Compound 4—4—0. This was later amended on 25th February to refer to *all* passenger engines again, but a P.S. on the letter that went to Beames (Crewe works) indicated that only 'Claughtons' and 'Prince of Wales' engines were to be done. A month later, the original decision of 7th February was reinstated and finally in late December 1928, the decision was made to paint the 'Prince of Wales' Class black after all.

Nevertheless, quite a number of interesting engines did manage to run for a while in the post-1927 red livery which was not scheduled for them. The red 'Crabs' have already been noted above but equally interesting were the first Fowler Class 4P 2—6—4 tank engines. The first twelve of these were given the red livery and of the next 13 built, one or two more also emerged in this style, the remainder being given the new lined black livery. Just how many years the red livery lasted on these few engines, or the 'Crabs' for that matter, is not known but three to five years would be a reasonable assumption. 2—6—4T No. 2313 was also interesting in being named *The Prince* in honour of a visit to Derby by HRH the Prince of Wales in 1928 and ran like this in service for some time. This engine was, however, one of the black ones and only had the name painted on, so lost its unique claim to fame at the first full repaint. Incidentally, these first 25 Fowler tanks all received small 10″ numbers (probably handpainted) when new, unlike the majority of the class which received 14″ Midland pattern numerals.

The 2—6—4Ts and 'Crabs' are, perhaps, the best-known examples of non-entitled red engines, but a few others also slipped through the net. According to one contemporary source, Derby as well as Crewe was quick off the mark after the change of style and many districts saw a complete change over of number position within a few weeks of the announcement. In order to do this, a considerable amount of local repainting must have been resorted to, no doubt with very peculiar results. Space precludes all examples but among the more interesting of them were Tilbury tanks Nos. 2147 and 2113 which were given red livery with handpainted numbers, the latter with a round topped '3' (!), while 0—4—4 tank 1415 was likewise treated and went to Skipton. How long the 4—4—2 tanks kept the red is not known but 1415 was repainted again in lined black only a few weeks later. 2—4—0 No. 208 had a similar history to 1415 while some other 2—4—0s (84/102/108/250) were also given the new red livery along with Class 2P 4—4—0 No. 545.

Details of the first repaints to the lined black livery from the red, other than new construction, are somewhat more fragmentary but the first *repainted* engines out of Derby, possibly the first on the system, were 2—4—0 No. 237 and 4—4—0s Nos. 562 (Class 2P) and 731 (Class 3P). On the Western Division where, as stated, there had been a considerable amount of lethargy in using the 1923 livery, it was by no means unusual to see the new type insignia used with the old LNWR lining during these early years and several passenger types were left black with LNWR tender lining and the LMS insignia hand painted in the erecting shop. Presumably this was in order to get the engines in service quickly without a full repaint and perhaps a last defiant fling by Crewe. Space again precludes mention of all, but interesting examples are 'Claughton' No. 5953 and 'George the Fifth' No. 5343.

Apart from special liveries, there are one or two other matters worthy of brief mention. Firstly it should be recorded that certain engines, by virtue of their configuration, could not be liveried in the usual way. Chief among the variants were the Garratts which carried the 14″ 'LMS' very closely spaced on the cabside and had two sets of running numbers, one at each end. Some ex-N. Staffs and North London tank engines were given post-1928 numerals in the pre-1928 position, often without company markings at all.

To list here all the oddities would merely duplicate information given elsewhere but mention ought to be made of the fact that from late 1939 onwards, engines with chimneys and/or domes too tall to allow them to pass onto the Northern Division, were painted with a 3″ diameter blue disc on the cabside. The classes concerned were LMS & MR Class 2P 4—4—0, Class 4P Compound 4—4—0, Class 4F 0—6—0. There were a few English and Welsh lines also included in this prohibition — Cockermouth, Keswick & Penrith; Cleator & Workington; Port Penrhyn; Dyserth Branch and Five Ways Branch (Conduit Jct. — Coppice Colliery).

ABSORPTION OF THE SOMERSET AND DORSET LOCOMOTIVES

As is well known, the S&D stock was absorbed by the LMS in 1930 and the locomotives seem to have been as hurriedly repainted with their new numbers as was the case with the whole stock in 1928. Again this was, for the most part, done at the sheds and in the case of the S&D took the form of a very neat handpainted numeral of a style rather like the new standard pattern but not quite the same. It was executed in yellow and varied in height according to the class of engine involved.

With these conversions, there was, initially, no new smokebox numberplate for the engines and they were, accordingly, given very neat painted smokebox numbers, some 4-5″ high in the same position as the plate would have been placed. The most interesting facet of the conversion was, however, the retention for a while by some of the engines, of the S&D lined blue livery with LMS insignia. It is not known how long they lasted in this form, or if all the blue engines ran like this but two immaculate 0—4—4Ts were so recorded, shortly after the take-over. These were 1202 and 1305. These, and other similarly liveried engines of different types are dealt with in later chapters.

EFFECTS OF THE 1936 VARIATION IN INSIGNIA

The introduction, in February 1936, of the non-serif style of insignia described on page 191, was to be the prelude to one of the more confusing periods of livery variation on the LMS system. As far as can be ascertained, the prototype for the style was LMS compound 4—4—0 No. 1094 and, oddly enough, it seems to have been the only engine of its class to be thus lettered.

This style of insignia was readily identifiable but was not widely used by comparison with other styles. Apart from a few repainted engines, it seems to have been confined mainly to new construction by outside contractors or by Crewe and Derby works. Of the types which initially received it, the Class 5s were probably the most numerous and the 1936 style was given to the whole of the Armstrong Whitworth batch of engines between 5225 and 5451. It was also applied to outside built Class 8Fs and 2—6—4Ts while Crewe put it on a batch of 'Jubilees' and Derby on another batch of 2—6—4Ts.

Although hardly experimental, the change was not deemed entirely satisfactory and did not last long. Derby does not seem to have been very impressed by it and as far as is known, neither Horwich nor St Rollox used it at all. Apparently in March 1936, the Northern Division expressed some difficulty with the style and a letter to H.G. Ivatt at St Rollox in that month implied that 10″ letters with 8″ numbers would be supplied in lieu. Presumably, some of the Scottish engines could not be fitted with the larger insignia, but no pictures have been located of these smaller symbols (although drawings of them do exist) and according to first hand evidence, the sans serif style was never used at all in Scotland, except by contractors building new locomotives.

Of the Company works which *did* use the 1936 style (probably only Crewe and Derby), Crewe may have employed it to a greater extent but not extensively. Contemporary evidence would suggest that the numbers were not as legible to the signalmen as were the older ones and it is known that Derby experimented in 1937 with variations in size and spacing to try and improve matters. This was clearly not a success for in January 1938, there was an official statement to the effect that reversion to the old type scroll and serif face was to be made. Supplies of the block transfers were to be used up but it is believed that because of their illegibility, many of them were in fact destroyed since little actual use seems to have been made of them after the reinstatement of the older pattern. Although all official sources refer to the block insignia as transfers, one observer at Crewe, not substantiated by Derby, claims that they were handpainted at the former works, but this has not been confirmed.

Coincident with the introduction of the 1936 block style, a change was also made to a similar style of number for the smokebox numberplates which had, hitherto, always been of standard Midland pattern. It is thought that this change may have been officially for new locomotives only but since several of the older engines also received them, they may have been employed whenever a new smokebox plate was needed. Even so, one can only conclude that a lot of new plates seem to have been needed on old engines if this was the explanation. The shape of these numbers is given at *Figure 7* but it has been quite impossible to say which engines carried them because, at a later date, reversion was made to the older type.

INDIVIDUAL WORKS VARIATION

Crewe Works

Prior to 1936, Crewe seems to have steadfastly refused to have much to do with the Midland pattern of numeral once the 1928 standard range was devised. Moreover, pictorial evidence tends to indicate that this works was more prone to disregard the official edicts from Derby than were others. Most of the unorthodox styles seem to have been given to ex-LNWR engines and one might be forgiven for assuming that while Crewe was quite willing to paint standard classes in the correct style, its beloved 'Premier Line' motive power deserved somewhat more individualistic treatment!

The most noticeable of these variations was a sort of hybrid pre/post-1928 style in which 14″ high *1928 pattern* numerals were applied in unshaded form to the side tanks of black tank engines which were otherwise unlined and carried the circular Coat of Arms on the bunker side. This practice seems to have been confined to passenger tank engines and considerable numbers of such classes as the 'Watford' 0—6—2Ts and the 2—4—2Ts were thus liveried. Some sources refer to these as left-over transfers from before 1928 but this does not stand up to close investigation when one considers that not only were these numbers not designed until 1928, but many of the engines concerned were *red* before that date*. As well as using this unique hybrid livery, Crewe was also prone to outshop many engines entitled to the red lining in plain black, while vast numbers of ex-LNWR goods engines were turned out with unshaded numerals, again of 14″ 1928 pattern. The correct colour of these numerals is in some doubt and although the whole question of colour is covered later this seems to be the best place to discuss this particular matter.

Sifting the available evidence, it appears that after a few months of using 10″ numerals, probably hand painted, Crewe made almost exclusive use of 14″ standard numerals for ex-LNWR engines. In fact, this variation was a Crewe speciality. Transfers of standard pattern were never supplied in the 14″ height and Crewe states that this variation of insignia was always applied by hand resulting from the policy of doing the bulk of non-passenger engine painting (except new engines) in the erecting shop. The method of application of the insignia was to make stencils of the number and letter patterns and to pounce through these with french chalk to leave an outline on the engine which was then hand painted, following this chalk outline. Because of this, the numbers were rendered in paint and not gold leaf, and were, as far as can be ascertained, the only examples of yellow lettering and numbering adopted by the LMS *as a matter of policy* until the more widespread

*Occasionally, Crewe did use left-over pre-1928 transfers of 18″ height with the 'hybrid' livery on such classes as the 4—4—2Ts and the 4—6—2Ts; but these were far less common than the 14″ standard pattern numerals.

Plate 339 Ex-LNWR 0−6−2T 2P No. 6869 in the Crewe hybrid style, Livery Code C9.   *Authors' Collection*

Plate 340 Ex-LNWR 'Precursor' Class 4−4−2T No. 6781 carries a further example of the Crewe hybrid style, Livery Code C7. Photographed at Watford in March, 1932.   *Photomatic*

Plate 341 Ex-NSR 0−6−0T No. 1597 depicts another example of the Crewe hybrid style, Livery Code C12; compare with Plates 339 and 340.
   L. Hanson

use of yellow insignia towards the time of World War II. The technique of applying the number would also explain the extreme regularity of shape which could have led them to be taken for transfers.

After considerable questioning at the works concerned, it appears that Crewe had instructions to paint these 14″ numerals in a shade as near as possible to gold leaf — i.e. to match the passenger engine transfers. This was done by using the pale yellow paint supplied for lining out red engines. This, after a few months in service would look very similar to weathered gold transfers and hence cause the confusion. Crewe also insist that on occasions when these 14″ standard numerals were used in black *shaded* form (e.g. on some 'Claughtons' and the odd 'Royal Scot' in the early thirties), they were also painted on in the pale yellow lining colour and not in gold. This handpainting technique was also used at Crewe on plain black engines when smaller number sizes were used (e.g. standard class 4Fs).

Why Crewe devised its own 14″ variation when this size of numeral was already available in Midland style is not known. However, from discussions at this works one gathers that the preferred method of lettering and numbering was hand painting. By contrast with Derby works, which even in 1965 was directly at variance with Crewe in this respect (!), Crewe maintains that it was quicker to paint numbers than to use transfers. This being so and the general policy being to use 14″ numbers where they would fit the engine, one can only presume that Crewe took the drawings of the 10″ and 12″ 1928 numbers and enlarged them for the 14″ stencils to be made, this probably seeming more logical than to use the existing 14″ Midland pattern as a guide. This would also fit in with the previously recorded statement that Crewe did not use the transfer method for the 1936 block style either. It seems not without significance that, after the 1936 block style was abandoned, many references make great play of the fact that Crewe began to use the 'new style' — i.e. yellow shaded red — scroll numbers in *transfer* form, the implication being that this form of applying insignia had not, hitherto, been wide-spread there. Certainly it is from this time that one begins to notice a great increase in the number of ex-LNWR engines, especially the lined black ones, carrying red shaded 14″ Midland type numbers.

Horwich and St Rollox Works

Reference is made in many sources to non standard practices at the above two works but this does not seem to have been as widespread as the policies at Crewe. Curiously, however, each was identified by contemporary observers. The style at each works took the form of the retention of the pre-1928 numerals on the tank side, usually the 18″ variety, but with the 'LMS' in post-1928 letters on the bunker. This method of livery treatment arose from a query by St Rollox in April 1931 asking what should be done with the obsolete 18″ numerals. The official answer was that they were to be used up by placing them on the tanks of tank engines with the 14″ initials 'LMS' on the bunker. Instructions were also given that the 18″ figures which were, of course, black shaded must not be altered to red shaded. This instruction went from E.J.H. Lemon to Derby, St Rollox and Horwich but only the last two seem to have been affected by it, Derby presumably having no 18″ stocks left.

As far as is known, at Horwich the style seems to have been confined to the 2—4—2 tanks of LYR origin more than any other class. It was most often used as a substitute for the correct 1928 mixed traffic livery and some examples have come to light which clearly show red lining present with the style. It may have been used on the occasional non-entitled red engine as well.

At St Rollox, it seems again to have been mainly confined to ex-CR tank engines although it is known to have also been used on a few ex-GSWR tanks as well but whether these latter were shopped at St Rollox or the style was also used at Kilmarnock is not certain. As far as is known, it was never used for standard engines either in England or Scotland, except for the odd Class 3F 0—6—0T.

Thanks to the kindness of Mr Duncan Burton of Edinburgh, it has been possible to obtain fairly comprehensive details of this livery at St Rollox and the following paragraph is based on his observations at that time.

The 18″ numbers were used in conjunction with unshaded gold 'LMS' tender letters on passenger tank engines while some of the freight tanks were given the pre-1928 cabside panel to use up. Passenger tanks were lined out in red (as were, of course some of the Horwich 2—4—2Ts). The ex-CR 4—4—0Ts were also given a lined black livery with 18″ tank side numbers but only had room for the Coat of Arms on the bunker instead of the 14″ gold 'LMS'.

The number of confirmed examples of the use of this style of painting is quite considerable and details will be found in the appropriate class chapters.

WARTIME PRACTICES

From 1939 onwards, the locomotives of the LMS gradually assumed a more sombre appearance as more and more were repainted in unrelieved black. During the first months of the war, an attempt was made to continue to paint the more important engines in the correct fashion but in June 1940, a decision was made that in the event of a complete repaint being necessary, only 'Royal Scots' and 4—6—2s would be repainted red, others to be unlined black. The new streamlined Pacifics were given the crimson and gold livery until 1941 but by April 1943, even the 4—6—2s had lost their privileged status when the CME agreed to the Crewe works' suggestion to paint the four new engines, shortly to be completed, in black without lining (6245-8). At the close of hostilities, virtually everything in steam was black, insofar as anything at all could be distinguished under the grime and filth resulting from years of inadequate wartime maintenance and cleaning.

Plate 342 Horwich style: ex-LYR 2—4—2T No. 10921 carries Livery Code B1 retaining its smokebox door numberplate.

Authors' Collection

Plate 343 St Rollox style: ex-CR 0—4—4T No. 15208 carries Livery Code B1 with the '8' cutting across the footstep on the tank-side.

Photomatic

Apart from the painting of all classes black, there was no change in the official company insignia during this period but the variety of styles continued to increase. Some engines were probably given the 1936 style of block letters as transfer stocks were used up while much more use was made of unshaded yellow characters than had previously been the case. Cabside windows were frequently blacked out to cut down glare from the fire. One point of confusion in official pictures at this time was the habit of putting chalk lines on engines as an aid to photography but, as far as is known, any engines carrying lining during the war were bearing unrepainted pre-1940 liveries.

What does seem clear is that, during this period, the different works were, of necessity, allowed to express much more individualism in the approach to lettering and numbering on engines. As the war progressed, an increasing number of engines came out with unshaded yellow numbers and letters of a bright 'old gold' shade, frequently painted on over the outlines of the old transfers (see p. 194). This seems to have been established policy at all works and frequently resulted in some very untidy-looking numerals. Nor was the practice confined to the works; such was the nature of cleaning difficulties that the running sheds themselves also resorted to renewal of the insignia by hand painting which added even more to the variety of styles.

Derby works still made considerable use of red shaded numbers — presumably transfer stocks — but it is not possible to say whether these were pre-1938 gold or post-1937 yellow. The probability is that they were almost if not exclusively the latter variety. Derby seemed to make more use of these red shaded characters during the war than anywhere else but, even so, it is felt that such transfers were mainly confined to full repaints and new engines and not to engines undergoing intermediate repairs, except, perhaps, for odd red engines. One or two 'Jubilees' were given fresh red shaded insignia during this period and although Derby did not generally shop 'Jubilees', it may have been that these engines were shopped there on this occasion, since Crewe had by this time stopped using red shaded transfers for the engines. One such example was

5628, still red, in 1946. Derby probably had a reasonable supply of transfers and was still using them on the newly constructed 2—6—4 tanks after the war, in 14″ Midland pattern. It is also believed that Derby supplied 10″ transfers with red shading to the LNER, GWR and SR for use on the newly constructed Class 8Fs which were being built by these companies, while 12″ transfers were often supplied to sheds for the renumbering of the returned Class 8Fs which were loaned from LNER stock.

Crewe did the vast majority of wartime repainting in the erecting shops but this was more in the nature of 'touching up' rather than full repainting which was so rare as to render the paintshop almost redundant at times. In this connection it is interesting to note that as early as 1940 an instruction had gone out to all works to the effect that all engines including the red ones should be patch painted wherever possible. If it was necessary to repaint them, only two coats were to be used, one of colour and one of colour with a little varnish — all lining to be discontinued.

Reverting to insignia at Crewe, one of the leading authorities on LMS engines can remember no examples of newly repaired Crewe engines being given new red shaded transfers from 1942 onwards and as far as can be ascertained, insignia applied during this touching up process in the erecting shop were always executed in hand painted pale yellow characters. The only known exceptions to this policy at Crewe were the 'Rebuilt Scot' and 'Coronation' Classes. The former were, of course, classified as new work, while the latter when losing the blue or red livery were fully repainted so both classes were treated in the paint shop. In spite of the repainting being in plain black, a touch of colour was given by polishing the nameplates and giving them red backgrounds while in addition, for these few engines, Crewe did use red shaded yellow transfers with 12″ standard numerals which were otherwise confined to brand new engines. Crewe clearly did not have a great supply of these transfers for, when the 1946 livery was announced, it was immediately adopted, all the 'Patriots' rebuilt before 1948 being given this 1946 style.

Other works had their own peculiarities at this time and a generally accurate summary of insignia styles for the whole company during 1943-7 would be as follows, *repainted engines only*:

Crewe: All classes unshaded yellow (except rebuilds) although there may have been the odd exception to the rule. Yellow still the pre-1935 lining colour.

Derby: All classes shaded yellow — transfers almost exclusively.

Horwich: Passenger classes shaded yellow transfers (including Class 5 2—6—0s — both Stanier and 'Crabs'). Goods classes unshaded yellow in 'old gold' paint. (LYR 0—6—0s 12″ figures, LYR 0—8—0s, LMS 0—8—0s and LYR 0—6—0STs all 10″.)

St Rollox: All classes 10″ shaded numerals, almost always transfers. This was very consistent throughout Scotland and was probably true of Inverness and Kilmarnock as well if any repainting was done there. One reliable source states that until 1940, gold numbers with red shading were in general use, also 10″ variety.

(Note: Bow tended to follow Derby practice but the buffer beams are reputed to have been a 'peculiar' shade of red.)

By 1945, the motive power of the LMS, although probably 95% plain black, was still decked out in a variety of insignia styles. A considerable number of red engines had managed to survive hostilities and indeed a score or more survived Nationalisation too. It is clear that the pre-war red livery was of high quality and it is interesting to note in passing that as late as 1944, all the 'Princess Royal' 4—6—2s, the first five non-streamlined 'Duchesses' (6230-4), two blue streamliners (6222/4), numerous red streamliners and a high proportion of the other red engines were still carrying the full colour liveries. Some of these had, doubtless, been patched up, but a considerable number were recorded at the time and although it is going slightly ahead of the period under discussion, this seems an appropriate point at which to list the known late examples of LMS red livery, most of which survived into the BR period. The full five figure BR number is given in those cases where the engine received it with the red livery. There may have been others but it is generally believed that 40934 was the last engine to carry LMS red livery and is reputed to have had it maintained in quite good state. The date should be assumed as 1948 unless stated otherwise.

'Princess Royal' 4—6—2:	46204; 46212
'Royal Scot' 4—6—0:	46106; 46123; 6130; 6156; 46165; 6167
'Jubilee' 4—6—0:	5594*; 45600; 45603(1950); 45604; 45630; 45637(1949); 5658(1947); 5665; 45669; 45670(1951); 5678; 45680; 45697; 45720(1950)
'Patriot' 4—6—0:	45516(1950); 45520; 45537
'Claughton' 4—6—0:	6004(1949)
Compound 4—4—0:	930(1946); 40934(1951); 1059(1946); 1081(1947)

*This engine was the only locomotive given a red repaint after the war — see page 199 and class chapter.

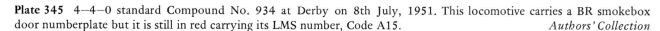

Plate 345 4—4—0 standard Compound No. 934 at Derby on 8th July, 1951. This locomotive carries a BR smokebox door numberplate but it is still in red carrying its LMS number, Code A15. *Authors' Collection*

Plate 346 'Patriot' Class 4—6—0 5XP No. 45516 *The Bedfordshire & Hertfordshire Regiment* hauling a troop special on 17th February, 1950. Still in red with 'LMS' on the tender. *BR LMR*

THE FINAL YEARS

The 1946 livery never achieved wide use because of Nationalisation but Crewe is known to have used it on all new engines and those given a full repaint. Since only the major passenger classes came into the latter category at this time, the livery was carried by relatively few locomotives before BR days. In the meantime, the older and, by now, obsolete scroll and serif insignia was still being applied to other repaired engines. A reliable source states that Derby made little use of the 1946 livery which, together with the extensive use it made of shaded numerals during the war by comparison with other works, suggests that this works really had a stockpile of transfers. This would not be altogether surprising since the general store for transfers for the whole Company was located at Derby. Horwich works put the 1946 insignia on a new batch of Class 5s from early 1947 onwards. Of these, No. 4997 (March 1947) was the first Class 5 to be built *new* with this style and all subsequent new Class 5 engines from Horwich received it. It is thought that St Rollox always used the red shaded scroll and serif transfers — at least as far as one of the officials can recall.

The official drawings of the 1946 numbers and letters describe them as transfers but it is believed that most, if not all the engines which carried them, received hand painted insignia. This would certainly help to explain why they were only seen on full repaints or new engines. The 1946 style of livery was, of course, perpetuated by the LM Region after Nationalisation until the new liveries were selected. This may cause a little confusion since pictures of engines carrying the livery with BR markings may not be of genuine LMS repaints with altered numbers and letters but post-1947 repaints which were done before the onset of the national liveries.

Thus at the end of private ownership, the approximate state of the LMS locomotive livery can be summed up as follows. The vast majority of engines were plain black and rather ill kept externally. There were probably residual survivors of the pre-war livery with plain gold insignia (plain black engines generally) or shaded gold insignia (lined black engines), but the majority which were not carrying the 1946 insignia were probably bearing yellow characters. These were one of three main types, namely red shaded yellow transfers (very evident in Scotland and on the Midland Division), bright yellow unshaded characters ('old gold' paint) and pale yellow unshaded characters (handpainted and generally confined to Crewe).

Remaining examples of pre-war lined out liveries (either red or black) were relatively few and many of them had probably had the insignia renewed during the war along with the possible obliteration of some of the lining as a result of wartime 'touching up'. There were also a few remnants of the short lived 1936 style of insignia still to be seen.

Examples of the 1946 livery were relatively few, mainly confined to express types and newly constructed standard engines and as far as is known, insignia of this 1946 style was always hand painted (see above). At the risk of undue repetition, it is probably worth re-emphasising that the post-war 'straw' shade of these 1946 characters (and the lining on the express engines too) was not an exact reversion to the pre-1935 lining colour, itself often also referred to as 'straw'. The post-war shade was almost devoid of any yellow element and appeared even lighter in tone than the pale pre-1935 yellow shade. This latter shade was perpetuated at Crewe of course (in scroll/serif insignia) almost to the end for plain black engines. *Table 10* gives a tabulated list of all LMS standard liveries and principal works variations.

It is not — and probably never will be — known when the last engine to carry any form of LMS livery was finally repainted. During the early years after 1947, many engines were renumbered with LMS type numerals but still retaining the Company initials while frequently the only repainting resorted to in the case of goods engines was to obliterate the company markings and replace with the BR version. This has been rather fortunate in a curious sort of way because it has enabled a certain amount of dimension checking to take place from the 'fossilised' outlines of the old insignia. Perhaps the best instance of this was the discovery, under years of grime, of some of the old tender side numerals on a Johnson tender in the year of grace 1965, almost 40 years after they were put there!

In 1948, BR conducted several experiments before adopting standard locomotive liveries and there was a reasonable number of LMS standard locomotives amongst the 'guinea pigs'. The principal classes involved were the Pacifics, 'Royal Scots', 'Jubilees' and Class 5s. Even after the decision to standardise certain liveries, many ex-LMS engines continued to be seen in non-entitled, albeit BR standard liveries. It was probably not until the middle 1950s that all LMS standard classes were carrying their appointed BR liveries.

It will be appreciated that the incidence of 'incorrect' livery styles on LMS locomotives of all kinds after 1947 is comparable with the similar state of affairs for LMS *pre-group* classes immediately following 1922. Most LMS standard classes had, of course, been outshopped from new in correct LMS standard liveries, so it was the first time for most of *these* machines that they had been seen in such widely differing styles. In the case of the LMS pre-group stock it was, of course, happening for the second and sometimes third time.

The number of locomotives carrying experimental or non-entitled liveries during the first few years of nationalisation was such as to make a full list in this chapter somewhat unwieldy — even assuming that such a list was complete. Moreover, to be fully comprehensive, such a list should also include the considerable number of 'hybrid' liveries seen immediately following 1947. These included LMS liveries with correct style BR numbers, LMS liveries with BR numbers in LMS style characters, plain locomotives with non-standard insignia and so forth. It has therefore been felt preferable to include all known details of these non-standard livery practices in the class articles and confine this chapter to a general discussion of BR livery as it applied to LMS steam locomotives.

The first sign of the new régime was probably the omission of any form of company identity on fully and correctly liveried new and repainted engines. For example, 4—6—2s were emerging from Crewe in January 1948 with completely unlettered tender sides but otherwise fully liveried in 1946 style. These blank tenders were quickly followed by those carrying 'BRITISH RAILWAYS' in full utilising straw painted letters of more or less 1946 LMS pattern. Coupled with this there was often an 'M' prefix to the old LMS number, shortly to be followed by the full five digit BR number — again often to be seen applied in quasi-1946 type figures.

As well as these changes, many locomotives retained their LMS initials but with their new BR numbers, in some cases the latter being applied in matching LMS characters.

During this transition period, the 'livery' adopted was usually plain black although most passenger types continued to be given the 1946 type LMS lining if they were of the classes entitled to receive it.

During the later part of 1948, experiments were carried out with various liveries for possible standardisation. Most of the more colourful varieties were permutations on the 'green' theme. GWR green, LNER green and SR green were all tried with a variety of lining alternatives. Three Class 5s (at least) were repainted, one each, in these three shades of green, some

Plate 347 This illustrates Class 5 4—6—0 No. 4762, the locomotive which was painted malachite green in the Southern Railway style.

BR LMR

Plate 348 Rebuilt 'Patriot' Class 4—6—0 No. 45531 *Sir Frederick Harrison* in apple green with LNWR lining. One of the authors recalls seeing this locomotive and felt the livery was not inspiring. *BR LMR*

Plate 349 This picture of 'Princess Royal' Class 4—6—2 No. M6206 *Princess Marie Louise* has been included to illustrate the 1948 policy of prefixing the original LMS number with an 'M'. This policy lasted only until the adoption of the British Railways renumbering scheme.

Authors' Collection

sources saying with different lining treatment on each side — not confirmed. A rebuilt 'Patriot' was painted LNER green with LNWR type red, cream and grey lining and there were others too.

Another departure in 1948 was the idea of two distinct express passenger liveries — one to be reserved for the most 'glamorous' classes. The logic behind this is hard to understand but it resulted in some experimentation with various blue shades. On LMS locomotives, the experiments seem to have been confined to the 4—6—2 'Coronation' class and resulted in several engines being painted dark blue with LNWR lining; while one at least was painted in so-called 'Coronation' blue with yellow and black lining.

A lined black livery was also being sought after and many locomotives were repainted this way. Most of these were given LNWR style lining and examples of all the principal LMS passenger tender classes were thus finished. One cannot be entirely certain that some of these were not turned out *after* the decision to paint the classes blue or green — after all Crewe works was only human and there was still the memory of 1923 to erase!

It became clear during the experimental phase that BR had opted for a Gill Sans style of insignia. Running numbers were applied in this style, coloured pale cream, while ownership was depicted in matching letters 'BRITISH RAILWAYS' on tank or tender. All locomotives were gradually fitted with LMS type front numberplates bearing the new BR number — generally in Gill Sans figures. It also became clear during this period that, whatever lined out livery was adopted, the lining would most probably be set in from the edge of the panels rather than be applied round the edges as in LMS days. In fact, none of the LMS lined liveries seem to have been seriously considered as BR standards — hardly surprising in view of the almost total lack of colour on the latter day LMS.

Plate 350 Fairburn 2–6–4T Class 4P No. 42109 in BR mixed traffic livery with 'British Railways' painted on the tank side.   *BR LMR*

Plate 351 'Princess Coronation' Class 4–6–2 No. 46243 *City of Lancaster*, the last streamliner to be converted, in 1949 carrying its first de-streamlined livery of BR blue with the early large emblem.   *Authors' Collection*

Arising from the experiments, the following BR liveries were adopted in January 1949:

Selected Express Passenger

Locomotives in this group were to be painted 'light blue' with black and white lining. The LMS standard classes involved were the Class 7P 4–6–2 locomotives of all types.

Remaining Express Passenger

This group was to be painted 'dark green', the GWR colour being officially specified. The lining was defined as yellow and black but seems to have usually been orange and black. The LMS standard classes involved were 'Royal Scot', 'Jubilee' and 'Patriot' 4–6–0s.

Other Passenger and Mixed Traffic

The livery adopted for this group was black lined red, cream and grey in LNWR fashion. The LMS standard classes involved were Stanier Class 5 4–6–0s, all standard 2–6–0 designs, Class 4P Compound 4–4–0s, Class 2P 4–4–0s, Class 4P 2–6–4Ts, all classes of 2–6–2Ts and Class 2P 0–4–4Ts.

Freight Classes

All engines in this group were to be unlined black.

Amplifying these details, it can be noted that the blue colour was very close to the old Caledonian Railway shade while the green was, most certainly, the GWR colour. On all classes carrying any form of lined livery, the boiler bands were all lined out (red lines only in the case of the mixed traffic livery but two colour lining for the blue and green liveries). Splashers, if present on the locomotive, were also lined out as were outside cylinders. However, the latter tended to be

Plate 352 'Silver Jubilee' Class 4—6—0 No. 45697 *Achilles* in the standard BR green livery adopted for this class and carrying the early BR emblem. *BR LMR*

black with all liveries rather than the main body colour. Tender backs were unlined as were step plates and tender side-frames.

Shortly after the decision to standardise the above liveries, the standard ownership markings were settled. A distinctive BR emblem was adopted which took the form of a stylised lion astride a locomotive wheel with the words 'British Railways' in a band across the centre.

Running numbers were standardised as Gill Sans in two heights (10″ and 8″) and the power class insignia was applied in small Gill Sans characters just below the running number. Two sizes of BR emblem were adopted to cater for the varying sizes of locomotives involved.

LMS pre-group classes were only given one of the two black liveries and details of the appropriate styles will be given in the pre-group chapters.

As far as LMS locomotives were concerned, only two significant changes took place in the original BR livery scheme. In 1951, the blue livery was abandoned — being apparently of poor wearing quality — and GWR green became the only express passenger livery. The change from blue was so soon after its adoption that not all the entitled locomotives received it.

The second livery change took place in 1957/8 and gave a welcome relief to the all pervading black and dark green. In late 1957, permission was given to repaint 20 ex-LMS 4—6—2s in red livery — this being associated with a general regionalisation of BR carriage liveries — and resulted in the re-appearance of LMS red on newly repainted locomotives for the first time in almost 20 years. The selected colour was matched to the pre-war LMS shade although officially called maroon — one gathers to avoid upsetting any lingering susceptibilities! Since the same shade had also been adopted for carriage stock, modern day enthusiasts could re-live a little of the pre-war scene for a few years.

Some of the first few red Pacifics were given BR style lining for comparative purposes in yellow and black set in from the panel edge but eventually, the red livery was lined in pure LMS style including step plates, tender frames and buffer beams. The yellow lining colour was quite a bright shade — rather more so than the running numbers which remained of the cream coloured standard Gill Sans style.

Other than changes to the actual livery, several sundry variations also took place in such matters as ownership markings and nameplate colours. In 1957, the first BR emblem was changed to a more heraldic device and as locomotives passed through shops, the new totem was applied. Cynics speculated whether or not the new device was symptomatic of the change in BR finances during the 1950s. In 1949, the locomotive wheel had carried the British Lion whereas in 1957, the British Lion was seen to be carrying the locomotive wheel!

Locomotive nameplates during the BR period reverted to the former LMS style of having polished letters and surrounds rather than the latter day LMS practice of painting both letters and background. At first, nameplates were black backed

Plate 353 Class 4F 0−6−0 No. 44203, photographed in 1953 carrying a 21A Saltley shedplate and in the condition in which one of the authors fired this locomotive. It has been included to show the first BR emblem.   *BR LMR*

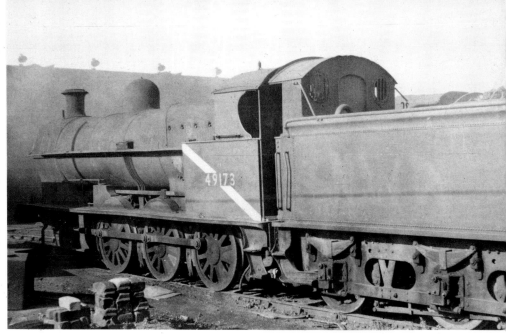

Plate 354 The final style of livery adopted by some ex-LMS locomotives. Ex-LNWR 0−8−0 No. 49173 with tender cab just prior to its withdrawal displays the yellow stripe painted on locomotives forbidden to work 'under the wires' of the electric system.
Authors' Collection

but red backed plates gradually came into vogue during the 1950s. However, most of the red Pacifics reverted to black backed nameplates.

Towards the end of the steam era (c 1964 onwards), repainted steam locomotives were devoid of all lining although still retaining the green or black colour as appropriate. From about the same date, and sometimes slightly earlier, nameplates began to be removed and classes prohibited 'under the wire' south of Crewe were given a broad yellow diagonal band on the cabside.

The final LMS express locomotives to run in BR colours were the handful of 'Jubilees' at Holbeck in 1967. All were in plain unlined green livery at withdrawal. However, several Stanier Class 5s, amongst them the locomotives destined to share the melancholy distinction of being the last standard gauge BR steam locomotives in service, retained the fully lined BR standard livery to the very end.

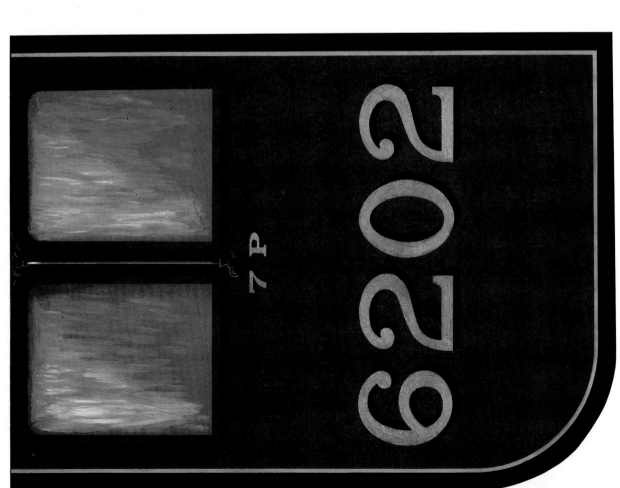

Facsimile cabside panels showing lining and number styles adopted with the post-1927 crimson lake livery. No. 6202 represents a Stanier 4—6—2 cabside (Turbomotive) with 12″ gold numbers, standard pattern, black shaded; while 6102 represents a Fowler Royal Scot cabside (*Black Watch*) with gold 14″ Midland pattern numbers, also black shaded. *Original panels prepared by the late G.L. Wilson.*

Facsimile cabside panels showing later variations in the post-1927 crimson lake livery with the darker lining colour. No. 5728 represents a Stanier 5XP cabside (*Defiance*) with the gold/red 1936 sans-serif style; while No. 5541 represents a Patriot cabside (*Duke of Sutherland*) in the post-1936 style with 12″ standard figures in chrome yellow with vermilion shading.

Original panels prepared by the late G.L. Wilson.

Chapter 14   Painting Methods and Colour Shades

In spite of the quite incredible number of non-standard items of equipment which it continued to possess, the LMS was very much a company of standardisation and in keeping with this policy, full and detailed schedules were laid down covering the painting of its locomotives. Thanks to the courtesy of the Carriage and Wagon Department at Derby which provided a copy of the schedules for 1935, it is possible to describe them here although in order to avoid confusing the narrative, the various shades of colour are merely referred to by name and identifying number, the full specifications being given afterwards.

PAINTING TECHNIQUE

Preliminary Stages — All Engines

The preliminary stages for both new engines and thorough repaints always took place before the locomotive went into the paintshop. In the case of repainting, the whole of the previous coat was burnt off or, if this was not the case, 'suitable arrangements must be made to deal with the areas not so treated'. It is felt that the 'suitable arrangements' were much more common than burning off! Needless to say, before applying the paint all rust and scale was removed from all components.

Before assembly, the first coat on boiler, axles and the insides of the frames was of *bauxite* (1). Wheels, except for the areas where polished metal was specified were painted *glossy black* (2) and the outsides of the frames in *common black* (3). The outer visible surfaces (boiler clothing, cab sheets, cylinder clothing) were given a first coat of *steel primer* (4) which was basically red oxide of iron.

After erection of the locomotive, but before entering the paintshop, all exterior surfaces were thoroughly scoured and given a second coat of steel primer.

Paintshop Work — Black Engines

(a)   Engine — Main Components

1st Day: All irregularities were filled with *hard stopping* (5) and all visible surfaces were then faced down with rubbing blocks and water until smooth when the engine was given one coat of *lead colour undercoat* (6), which was basically two parts of white to one of black.

2nd Day: The engine was faced down again with Grade I sandpaper and given one coat of *drop black* (7), followed by one coat of *exterior finishing varnish*.

3rd Day: The engine was flatted with pumice dust and water and the lining, if present, was applied in *vermilion* (8), together with the transfers. One coat of exterior finishing varnish was then applied, together with a coat of common black on the footplate and cab front.

The locomotive was then allowed to stand for as long as possible for the varnish to harden.

(b)   Engine — Details

Cab interior: The cab roof interior received two coats of *white* (9) and the upper parts of the sides and front were given two coats of *buff undercoat* (10) and one of *graining colour* (11), the whole then being grained. The bottom portion of the cab interior was given two coats of drop black and then the whole of the inside of the cab was given two coats of exterior finishing varnish.

Smokebox: This was given one coat of common black on top of which went a coat of *finishing black enamel* but no varnish was used.

Fittings and frames: With the exception of the polished metal areas and the inside of the frames, all remaining areas were given one coat of common black. The insides of frames, axles, motion were given one coat of vermilion (lining colour) and one coat of a 50/50 mixture of vermilion and mixing varnish.

Buffer beams: These had two coats of vermilion, edged with one coat of drop black and finished with two coats of exterior finishing varnish.

Lettering: All lettering on fittings (lubricators and hand brake, etc.) was done in white except for the lamps which were painted in *spirit black* and letters 'LMS' in vermilion.

(c)   Tender

The tender was painted in the same manner as the engine except for the following details:

Insides of frames — before erection: These were finished with one coat of *tar varnish* and the springs and boxes painted in common black.

Tender top: Tar varnish was also used for this part of the tender unless it was visible to the public when it was painted as for the sides!

Tender front: This was given one coat of drop black and one of finishing black enamel.

Inside of water tank (when engine was new only): This was given one coat of bauxite.

Paintshop Work — Red Engines
(a)   Engine — Main Components

1st Day: As for the black engines.

2nd Day: The engine was faced down with Grade I sandpaper and then given one coat of *brown undercoat* (12), followed by one coat of *standard crimson lake* (13).

3rd Day: The edging was applied in drop black followed by one coat of exterior finishing varnish.

4th Day: The whole engine was flatted with pumice dust and then the lining was applied in *yellow* (14), together with the transfers and a second coat of exterior finishing varnish.

5th Day: The engine was again flatted with pumice dust and water and given a third coat of exterior finishing varnish. The footplate was then finished in common black and the bright work polished.

The locomotive was then allowed to stand for as long as possible for the varnish to harden.

(b)   Other Details

Buffer beams: These were given two coats of vermilion, picked out with drop black and then lined inside the black with yellow before being completed with two coats of exterior finishing varnish.

Tender front: This was given one coat of common black and one of finishing black enamel.

The rest of the tender was painted in the same manner as the engine and all other details were exactly the same as specified for the black engines.

PAINT SPECIFICATIONS

The above description of paintshop technique refers to the methods current in 1935. These were probably representative of a fairly lengthy period and are, in any case, the only full surviving records which have been located. The following specifications were used for the various paints employed, the numbers referring to those quoted in the text. Where a paint quoted in the text is not specified below it is because the details of it were not given in the 1935 schedules.

Shade Number 1 — Bauxite Paint
Boiled Linseed Oil	8 lbs
White Spirit	6-10 lbs
Liquid Drier	2-4 lbs
Bauxite residue in oil	82 lbs

Shade Number 2 — Glossy Black Paint
Common Black Paint (see No. 3)	60 lbs
Finishing Black Enamel	46 lbs
Liquid Drier	2-4 lbs

Shade Number 3 — Common Black Paint
Black in oil	55 lbs
Boiled Linseed Oil	22 lbs
Liquid Drier	18 lbs
White Spirit	7 lbs
Gold Size, Type A (Dark)	30 lbs

Shade Number 4 — Steel Primer
Oxide of Iron, in oil, Type R, (Red shade)	88 lbs
Zinc Oxide White, in oil	2 lbs
Aluminium Powder (Fine varnish powder)	10 lbs
Raw Linseed Oil	10 lbs
Mixing Varnish	26 lbs
Genuine Turpentine	16-20 lbs
Liquid Drier	Not more than 4 lbs

Shade Number 5 — Hard Stopping

Enamel Filling	112 lbs	
Gold Size, Type A (Dark)	4 parts	} This 4 : 1 mixture to be added sufficient
Genuine Turpentine	1 part	} to bring to right consistency

Shade Number 6 — Lead Colour Undercoat

Zinc Sulphide White, composite pigment in oil	50 lbs
Black in oil	25 lbs
Liquid Drier	6-8 lbs
Genuine Turpentine	18-20 lbs
Gold Size, Type A (Dark)	10 lbs

Shade Number 7 — Drop Black Paint

Drop Black in Turpentine	78 lbs
Gold Size, Type B (Light)	23 lbs
Genuine Turpentine	8-12 lbs

Shade Number 8 — Red Lining Colour for Locomotives

Vermilion Substitute in oil	100 lbs
Mixing Varnish	4-6 lbs
Liquid Drier	8-10 lbs

Shade Number 9 — White Paint for Cab Roofs

Zinc White, composite pigment in oil	78 lbs
Paste Driers in oil	12 lbs
Mixing Varnish	6 lbs
Genuine Turpentine	12-16 lbs
Ultramarine Blue in oil	6-7 ounces

Shade Number 10 — Buff Colour Undercoat

Zinc White, composite pigment in oil	78 lbs
Paste Driers in oil	11 lbs
Yellow Ochre in oil	8 lbs
Genuine Turpentine	12-16 lbs

Shade Number 11 — Graining Colour

Yellow Ochre in oil	48 lbs
Burnt Turkey Umber in oil	3 lbs
Paste Driers in oil	12 lbs
Liquid Drier	24 lbs
Genuine Turpentine	24-28 lbs

Shade Number 12 — Brown Undercoat for Lake

Oxide of iron in oil, Type R, (Red shade)	100 lbs
Liquid Drier	4-6 lbs
Mixing Varnish	28-30 lbs
Genuine Turpentine	12-14 lbs

Note: 95 lbs of this mixture was put with 5 lbs of black in oil to get the correct shade for locomotives.

Shade Number 13 — Standard Lake

Standard LMS Lake (Paste Form)	12 lbs
Mixing Varnish	4 lbs
Genuine Turpentine	3-5 lbs
Liquid Drier	1-3 lbs

Shade Number 14 — Yellow Lining Colour

Lemon Chrome in Oil	18-20 lbs
Orange Chrome in Oil	2-3 lbs
Zinc White, composite pigment in oil	15-20 lbs
Genuine Turpentine	2-5 lbs
Liquid Drier	6-10 lbs

Note: This mixture was intended to match British Standard Colour No. 56 and slight adjustments to quantities were permitted in order to get a good match. B.S. Colour 56 became BS 356 in the 1948 British Standard list at which time it was called 'Golden Yellow'.

THE COLOUR OF LMS LAKE

Knowledgeable readers will detect some differences in the application of the 'crimson lake' livery to LMS engines in relation to the classic method adopted by the Midland Railway when Samuel Johnson first introduced the shade. According to Hamilton Ellis in his book on the Midland Railway, 'Midland red' for engines was obtained by applying four coats of 'purple brown' undercoat on top of which went one coat only of 'crimson lake' (with a small admixture of 'purple brown'), followed by no less than *five* coats of varnish. When this practice ceased is not known but one might presume that it gradually evolved to the more economical but still very thorough specification quoted above. Unquestionably, the red engines of the LMS were thoroughly well finished and the fact that the livery is known to have lasted for over ten years on more than one engine without repainting is adequate testimony to its high quality.

At the same time, considerable controversy surrounds the topic of 'crimson lake' as a shade. Many reputable publications consistently refer to the colour as maroon but this is not correct, for the LMS first specified maroon as a colour for lining engines and painting coaches as late as 1946. Moreover, maroon to many people implies a darker shade than true crimson, although in truth, there may not be much in it. The quoted painting specifications are dated 1935 and in 1937, no less an authority than the late J.N. Maskelyne wrote in the *Model Railway News*:

> I now have official information to the effect that the colour is 'Crimson Lake' and has *never* changed, officially, since Mr. S.W. Johnson introduced it on the old Midland Railway, fifty years ago. If any change has occurred in the meantime, it has been due simply to varying methods of manufacture by different makers, from time to time. No order has ever been issued by Derby or Crewe, authorising a change.

Furthermore, the official specifications for the new 4–6–2s in 1938-40 were still referring to the colour as 'Midland red' so it would seem on all counts that the colour did remain crimson right through until 1946. Nevertheless, since there does seem to be this controversy about the shade, it has been felt desirable to rationalise the argument if only to prevent it from developing into yet another bone of contention such as that which periodically breaks out over 'Caledonian blue'.

The one common factor on which all authorities are agreed is that 'Midland lake' had a certain undefinable 'warm glow' in its outward effect on the viewer. The general concensus seems to be that it probably got a little darker (slightly) during LMS days but this, as suggested by Maskelyne, may have been nothing more than a result of changed paint manufacturing methods. At all times it was unquestionably a rich shade of red, probably lighter than most memories will admit and certainly not the dark muddy red-brown as so often thought.

It is interesting to note that in both the LMS and Midland Railway specifications, only one coat of the finishing colour was applied which means that the undercoat colour must have contributed considerably to the overall effect, red in any shade being a semi-transparent pigment. It therefore seems not without significance that the undercoat had a large brown element which would have the effect of giving 'warmth' to the red — unlike a grey undercoat which would make the shade 'colder'. Therefore, given a shade like crimson, the 'purple brown' undercoat of Midland days or the oxide of the LMS would explain part of the elusiveness of the shade. Also interesting is that the Midland mixed a small amount of 'purple brown' in the final coat (would that we knew more precisely the proportions), but the LMS apparently used unmodified crimson. This may have been because the LMS oxide undercoat had a larger brown content than the 'purple brown' of the Midland, thus alleviating the need for any brown in the final coat of red to get the same shade. What does seem very apparent is that the two methods of painting would each produce a very similar end product, the edge in quality probably being with the Midland technique if only because of the greater care bestowed on things in those days.

Several other imponderables must, however, be taken into consideration if one is to arrive at the correct assessment of what this elusive colour really looked like for red is probably one of the world's worst colours for retaining its original shade. Once out of the paintshop, continual oxidation would tend to brown the pigment which, combined with the bleaching effect of strong sunlight would cause a gradual deterioration from brilliant red to a rather indeterminate faded brown/red. As this fading and oxidation took place, the colour would suffer additional modification by any subsequent varnishing and cleaning processes it might have received. Further varnishing would continue to yellow the finish while oil or vaseline would dull it. At the same time, varnishing and oiling would, in time, impart a depth to the finished product rather akin to a wood surface under a good layer of french polish. There was a story some few years ago that some BR 2–6–2Ts were turning up at Waterloo in LNWR 'blackberry' black. Apparently an ex-LNWR man was shed foreman and had enough cleaners to properly clean his locomotives with engine oil. If there was enough blue in this to affect black, then similar methods applied to red engines might give them a slight purple hue.

What does, therefore, seem abundantly clear is that there could have been no one shade that, above all others, could be said to be the only true 'Midland red'. It seems more than probable that any group of red engines at any time would have exhibited a variety of shades depending on the time out of shops, the method of cleaning adopted and so on. That this could have been so is well exemplified by the variety of shades visible on any train composed of a mixture of coaches outshopped at different times. Moreover, complete colour perception is a rare quality in any individual and we all probably 'see' colour in a slightly different manner from our neighbours — which certainly does nothing to help when trying to assess the validity of personal recollection.

Our view, therefore, which admittedly does not necessarily prove anything, is that there was a spectrum of colour within which any shade could be acceptable as 'Midland red', excluding of course the quasi-vermilion or deep maroon. Fortunately, since this information was first published some 14 years ago, more information has been garnered. It now seems certain that BR maroon, in use until 1964 on coaches and ex-LMS 4–6–2s, was, in spite of its name, a deliberate attempt to match the pre-war LMS red. This is confirmed when comparing restored locomotives and coaches of which many more examples exist than was the case in 1967. The authors have been privileged to be able to advise on several examples of LMS locomotive restoration and we have had considerable opportunity to check and double check on precise paint colours. We are, in consequence, happy to be able to record that there are now several examples of preserved locomotives which, within the acceptable degrees of tolerance, do accurately depict the correct LMS shade of red. Space precludes us from giving full details, but the following examples are particularly noteworthy: MR Compound 4–4–0 No. 1000 (with MR insignia); LMS 4–6–2s No. 6201 and 6233 (the latter with the correct gold/vermilion lining); LMS 4–6–0s No. 5593 (with countershaded insignia) and 5690. We hope that this list will grow longer as time goes by.

YELLOW LETTERING AND LINING

From the uncertainties of MR/LMS red, it is necessary now to turn to an almost equally contentious shade, namely yellow. The LMS used yellow for its lining on red engines and, sometimes, for its letters and numbers as well. Some sources refer to the shade as middle chrome yellow but this is felt to be an oversimplification and only strictly applicable to the shade of yellow specified in the 1935 schedules. This was indeed a chrome yellow colour and was the same hue as the red shaded yellow insignia introduced in 1938 – see p. 194. However, prior to these 1935 schedules, the lining on red engines had been executed in a paler shade which, when used as it was for handpainted insignia in the Crewe erecting shop (p. 214), must have been difficult to distinguish at any distance from gold leaf proper. In fact, expert opinion at Derby works states that this paler lining colour was a deliberate attempt at a shade which was as near identical to gold leaf as could be obtained, bearing in mind the difference in texture.

Just when this paler lining colour was changed to the darker shade specified in 1935 is not known – in fact the schedules themselves may well have introduced the change. What does seem likely is that the change from gold to yellow *insignia* did not take place at the same time. The 1936 block pattern transfers were gold leaf and Derby Works is not positively recorded as having used the yellow type of insignia until late 1937/early 1938 on a batch of 2–6–2Ts. Thus, between 1935 and 1937/8 red engines were painted with gold insignia but chrome yellow lining. Things were not made easier by the fact that this chrome yellow shade was often called 'golden' yellow.

At the same time Crewe works continued to use the paler shade for the hand painted insignia in the erecting shop. Thus, during this period, both shades were visible depending on the type of engine, not to mention the black shaded gold leaf transfers which were still in use and gave the finished appearance of plain insignia on black engines. After a few months in service, these gold leaf transfers would be almost indistinguishable from the pale yellow paint applied at Crewe.

This has, therefore, made it impossible in some cases to deduce the colour of insignia from black and white pictures. Observation of the preserved No. 1000 confirms this view. From a short distance away, the gold leaf numbers look the same shade as the pale yellow lining and only close inspection reveals the more metallic finish of the numbers – which is not very pronounced anyway and even less so under the varnish.

During the war, however, much use is known to have been made of *painted* yellow numerals in which case the colour was as bright if not more so even than that specified in 1935 (see p. 228) – almost 'old gold' to quote a reliable source. This very bright yellow was apparently introduced after experiments to find a colour which would be as near as possible to the 1935 chrome yellow but which would cover adequately in one coat during wartime 'touch-up' repaints. In the event, it emerged as a rather more orange colour and this fact was confirmed by investigation of several withdrawn tenders where, revealed beneath some 17 years of grime, the old LMS lettering was discovered to have been painted on in this bright orange/yellow shade.

It would therefore seem that except at Crewe, plain *yellow* numbers and letters were, if they existed, rarely used until about 1938/9 and that when they finally were adopted during the Second World War they were painted on in this bright 'old gold' shade. It seems most probable that before this the vast majority of unshaded letters and numbers were black shaded gold transfers which might well have appeared as pale yellow from any position except close to the engine. This was certainly the case at St Rollox where, according to first hand evidence, it was extremely rare before 1938/9 to have a goods engine shopped in any other insignia than plain gold. There seems to be no reason to assume that the other works (except Crewe), were substantially different.

Needless to say, these arguments do not apply to the Crewe shopped black engines which, as far as can be judged, continued to receive handpainted insignia in the same shade as the pre-1935 lining colour if the work was done in the erecting shop where, according to one correspondent, transfers were not allowed. Even so, this did not seem to prevent Crewe from shopping the odd plain black engine with Midland pattern transfer figures just to make confusion complete. Thus, summarising the situation, it appears that the following 'Calendar' of events fits the known facts:

Pre-1928: Always black shaded gold insignia for all engines together with pale yellow lining on red ones.

1928-35: Gold transfer insignia (red or black shaded) at all works, except for unlined black engines shopped at Crewe, which almost always received pale yellow painted insignia. Lining on red engines – pale yellow.

1935-8: Insignia colour generally as for 1928-35 but lining on red engines changed to chrome yellow (1935 specification).

1938-47: Insignia chrome yellow shaded red at all works when transfers were used, but even brighter 'old gold' paint when 'touched up' in unshaded form by hand during the war. Crewe continued to use pre-1935 pale yellow for handpainted insignia on black engines. Red engines lined in chrome yellow. Engines given the correct 1946 livery received straw coloured letters, numbers and lining, but of even paler shade than that which had always been used at Crewe for plain black engines.

ACKNOWLEDGEMENTS

We are very conscious that although our names appear as the authors of this work, the task would have been impossible without the cheerful and willing backing of the publisher and the magnificent co-operation of our friends in the LMS Society, many of whom have lent notes and photographs, not to mention helping to check vast amounts of detail. We must also thank those who have written to us over the years since the first book was published, with much extra detail, confirmatory evidence and so forth. This has enabled us to make much firmer statements in this revised compilation.

Of all involved, however, we would like to single out for especial thanks several individuals by name. Firstly, to John Hinchliffe and Arthur Whitehead go our thanks for preparing all the insignia drawings — we know from subsequent statements that the shapes were anything but simple to reduce to the size of a drawing board. Secondly, we would like to thank John Edgington, Ken Hopkins, Don Rowland and David Tee for casting their critical and eagle eyes over the manuscripts and trapping many errors in the process — David Tee must also be thanked for preparing *Tables 1, 2* and *9*. Thirdly, we would like to acknowledge, posthumously, the work of the late Alex McNair and Gavin Wilson, two of our very dear friends without whom life will always seem much duller. Alex worked for all his early railway life with LMS engines including a spell in the Derby drawing office and his comments and observations have made a material contribution to the introductory chapters. Gavin undertook part of his training as an engineer on the LMS before the Second World War and was responsible for preparing all the original colour samples which are reproduced in this book.

Finally, we must thank all the photographers, known and unknown, whose work has been incorporated in the book. Many of the pictures were provided way back in the early 1960s by BR(LMR) and our renewed thanks go to Euston House for the co-operation received. Most of these official pictures have now been transferred to the care of the National Railway Museum and we must therefore now extend our thanks to this institution for continuing to make the material available. Private sources of pictures are acknowledged in the captions and if we have made any mistakes in attribution may we apologise now and ask readers to let the publisher know.

BIBLIOGRAPHY

To list every book which mentions LMS locomotives would probably be impossible but the following list of titles gives, we think, a good cross section of those titles which are either still readily available from booksellers or which should not be too difficult to obtain via a library. They are listed in no particular order of preference but do encompass a considerable variety of approaches and styles.

Reference Books specific to LMS types

L.M. Pacifics	Higson	Roundhouse 1967
Engines of the LMS 1923-51	Rowledge	OPC 1975
Locomotives at the Grouping	Casserley/Johnson	Ian Allan 1966
LMS Steam	Nock	David & Charles 1971
The LMS Duchesses	Doherty	M.A.P. 1973
Stanier Locomotives	Haresnape	Ian Allan 1970
Fowler Locomotives	Haresnape	Ian Allan 1972
Royal Scots of the LMS	Doherty	Ian Allan 1970
Jubilees of the LMS	Clay	Ian Allan 1971
The Stanier Black 5s	Clay	Ian Allan 1972
West Coast Pacifics	Clay/Cliffe	Ian Allan 1976
Power of the Duchesses	Jenkinson	OPC 1980
Firing Days at Saltley	Essery	Bradford Barton 1980
More Firing Days at Saltley	Essery	Bradford Barton 1980
LMS Engine Sheds	Hawkins & Reeve	Wild Swan 1981
Reflection on a Railway Career	Dunn	Ian Allan 1966
Mendips Engineman	Smith	OPC 1972
Midland Compounds	Tee	RCTS 1962

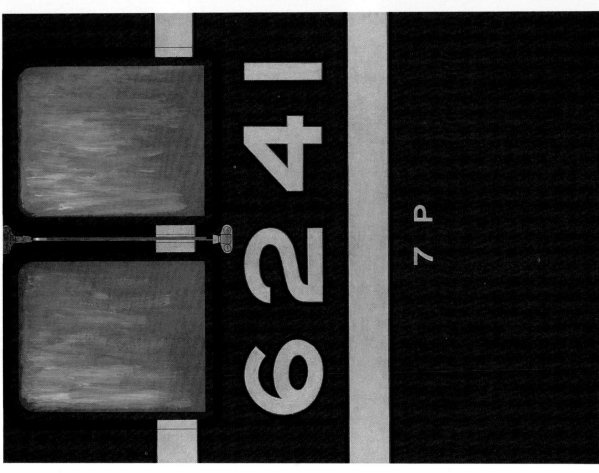

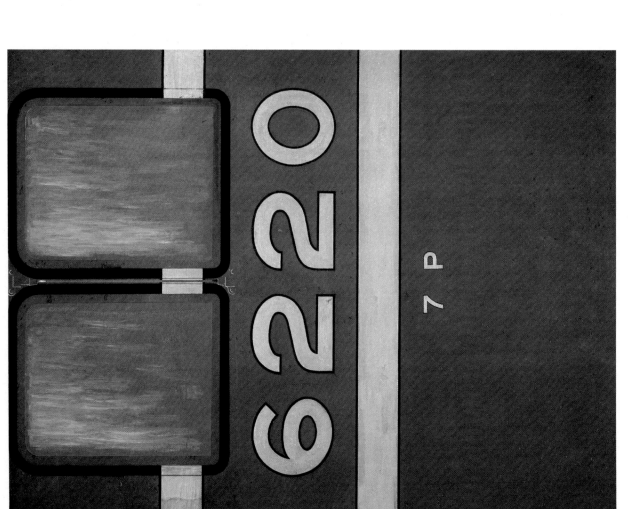

Facsimile cabside panels of the two variations of the special livery on the streamlined Stanier 4—6—2s; No. 6220 *Coronation* in blue and silver with dark blue edging and No. 6241 *City of Edinburgh* in crimson lake and gold with black/vermilion edging.

Original panels prepared by the late G.L. Wilson.

Facsimile cabside panels of Stanier 4–6–2 No. 6231 *Duchess of Atholl* in original 1938 crimson lake with gold/vermilion numbers and special gold/vermilion lining (left) and in standard 1946 black livery with maroon/straw decoration (right).

Original panels prepared by the late G.L. Wilson.

Personal Accounts, Biographies etc.

Locomotive Panorama Vol I	Cox	Ian Allan 1965
Vol II	Cox	Ian Allan 1966
Chronicles of Steam	Cox	Ian Allan 1967
Speaking of Steam	Cox	Ian Allan 1971
The Last Steam Locomotive Engineer — R.A. Riddles	Rogers	Allen & Unwin 1970
Master Builders of Steam	Bulleid	Ian Allan 1963
William Stanier — a biography	Nock	Ian Allan 1964
London Midland Fireman	Higson	Ian Allan 1972
A Breath of Steam	Thorley	Ian Allan 1975
A Lifetime with Locomotives	Bond	Goose & Son 1975
Gresley and Stanier — a centenary tribute	Bellwood/Jenkinson	HMSO 1976
Living with London Midland Locomotives	Powell	Ian Allan 1977

General References

British Steam Railway Locomotive Vol I	Ahrons	Re-issued Ian Allan
Vol II	Nock	Ian Allan 1966
The Locomotive Exchanges	Allen	Ian Allan 1950
British Pacific Locomotives	Allen	Ian Allan 1962
Locomotives in Profile Vols I-IV and No. 37	Reed	Profile Pubs. 1971-5
London Midland and Scottish	Hamilton Ellis	Ian Allan 1970
Salute to the LMS	Allen	Ian Allan 1972
British Internal Combustion Locomotives	Webb	David & Charles 1973
Nameplates of the Big Four	Burridge	OPC 1975

Pictorial Albums etc.

LMS Album I	Dorman	Ian Allan 1967
II	Stephenson	Ian Allan 1971
III	Stephenson	Ian Allan 1973
Portrait of the LMS	Anderson/Essery/Jenkinson	Peco Pubs. 1971
LMS Steam	Casserley	Bradford Barton 1975
LMSR Locomotives I, II and III	Casserley	Bradford Barton 1976
The LMS Remembered	Whiteley/Morrison	OPC 1979

Pre-group LMS Locomotives

LNWR Miscellany Vol 1	Talbot	OPC 1979
Vol 2	Talbot	OPC 1980
North Western Album	Dorman	Ian Allan 1965
North London Railway	Atkins/Edgington	NRM 1979
North Staffordshire Album	Dow	Ian Allan 1970
Lancashire & Yorkshire Album	Coates/Waters	Ian Allan 1971
Lancashire & Yorkshire Railway	Marshall	David & Charles 1977
Highland Railway Album Vol 1	Lambert	Ian Allan 1974
Vol 2	Lambert	Ian Allan 1978
LNWR Scene No 3	Nock	Ian Allan 1980
The Furness Railway	Sankey/Norman	Dalesman 1977
North Western Steam	Tuplin	Allen & Unwin 1963
Midland Steam	Tuplin	David & Charles
The Midland Railway	Hamilton Ellis	Ian Allan 1953
Derby Works & Locomotives	Radford	Ian Allan 1971
My Life with Locomotives	"Rivington"	Ian Allan 1962
LNWR Locomotives of Bowen Cooke	Nock	Bradford Barton 1977
London, Tilbury & Southend Album	Dow	Ian Allan 1981
LNWR Precursor Family	Nock	David & Charles 1966
Midland Compounds	Nock	David & Charles
Caledonian Dunalastairs	Nock	David & Charles 1968
Scottish Locomotive History	Highet	Allen & Unwin 1970
Scottish 4-6-0 Classes	Atkins	Ian Allan 1976
Forty Years of Caledonian Locomotives	Campbell Cornwell	David & Charles 1974
Locomotives of the GSWR	Smith	David & Charles 1976
Aspinall Era	Bulleid	Ian Allan 1967
Somerset & Dorset Locomotive History	Bradley/Milton	David & Charles 1973
Highland Locomotives	Tatlow	OPC 1979
North Wales Steam	Kneale	OPC 1980
Forty Years of Steam	Flowers	Ian Allan 1969
Scottish Steam in the 1920's	Stephen	Bradford Barton 1975
London Midland Steam on Shed	"45562"	Bradford Barton 1978
LMS Days	Cooper	Ian Allan 1979
Caledonian Cavalcade	Glen/Dunbar	Ian Allan 1979
The Midland Railway	Radford/Smith	Bradford Barton

Index